MURDER, CULTURE, AND INJUSTICE

SERIES ON LAW, POLITICS AND SOCIETY

MURDER, CULTURE, AND INJUSTICE

FOUR SENSATIONAL CASES IN AMERICAN HISTORY

WALTER L. HIXSON

 **THE UNIVERSITY OF AKRON PRESS**
AKRON, OHIO

All inquires and permissions requests should be addressed to the publisher,
The University of Akron Press, Akron, OH 44325-1703

Manufactured in the United States of America

First Edition 2001

Designed and produced by Kachergis Book Design, Pittsboro, NC

LIBRARY OF CONGRESS CATALOGING-IN-PUBLICATION-DATA
Hixson, Walter L.
Murder, culture, and injustice : four sensational cases in American
    history / by Walter L. Hixson.— 1st. ed.
        p.   cm. — (Series on law, politics, and society)
    Includes bibliographical references and index.
    ISBN 1-884836-67-4
        1. Murder—United States—Case studies.   2. Murderers—United
States—Case studies.   3. Murder victims—United States—Case studies.
4. Celebrities—United States—Case studies.   5. Trials (Murder)—
United States—Case studies.   6. Mass media and culture—United States.
I. Title.   II. Series.
HV6529 .H59 2000
364.15'23'0973—dc21

                                        00-010635

The paper used in this publication meets the minimum requirements of American National
Standard for Information Sciences—Permanence of Paper for Printed Library Materials,
ANSI Z39.48-1984

CONTENTS

INTRODUCTION

The four murder cases and the subsequent criminal trials analyzed in this book are among the most sensational in American history. As primordial dramas involving murder within or against a socially prominent family, the Lizzie Borden, Lindbergh baby, Sam Sheppard, and O. J. Simpson cases riveted the public.

These murder cases, scattered across a century, were not merely sensational but highly revealing as well. While historians have long recognized the significance of famous political trials, such as the Sacco and Vanzetti case, the Scottsboro boys, or the Chicago Seven, they have paid less attention to sensational murder cases. In fact, however, such cases have a great deal to teach us about American history, culture, and jurisprudence.

These dramas converge at an intersection of crime, law, journalism, and culture. All four cases spurred feverish public interest and saturated media coverage. Each represented—in varying degrees—a miscarriage of justice.

All four cases offer insight into the evolution of the American criminal justice system, the role of the media, and the larger cultural milieu. The four case studies demonstrate how deeply issues such as gender, ethnicity, class, and race influence high-profile judicial proceedings. They underscore the prevalence and implications of police and judicial incompetence. They show us, in short, just how fragile American justice can be, especially in high-profile cases.

The Lizzie Borden case reveals the extent to which patriarchal culture influenced criminal justice in late-Victorian America. In the Lindbergh case, New Jersey officials denied Bruno Richard Hauptmann legal protections and access to the evidence against him—legal rights of criminal defendants that are taken for granted today. The Sheppard case, conducted in a McCarthy-era witch-hunt atmosphere, became a "trial by newspaper," ultimately spurring a landmark 1966 U.S. Supreme Court decision. The O. J. Simpson case became a referendum on American race relations, while at the same time calling into question for many the very legitimacy of the U.S. criminal justice system.

The Simpson case, perceived by millions of (mostly white) Americans as an outrageous perversion of justice, was not nearly as anomalous as contemporary observers seemed to believe. The comparative historical analysis offered in this study reveals that the Simpson case was rather typical of celebrity trials. In the Simpson investigation and trial, as in the other three cases analyzed in this book, pressures flowing from overwhelming public attention upset the delicate processes of justice. The actors in the criminal justice system—police, prosecutors, defense attorneys, judges, and juries—succumbed in varying degrees to the external pressures that roiled the administration of justice.

Publicity played an enormous role, heightening both the hype and the controversy surrounding all four cases. Sensational media coverage inundated the courtroom proceedings, requiring each trial to be conducted in a carnival-like atmosphere. Popular trials such as the four studied here contain all the features that captivate the public: drama, narrative, rhetoric, and advocacy. Such cases tend to obscure the criminal or legal issues in question, as they provide an opportunity to advance other causes before, during, and after the courtroom proceedings. As Robert Harriman has pointed out in *Popular Trials: Rhetoric, Mass Media, and the Law* (1990), "Trials function in this way as forums for debate, as symbols of larger constellations of belief and action, and as social dramas used to manage emotional responses to troubling situations."

These cases became mesmerizing national dramas because they brought to the surface cultural tensions that transcended the courtroom. The Lizzie Borden case cannot be understood absent consideration of class and gender roles in Victorian America. Similarly, nativism and xenophobia served to condemn Bruno Richard Hauptmann well before his trial began. Dr. Sheppard's fate stemmed from class anxieties and disgraceful journalism in Cleveland. Finally, a long history of arbitrary authority, police violence, and discrimination under the law against African-Americans enabled Simpson's defense team to win his freedom by exploiting popular black perceptions of racial injustice.

Although the verdicts in these cases were issued in a hall of justice, in reality they were decided in the proverbial court of public opinion. In each case community sentiment—American culture writ large—overwhelmed the judicial process. As a result, all four cases represented (to one degree or another) a perversion of the processes of criminal justice. If the history of these murder cases offers any guide, we may conclude that sensational trials almost invariably invoke broad cultural issues that threaten the administration of justice on its own merits.

While these cases offer insight into the history of American culture and jurisprudence, at the same time they tap into the natural human fascination with mystery and evil that lies at the core of public interest in murder narratives. Moreover, these cases are fascinating whodunits—even if, as is usually the case, the answer to that question is clear. One of my purposes is to put to rest some of the alternative theories that proliferate about these four sensational crimes. A few years back, while writing a biography of Charles A. Lindbergh, I thumbed through some of the popular literature on the kidnapping and murder of the Lindbergh baby. I was appalled at the prospect that large numbers of people might actually believe some of the fatuous theories about the Lindbergh crime that had found their way into print.

Looking into the Lizzie Borden case, I discovered another collection of schlock literature on those infamous murders. Meanwhile, as a resident of northeast Ohio, I followed with fascination revelations about the Sheppard murder case. And like many Americans, I was captivated by the Simpson trial, with all its implications for race relations and criminal justice administration in the United States.

As a result of the enduring public interest and cultural significance of these cases, all four have secured a place in American history, legend, and folklore. The Borden murders have generated thousands of articles, scores of books, plays, novels, movies, and even an entire journal devoted to Lizzie Borden and the crime. The Lindbergh crime has spurred a large and still growing popular literature as well as movies and documentaries. In the mid-1960s, the Sheppard case inspired the famous television series *The Fugitive,* starring David Janssen as Dr. Richard Kimble, a physician who escaped prison for a life on the run after being falsely accused of murdering his wife. The Sheppard case was still being litigated in 2000, as the Cleveland physician's son pursued a wrongful imprisonment suit against the State of Ohio. The Simpson case prompted a shelf full of memoirs, legal analyses, reflections on racial injustice, and a spate of television docudramas.

As the stuff of history, legend, and folklore, the Borden, Lindbergh, Sheppard, and Simpson cases will continue to attract public attention and scrutiny. The interpretive history that follows thus enters into a collective national discourse on some of the most sensational crimes of the century.

In order to make this book more accessible, I have not used footnotes. The critical bibliography at the end of the book addresses the primary and secondary sources upon which my account rests.

Since no one (other than the killers and their victims, of course) was present when these crimes took place, the precise train of events that occurred in each incident will never be known. I do not know exactly how or when the Lindbergh baby was killed, nor what tool (probably a screwdriver, but perhaps a flashlight) Marilyn Sheppard's killer used to subdue her. For the purposes of dramatic effect, however, I have taken the liberty in the first few paragraphs of each case study to exercise my historical imagination as to how these murders might have been committed. These paragraphs represent a plausible reconstruction, but the technique employed is essentially that of the novelist rather than of the historian.

Except for those opening paragraphs of each chapter, however (those appearing in italic type) this is a work of history. Evidence supports the facts as I present them. Interpretations, of course, are strictly my own.

Although none of the persons listed below bears responsibility for the book's content, I would like to acknowledge the following individuals for their critical reading of all or parts of the manuscript: Abel Bartley, T. J. Boisseau, Michael J. Carley, Barbara Evans Clements, J. Richard Downey, Mark W. Falzini, Mindy Nelle Fetterman, Emma Hixson, Kandy L. Hixson, Sheryl Stevenson, and two anonymous reviewers for the University of Akron Press.

Lizzie Borden, at age 33, as she appeared a year after the murders. She was active in the Central Congregational Church, Christian Endeavor, the Women's Christian Temperance Union, and the Fruit and Flower Mission. Given Miss Lizzie's appearance of schoolmarmish normality, most residents of Fall River found it difficult to conceive of her carrying out the brutal hatchet murders. Courtesy Fall River Historical Society

I GENDERED JUSTICE

LIZZIE BORDEN AND VICTORIAN AMERICA

The old woman crashed to the floor, face first, with a reverberating thump. The killer sprang over her, wielding the hatchet maniacally. Blood and clumps of scalp flew in the air.

The corpulent old woman lay still now, her arms trapped awkwardly under her body, but still the blows of rage came down, nineteen in all. A puddle of blood flowed from her head as she lay dying between the framed bed and a large mirrored bureau on the far side of the upstairs guestroom.

There was no time to waste. The killer straightened up, dripping with perspiration as it was another hot summer day—August 4, 1892—in Fall River, Massachusetts.

The killer hurried downstairs, wiping off the blood-soaked weapon—for the killer intended to strike again.

After more than an hour, an interminable ticking away of the minutes, the dead woman's husband came home at last. Old man Borden went upstairs for a few moments, but he used a separate set of stairs on the other side of the house and was in no position to discover his wife's corpse. Knowing well the old man's habits, the murderer was not surprised when he came back downstairs and made ready to lie down on his couch in the parlor for a habitual midday nap. It would be his last.

The old man was already breathing rhythmically as the killer crept behind the door that opened into the parlor. Old man Borden's arms lay folded at his midsection. His legs, too long to rest comfortably on the upholstered mahogany couch, angled to the floor. The killer took a deep breath and drove the hatchet into the center of the old man's face. He never budged from his recumbent position.

The killer's rage took hold again as the blows, twelve in all, crashed into the victim's head with a sickening sound. The killer continued to strike, even after the blade ripped one of the old man's eyes from its socket and left it dangling on his cheek. Heart pounding with an almost surreal excitement, the killer disposed of the weapon.

Moments later, the old man's daughter appeared at the parlor door and screamed for the family maid, who was resting upstairs: "Maggie! Come down quick," she wailed. "Father's dead . . . Someone came in and killed him!"

Despite the passage of more than a century, the Lizzie Borden case remains one of the most notorious crimes in American history. The allegation of female parricide, with a hatchet no less, immediately made the case a national sensation. At first, however, the sheer brutality of the murders was enough to convince most people that no woman could have been responsible for such crimes. Most of the public rejected the possibility that the daughter of the elderly dead couple could have been responsible for the murders.

At the time of the murders Lizbeth Andrew "Lizzie" Borden was thirty-two years old. She was five-feet, four-inches tall with light hair, typically parted in the middle and kept in a bun. Lizzie's most distinctive feature, however, was her protruding gray eyes.

Neither Lizzie Borden nor her sister Emma, aged forty-two at the time of the killings, ever married or even appears to have come close to the altar. Unmarried women today are not remarkable enough to be burdened with such an unflattering appellation as "spinster," but the same was not true in their era.

The culture of Victorian America not only denied women the vote and the right to hold political office, but defined their very identity in terms of their relationship to a man. A married woman's place in nineteenth-century America was in the home in service of husband and family, as clergymen and society columnists repeatedly reminded them. Without husbands, spinsters such as Emma and Lizzie, though mature adults, were nonetheless relegated to a life-long existence under the roof of their father, Andrew Jackson Borden.

The Victorian "cult of domesticity," widely perceived as biologically determined, confined women's activities to the home, church, and female social clubs. Although denied citizenship and political rights, women were viewed as morally superior to men, whose aggressive, amoral instincts they were charged with tempering in the domestic sphere. By the late nineteenth century, however, as urban-industrial growth began to sever traditional bonds of community, many women began to challenge Victorian norms. Such desires played a pivotal role in the Borden case.

Lizzie, to be sure, took advantage of the few opportunities that were available to her outside the home in the Victorian cultural milieu of Fall River. After attending but apparently not completing high school, she became active in the Central Congregational Church, Christian Endeavor, the Women's Christian Temperance Union, and the Fruit and Flower Mission. Despite her involvement with these groups, Lizzie maintained only a small circle of friends. Those who knew her often described the younger Borden sister as eccentric and retiring.

Lizzie and Emma certainly had been left scarred by the death of their mother in 1862, when Lizzie was just two years old. Sarah J. Morse had married Andrew Borden in 1845 and the couple had had three daughters, one of whom, Alice, had died in infancy.

Two years after his wife's death, following an altogether proper interval of mourning, Andrew Borden proposed marriage to another Fall River spinster, thirty-eight-year-old Abby Durfee Gray, who promptly accepted. In Abby, Andrew had found a wife to manage his home as well as a mother to care for his daughters. But neither Emma nor Lizzie developed a deep bond of love with their stepmother. Emma, smaller and plainer looking than Lizzie, never called Abby "Mother." Although Lizzie, ten years younger than her sister, did for a time refer to Abby as "Mother," she soon renounced use of all terms of endearment for her stepmother.

While tensions simmered beneath the surface in the Borden home, in Fall River society Andrew and Abby were a respected, if not particularly appealing, couple. The Borden family name had long been known in with Fall River. Andrew's forbears, English immigrants Richard and Joan Borden, had arrived in Portsmouth, Rhode Island, in 1638. The family later moved to Fall River. In 1892, there were listings for 131 Borden households in the Fall River city directory.

Andrew Borden, approaching age seventy at the time of his death, was tall and austere. He dressed in black cloth, typical of men in the era, and wore a thin white beard that wrapped around his chin from sideburn to sideburn. He was well known in Fall River as a successful but notoriously tight-fisted businessman. "No other man knew the worth of a dollar better than he," wrote Fall River journalist Edwin Porter.

Abby Durfee Borden, approaching her sixty-fourth birthday at the time of the murders, was a decent but dull and plodding individual. While Andrew accumulated wealth, Abby accumulated girth. Though small of stature, she weighed more than 200 pounds at the time of her death.

Both Andrew and Abby came from good stock. Indeed, their marriage was typical of the way that a handful of families maintained control of the economic and social structure of Fall River. The Bordens, Durfees, Buffingtons, Chases, and other prominent families owned the mills and the shops that dominated the community's economic life.

Providentially situated along water routes to the sea, Fall River emerged at the center of New England textile milling at a time of transformation of the United States from a predominantly agrarian to a predominantly urban-industrial society. The city's population growth and economic development had been little short of phenomenal. From a population of 56,870 in 1885, the city grew to 74,398 in 1890 and 104,864 in 1900. By that time immigrants comprised more than half the city's population. English and Irish immigrants came first to work in the city's textile mills and in the related dyeing and finishing industries. Large numbers of Portuguese immigrants followed. By the time of the Borden murders the largest wave of immigrants were French Canadians who flocked south for work in the Fall River mills. Although Jewish immigrants, mostly from eastern Europe, had "proved good citizens," the *Fall River Daily Globe* observed that "it is doubtful if additions to their numbers by thousands or even hundreds would be welcome."

The textile mills lured immigrants (including child laborers), fueled Fall River's growth, and helped insulate the city from the boom and bust cycles of late-nineteenth-century American capitalism. Indeed, the mills so dominated life that some referred to Fall River as Spindle City or the Manchester of America.

A city still characterized by wide streets filled with dirt, mud, and horse dung, Fall River was nonetheless modernizing rapidly. A magnificent new high school opened in 1886 and three years later the city's Iron Works factory boasted the tallest smokestack in the nation. In 1890 more than two million passengers rode on horse-drawn street railway cars. Tennis and baseball were the most popular sports.

Through the hard work and discipline that personified the age, Andrew Borden had capitalized on Fall River's growth to amass a fortune. Starting off as a fish peddler, Borden branched off into undertaking, then mill works, banking, farming, and real estate. He was president of the Union Savings Bank and well connected in other banks and mills in the community. Respected for his keen business judgment, Borden was frequently called on to appraise land and property. At the time of his death the value of Andrew Borden's savings, investments, and real properties approached half a million dollars, a vast sum in 1892.

The problem with her father's wealth, as far as Lizzie Borden was concerned, was his unwillingness to part with the money he made. As writer Victoria Lincoln once observed, Lizzie "loved money to spend as much as her father loved money to keep." As Fall River grew and prospered Lizzie and Emma longed to make the most of their prescribed roles as homebound spinsters. Lizzie aspired to live in comfort, dress in the latest fashions, entertain her small circle of friends, and travel regularly in both in the United States and abroad. She longed to take her rightful place as an elite member of provincial society, and to do it in style.

Nothing better symbolized Andrew's old-fashioned contempt for such aspirations as the Borden family home at 92 Second Street in Fall River. In a city whose neighborhoods were rigidly divided along class lines, Andrew insisted on remaining in the home that the family had inhabited since 1871. The narrow two-and-a-half-story frame dwelling in downtown Fall River was close to the mills and to neighborhoods teeming with immigrant working-class families. Their wealthy father's refusal to better their surroundings left the Borden women to endure the dust, the putrid odors of raw sewage and horse manure, and the noise and bustle of the inner city.

Originally built for two families, the Borden home itself had no hallways and required separate stairways to access the upstairs bedrooms. In order to reach the Bordens' bedroom, one had to take the stairs off the kitchen. To reach the rooms of Emma, Lizzie, and the guest quarters, one would have to mount a separate set of stairs off the front entrance. A locked door between the two large upstairs bedrooms sealed the division of the family home.

The Borden home was adequately furnished but Andrew, ever the stubborn traditionalist, eschewed the modern comforts of central plumbing and electric or gas lighting. The Bordens relieved themselves in "necessary pots," or in a single basement water closet. Refusing to hook up to the gas main, Andrew lit the

The Borden home, 92 Second Street, in Fall River, Massachusetts. Although Andrew Borden could easily have afforded to purchase an upscale home in the city's Hill district, he refused. Lizzie Borden resented having to live in the traditional downtown dwelling. Inside the home, the Borden "family" divided itself with locked doors, separate stairways, and separate meal services. Courtesy Fall River Historical Society

home with kerosene lamps or, as he often preferred, simply sat in the dark at night.

While the 1890s were an exciting time for many, with new conveniences and consumer goods becoming available, Andrew Borden typically disdained such amenities. As the American frontier closed, and a modern urban society began to emerge, the old man clung to the past. Lizzie, who wanted nothing more than to use the family wealth to enjoy a comfortable modern lifestyle, languished in the old home with its frayed carpets, outmoded furniture, and scratchy horsehair upholstery.

Their father's parsimony, and his refusal to change with the times, infuriated Lizzie Borden. Although Emma, too, bitterly resented the situation in the Borden household, it was Lizzie—by far the more stubborn, outspoken, brooding, and volatile of the sisters—who took action to liberate herself from an oppressive existence.

Lizzie longed to live on the Hill, the elite northern part of the city whose high ground provided a spectacular overlook to Mount Hope Bay and the wide, deep blue Taunton River. Relegated to a life under their father's roof, the status-conscious Borden girls continually pressed the old man to purchase one of the sturdy Victorian homes on the Hill so that they might take their rightful place in Fall River society. Andrew Borden steadfastly refused and angrily dismissed his daughters for their meddling. After all, it was not the place of the girls to interfere with the decisions of the family patriarch. Besides, his daughters enjoyed the benefit of a live-in maid and lacked for no essentials. Both Lizzie and Emma received a weekly allowance, though, typical of their father, it was a miserly sum amounting to about $200 a year.

As if the denial of their proper station in life had not been grating enough, Lizzie and Emma became convinced that their father had begun to favor their stepmother over his own daughters. The incident that ignited a jealous rage within Lizzie occurred in 1887, when the daughters learned that their father had purchased a dwelling for Abby's sister and her husband, who had fallen on hard times. When the girls discovered that their normally tight-fisted father had deeded the modest property to Abby, they were livid.

Darkly suspicious of their father's alleged favoritism toward their unloved stepmother, Emma and Lizzie now suspected that Abby and their uncle, John Vinnicum Morse, sought to deny them their rightful share of the Borden property in their father's will. Morse was the brother of Sarah, Andrew Borden's first wife, but the daughters were not close to Uncle John, who had lived "out West" (in Iowa) for most of their lives.

The sisters complained bitterly to their father that they had never received a gift comparable to the dwelling purchased for Abby's family members. Andrew responded to his daughters' angry protests by deeding to them a roughly equivalent piece of property once owned by their grandfather. They were not mollified, however.

The incident wounded Lizzie deeply. She felt betrayed by the only man she had ever loved, her father. Not even a trip to Europe on a church mission improved her disposition. The damage had been done and the dysfunctional relationships inside the Borden household cascaded toward tragedy.

From the moment the home was purchased and put into Abby's name, Lizzie pointedly refused to call her "Mother." She now referred to Abby only as "Mrs. Borden." When an acquaintance made reference to her mother, Lizzie promptly interjected that Abby was not her mother, but her stepmother, and "a mean old thing" at that. Even more ominous, the family ceased to eat their meals together, as Emma and Lizzie insisted on being served separately. These tensions required the family maid, Bridget Sullivan, a twenty-six-year-old Irish immigrant who the family referred to as "Maggie," to offer separate meal services at breakfast, dinner, and supper. Aided by their individual stairways and locked doors, the Borden family was irrevocably divided against itself.

Lizzie continued to display compulsive anger not only in bitter arguments with her father, but through her actions outside the home. Most people knew Lizzie as a good Christian and active club woman, but others knew her as something else: a shoplifter. According to Victoria Lincoln, herself a lifelong resident of Fall River and a noted chronicler of the Borden murders, Lizzie regularly pilfered items from downtown department stores. Borden scholar Joyce G. Williams reports that Fall River sources confirmed to her that Lizzie was a known shoplifter.

The depiction of Lizzie as a shoplifter appears credible. Shoplifting from modern department stores by middle-class women in fact emerged as a significant social phenomenon in the late nineteenth century. The issue was inextricably linked with gender. The modern department store, with its array of appealing and colorfully displayed merchandise, catered to the needs and fantasies of women such as Lizzie, whose lives in reality were rigidly controlled by patriarchal norms. The physical environment of the department store represented freedom and escape. The removal of its goods was a tangible reward in defiance of the limitations imposed on women, like Lizzie, who lacked economic autonomy and control over their own lives.

Forced to grapple with female shoplifting, department store managers, police, judges, physicians, clergy, and others determined that kleptomania—a new term that purported to explain the phenomenon—stemmed not from women's deprivations, which the male power structure refused to acknowledge, but from biology. This "mania" was part of the peculiar female life cycle, including the stress of monthly menstruation, that explained women's often-irrational behavior, according to Victorian pseudoscience on womanhood. As Elaine S.

Abelson explains in a fascinating book on the subject, shoplifting became "part of the collective identity of middle-class women" and as such "legitimated existing notions of gender and the structural inequality of Victorian society."

The uniquely female medical condition of kleptomania provided a quasi-medical rationale to avoid depicting women as mere thieves, a charge that would have violated the Victorian image of women as pious and pure. Instead, female shoplifters were depicted as childlike, unstable, and unable to control their urges when confronted with shelf after shelf of so many colorful and desirable products.

While the theft of property by women could be so explained, it could hardly be overlooked. As a result, cases were often dealt with in the manner that characterized the thefts committed by Lizzie Borden. The man "in charge" of the woman, sometimes a husband but in this case Lizzie's father, Andrew Borden, would be quietly contacted to make good on his daughter's "charges" in such a way that no criminal action needed to be taken and a public scandal could be avoided.

Professor Williams notes that psychologists have identified several motivations for shoplifting that Lizzie Borden seemed to share. These include feelings of deprivation, suffering of real or imaginary injustices, and lack of parental love and support. "I think Lizzie Borden shoplifted early because she thought she was badly treated at home and that she deserved nice things," Williams writes. "I think she thought the world owed her and she was balancing the score."

As the family crisis escalated in the months leading up to the murders, Lizzie exported her criminal behavior from the department stores to her own home. She was the only logical suspect in a supposed burglary of the Borden home in the early summer of 1892. Some money, streetcar tickets, and jewelry belonging to Abby—increasingly the target of Lizzie's wrath—disappeared, but no one saw anything or had a clue as to how a burglar could have entered into a notoriously well-fortified home in daylight, penetrating a series of double and triple-locked and barred doors through Lizzie's own bedroom and all the way to her parents' chambers. Andrew at first summoned the police, but discontinued the investigation when he realized that only his youngest daughter could have committed the crime.

The tensions inside the Borden home were reaching a critical mass. But what precipitated the homicidal outburst of August 4, 1892? Historians and Borden murder case aficionados have been asking that question for more than a century.

Some theories have more credence than others. Some are highly creative. The writer Victoria Lincoln argued that Lizzie had been dreaming of killing Abby, but actually did so only in the grip of an epileptic seizure that coincided with her menstrual cycle. Lincoln explains that Lizzie suffered from "peculiar spells" and notes that some epileptic seizures are medically associated with female menstruation. While intriguing, this theory of the Borden murders is not, however, bolstered by evidence.

Another theory holds that Lizzie was a victim of sexual abuse by her father. She may have blamed her stepmother for allowing her father to abuse her, hence the attack on Abby as well as on Andrew. The locked doors, familial sep- aration, and the fact that Lizzie and Emma had swapped bedrooms at one point are cited as evidence to bolster this argument. This theory is intriguing. A histo- ry of sexual abuse might account for the rage that Lizzie displayed in bashing in the skulls of her elderly parents. Certainly such abuse was not unknown in Vic- torian families. No evidence of sexual abuse exists, but we would expect none in an era which disdained public discussion of even "normal" sexuality. From all that we know, however, it seems clear that accumulation of money, not sexual gratification, was Andrew Borden's driving obsession.

The impetus for the Borden murders appears to have been a combination of avarice, status anxiety, and accumulated rage on the part of an unstable young woman over her powerlessness in a patriarchal world.

The Borden household reached a crescendo of contentiousness in the weeks before the murders. Still bitter over their financial limitations, Lizzie and Emma complained that the rental property their father had deeded them in compen- sation for the house put in Abby's name was more trouble than it was worth. The sisters made only a pittance on the rents. Two weeks before the murders Andrew bought the rental property back from his daughters for $5,000, some $2,000 more than it was worth.

The settlement with Andrew left a bitter taste, but what is more, Lizzie apparently feared that her aging father intended to turn over still more of his wealth and property to her stepmother. Lizzie might have suspected that Andrew planned to sign over to their stepmother the family farm, just across the Taunton River to the west in Swansea, where Lizzie and Emma had frolicked in their youth. Uncle John Morse, who arrived at the Borden home the night before the murders, may have been summoned to discuss that very issue.

No doubt adding to the tensions in the Borden household were the discomforts of a brutal summer heat wave. The local press reported that the heat wave killed ninety persons—sixty-five of them children, mostly of poor immigrant families—in Fall River alone in the weeks before the Borden murders.

With Emma on an extended visit with a friend in Fairhaven, some fifteen miles away, Lizzie was left alone to contemplate the prospect of the family fortune slipping from the sisters' grasp. She may have feared being completely disinherited by her father, who had grown fed up with the antics of his contentious younger daughter.

Like Lizzie herself, Andrew Borden was stubborn and vindictive. He was a man who enjoyed collecting his rents on time and in person. Lacking sentiment, he ignored tenants' sob stories and was more than willing to boot them out with little notice for failure to make their payments. At the time of his death the wealthy Borden patriarch still sold eggs on the street for a few pennies.

Andrew Borden was the man of the house and determined not to give in to Lizzie's demands. Given the absence of communication in the Borden family, Lizzie may not have known what, if anything, Andrew had in mind concerning the family property, but she would have been inclined to assume the worst. Still bitter over the previous transfer, Lizzie clearly was not the type to idly stand by while her father perfidiously shifted his wealth into the hands of her contemptible stepmother.

It appears that Lizzie first tried to poison her parents on the evening of Tuesday, August 2, and Wednesday, August 3. Both Mr. and Mrs. Borden suffered from severe cramps and vomiting. Maggie (Bridget), who lived in a cubicle in the attic, also became ill. Lizzie claimed that she, too, had fallen sick. It is always possible, but not likely under the circumstances, that the hot weather had spoiled something they had eaten—certainly not an uncommon occurrence in the absence of home refrigeration. Abby did not think that was the case, however.

On August 3 Abby summoned Dr. Seabury Bowen, a physician and family friend who lived across the street. While Mrs. Borden insisted they had been poisoned, Andrew, penny-pinching to the end, blasted the doctor for appearing at the family home without his personal authorization and let him know in no uncertain terms that he would not be paid for a house call. Once again, Andrew may have known or suspected that Lizzie lay behind the incident. He may have been trying to keep the crisis within the family, even though the Borden family was pathetically ill equipped to cope with its tragic dysfunction.

That same day, Wednesday, August 3, Uncle John Morse, sixty-nine years old, tall, white haired, and mustached, arrived at the Borden home. Morse, after moving back to Massachusetts from an Iowa farm, managed some of Andrew Borden's properties. Andrew counted Morse as one of his few close friends. Both were hard-working and frugal men of the old school. Lizzie may have gotten wind of Uncle John's impending visit or it may have taken her by surprise.

Having failed in the first effort, Lizzie tried to buy a more deadly poison, in the form of the highly toxic prussic acid, on Wednesday. She was unsuccessful. That evening Lizzie visited a friend, Alice Russell, well known to both Borden sisters but actually a closer friend of Emma's.

The purpose of Lizzie's visit appears to have been a crude effort to cast suspicion for the impending premeditated murders onto someone else. Lizzie told Miss Russell of the illnesses, claiming that the family's milk had been poisoned by some dark external force. "I feel afraid sometimes that Father has got an enemy," she explained. The Borden barn had been broken into, she added breathlessly, and people had been seen lurking around the house. "I am afraid somebody will do something!" Lizzie concluded dramatically.

When Lizzie returned home that evening, she came through the front door and went straight up to her room. She did not speak to her father, her stepmother, or Uncle John, all of whom sat conversing in the dark in the adjacent front room.

It must have been a strange night indeed in the Borden home. Abby and Andrew may have suspected that Lizzie had attempted to poison them. Andrew, in a rare outburst of loquaciousness, had told a business associate that week that there was "a lot of trouble in the house." The Bordens and Uncle John undoubtedly discussed these matters, perhaps even including what to do about Lizzie, even as she lay alone upstairs plotting a course of her own.

The conditions were ripe for violence. Emma, still away on her visit at the home of a Mrs. Brownell in Fairhaven, was not there to exercise a calming influence on her volatile younger sister.

The extreme heat wave had begun to abate but it was still a hot summer morning when Lizzie came down from her room between 8:50 and 9 A.M. on August 4. Maggie served Lizzie a cup of coffee as she sampled a cookie in the kitchen. The Bordens and Uncle John had arisen earlier. Morse had left to visit relatives, who would later attest to his whereabouts at the time of the murders. Andrew, as was his custom following breakfast, went downtown to attend to business matters. Only Abby, Lizzie, and Maggie now remained in the Second Street home. Maggie, apparently having eaten some of the poisoned or spoiled food, became ill and went out to the backyard to vomit. When she returned inside, she went to work washing the lower-floor windows, inside and out.

Sometime between 9 and 9:30 Abby was attacked in the upstairs guestroom where Uncle John had slept. She received nineteen blows to the head and back. There was no sign of a struggle and relatively little blood spattering considering the savagery of the attack.

Later, neither Maggie nor Lizzie, of course, reported hearing the corpulent Mrs. Borden's body hit the floor. Maggie remained outside washing windows, though she had passed some time chatting across the fence with the domestic servant of the neighboring Mrs. Kelly. By the time Maggie returned inside the killer would have had time to clean up and conceal the murder weapon.

As Maggie began cleaning the windows on the inside of the house, Andrew Borden returned home at 10:40 A.M. He found the side door not only locked from the outside, as was customary, but bolted on the inside, as was not customary. Hearing the old man grousing and fumbling with his keys, Maggie rushed to let him in. As she opened the door Lizzie stood on the stairway above . . . and laughed.

Lizzie came down the stairs and asked Mr. Borden a question about the mail. He mumbled a response and queried Lizzie as to the whereabouts of Mrs. Borden. Maggie heard Lizzie explain that Abby had received a note from a friend who had fallen ill and had gone to attend to her. Andrew went up to his bedroom through the back stairway, making the familiar trek for the last time in his life, before returning to the front sitting room. He had no reason to check the upstairs guestroom at the top of another set of stairs on the other side of the house, where Mrs. Borden lay dead in a pool of congealed blood.

Andrew Borden was old, tired, still recovering from the vomiting illness, and it was a hot summer day. He lay down for his customary noontime nap, almost an hour earlier than usual. Andrew put a pillow under his head, let his legs fall to the floor, and closed his eyes for the last time.

As Maggie washed windows in the dining room, Lizzie accommodated her nervous energy by setting up an ironing board on the dining-room table. While ironing a few handkerchiefs, she suggested that Maggie might wish to go shopping—there was a sale downtown on yard goods. Maggie allowed that she would go instead to her room in the attic for a short rest, as was her habit before returning downstairs to prepare the midday meal.

Only a few minutes later, Lizzie screamed for Maggie. The maid came rushing down the stairs, but did not go into the room where Lizzie's father lay bludgeoned to death. Lizzie ordered Maggie to run across the street to summon Dr. Bowen.

In so doing, Lizzie displayed no fear, as her accusers later pointed out, that a hatchet-wielding maniac might still be about the premises. Such fear, if not outright terror, would have been the normal reaction for a daughter suddenly confronted with the macabre spectacle of her father bludgeoned to death, his eyeball hanging on his cheek and his head oozing blood.

As Maggie prepared to go and summon Dr. Bowen, she thought to ask the logical question: "Miss Lizzie, where were you when this happened?"

"I was in the yard and heard a groan," Lizzie replied, "and came in and the screen door was wide open."

As the frightened maid ran from the home to the doctor's house across the street, the Borden's next-door neighbor, Mrs. Adelaide Churchill, returning to her home on foot, witnessed the chaotic scene. Seeing Lizzie standing in the screen door, hands on her head and looking "distressed," Mrs. Churchill called out to ask Lizzie what was wrong.

"Oh, Mrs. Churchill, do come over," Lizzie replied. "Somebody has killed father."

Dr. Bowen entered the Borden home shortly after Mrs. Churchill and quickly confirmed that Andrew Borden was dead. Noting no sign of a struggle, the doctor concluded that the old man had obviously been attacked in his sleep. "Murdered," he declared. "He's been murdered." The police were called at 11:15 A.M.

Maggie, who had heard Lizzie tell her father that Mrs. Borden had gotten a note and gone out, raised the question of informing Abby of her husband's

Andrew Borden never moved from the awkward recumbent position, legs dangling to the floor, that he had adopted for his midday nap on August 4, 1892. The killer struck from behind and delivered twelve blows with a hatchet to the old man's face. Andrew Borden's wife, Abby Durfee Borden, already lay dead upstairs, having absorbed nineteen blows to the head. Altogether, the killer struck 31 times, rather than the "forty whacks" of the popular ditty. Courtesy Fall River Historical Society

death. At this point, Maggie recalled, Lizzie "said she was positive she [had] heard [Mrs. Borden] coming in, and would we not go upstairs and see." Mrs. Churchill, too, clearly recalled hearing Lizzie make this statement.

Lizzie's claim that she had heard Mrs. Borden return raises the question as to why Lizzie had called out to the maid in the attic rather than her stepmother on the second floor, who presumably would have been the logical person to inform about the discovery of her dead father.

At the time, Maggie, displaying the rational fear of a murderous intruder that Lizzie so notably lacked, refused to ascend the stairs alone in search of Mrs. Borden. She consented to Lizzie's request only when Mrs. Churchill agreed to go with her.

As the two of them reached the turn of the stairs—where Lizzie had stood laughing when her father arrived home—they saw Abby's body on the other side of the bed. Dr. Bowen, who had left the house briefly to place a call to Emma, now returned to examine the body of the second—though actually the first—murder victim. He immediately noticed that Abby's blood had coagulated, whereas Andrew's still dripped from his battered skull.

On the day of the most sensational crime in Fall River's history, two-thirds of the city police were out of town for their annual clambake. Nonetheless, City Marshal Philip Harrington remained on the job and quickly dispatched officers to the scene of the carnage.

In a city filled with poor immigrants and underpaid workers, the police immediately looked for signs of robbery or forced entry. There were none. The police found the house in "perfect order." All doors and windows were locked and there was no evidence of struggle. Andrew Borden's watch and cash remained on his body. Indeed, as Lizzie herself confirmed, nothing was missing from the home.

Marshal Harrington arrived at 12:20 and, after surveying the scene, questioned Lizzie Borden in her upstairs room. He noted that Lizzie remained the calmest person on the scene. Indeed, police reports show how Victorian gender mores, which Lizzie would later exploit to her benefit in the courtroom, at first served to cast suspicion on her. One police officer searching the scene recalled that he was "surprised at the way she carried herself and I must say that I admire her nerve. I did not think that a woman could have so much . . . I have wondered why she did not faint upon the discovery of the dead body of her father."

In response to Harrington's questions, Lizzie stated that she had not seen or heard anything suspicious that morning. She added, however, that her father had had a heated argument over a business dispute with an unknown man in the Borden home "a few weeks ago."

What aroused Harrington's suspicions about Lizzie herself was not only her remarkably calm demeanor, but her story that she had been out in the barn loft for twenty minutes that morning. The loft, Harrington reasoned, was just about the last place anyone would choose to be in the August heat, and Lizzie's reasons for being there were contradictory.

By the time Harrington questioned Lizzie a huge crowd had gathered outside the Borden home. Many mill workers simply walked off their jobs when news of the savage murders filtered through the community. As Edwin Porter later wrote, "At high noon on Thursday the fourth day of August, 1892, the cry of murder swept through Fall River like a typhoon on the smooth surface of an eastern sea." Talk of an axe-wielding madman on the loose permeated the streets of Fall River. People stood outside the Borden home and "stared with open-mouthed amazement."

During the 1890s, an era known for its sensational yellow journalism, it was not uncommon for newspapers, the sole source of mass communication, to report rumors and unconfirmed allegations. This was especially true in towns like Fall River where the papers competed with one another for readership. On the evening of the murders the *Fall River Daily Herald* headlined the "shocking crime . . . at the hands of a drunken park hand."

The newspaper report reflected the widespread view on the part of the middle-class citizens of Fall River that a crime so foul could only have been committed by a person of the lower orders, probably one of the city's dark-skinned Portuguese immigrants. Many whites of old New England Puritan stock, unnerved by the unprecedented wave of immigration in recent years, had embraced racist and nativist attitudes. That a woman might have committed such vicious crimes was far from almost everyone's thoughts.

On August 5, however, the *Daily Herald* acknowledged that the initial reports "that a Portuguese had done it" were now "looked on with suspicion." Still, "nothing but the murder was talked about on the streets." The newspaper contained an offer of a $5,000 reward by Emma and Lizzie Borden for information about the murder of their parents.

Although the press reported "no clue yet as to perpetrator," in fact suspicion gradually began to fall on Lizzie Borden. On the streets people talked about the poor relations between Lizzie and her parents, noting that Lizzie had been at the home at the time of the murders and thus had had opportunity as well as motive.

Another even more bizarre night had passed in the Borden home, with

Lizzie, Emma, their friend Alice Russell, and Uncle John Morse all sleeping upstairs while the two dead bodies, stripped and covered with sheets, lay downstairs.

Some seventy-five persons attended a private service the next morning in the Borden parlor. There was a reading of Scriptures and prayer, but no singing or remarks. After the service, police set up barricades to control a throng of three to four thousand as the bodies were taken to the Oak Grove Cemetery.

Lizzie herself continued to appear strangely unaffected by the train of events, but a growing legion of defenders energetically dismissed what they perceived as vicious rumors sullying the reputation of a good Christian woman. To their minds, the notion that a woman, let alone a daughter, could perpetrate such violence against her parents was simply illogical. Victorian culture did not allow the possibility that a woman of Lizzie's standing in the community could commit such a crime.

The majority of Fall River residents was appalled that poor Lizzie had to endure such baseless charges on top of the shock of discovering her parents slaughtered by a madman. Lizzie's defenders repeated her own suggestion that the murders must be connected with the previous break-in and the threats against her father by either an angry business associate or one of the old man's tenants. Lizzie's partisans emphasized the Borden sisters' prompt public offer of the $5,000 reward for identification of the murderer. The Borden family attorney, Andrew Jennings, rejected rumors of any involvement by Lizzie, noting "the improbability that any woman could do such a piece of work."

Lizzie's defenders also noted that Jennings had hired O. M. Hanscom, from the Boston office of the Pinkerton Detective Agency, to look into the murders. The Pinkertons were the most respected, and feared, law enforcement entity in the country. Hanscom spent the weekend investigating, but Lizzie's defenders later neglected to point out that the Borden sisters relieved him of his duties when his persistent questions and desire to comb the house for clues threatened to implicate Lizzie. Porter wrote that "Detective Hanscom remained in Fall River for two days and then disappeared as mysteriously as he came."

The tension at the heart of the case—the mounting evidence against Lizzie in opposition to the Victorian notion that a woman could not commit such a heinous crime in the sanctity of the home—permeated press coverage. Much of the public clung to crude applications of social Darwinism, which held that violent criminals, invariably male, were badly evolved primitives who could be identified through such physical characteristics as low brows, ill-shaped craniums, and small brains. Such theories, associated with the Italian psychiatrist Cesare Lombroso, were typical of highly racialized nineteenth-century pseudoscience.

The Borden family doctor, Seabury Bowen, held the widespread view that ruled out a woman, any woman, as the perpetrator of such savage murders. Certainly no daughter could bludgeon to death a "a defenseless old woman" and then proceed to rain blows on her mortally wounded father, the physician told the *Daily Herald*. "I am a surgeon, and have been in active practice for years," he explained, "and the first view of the old man's body staggered me. I could not inflict upon a dead dog the additional 11 blows with the manifest precision and care that were driven into the victim's head."

While it was true, the doctor added, that there had been "occasional family differences between Mr. Borden and the girls," intra-family relations as a whole had always been "cordial." Since Lizzie was a "a person of undisputed virtue and Christian living . . . I do not believe it right to insinuate a word against so good a woman as Miss Lizzie. She possesses our confidence and we believe in her."

The next day's *Daily Herald*, however, delivered a bombshell in the form of an interview with Hiram Harrington, the husband of Andrew Borden's only sister. "For nearly ten years," Harrington revealed, "there have been constant disputes between the daughters and their father and stepmother." He allowed that his murdered brother-in-law was "an exceedingly hard man concerning money matters, determined and stubborn, and when once he got an idea nothing could change him."

Harrington called attention to the bitter disagreement over the house purchased for Abby's sister, adding that Emma and Lizzie had not been mollified by the rental property purchased for them. "The dispute about their not being allowed enough went on with equal bitterness," he explained, adding that "Lizzie did most of the demonstrative contention." Whereas Emma was "very quiet and unassuming," Lizzie was "haughty and domineering with the stubborn will of her father and bound to contest for her rights." She and her father had many bitter disagreements and often went days without speaking, he added.

Harrington summed up Lizzie's motive for the murders. "She moved in the best society in Fall River, was a member of the Congregational church, and is a brilliant conversationalist. She thought she ought to entertain as others did, and felt that with her father's wealth she was expected to hold her end up with others of her set. Her father's constant refusal to allow her to entertain lavishly angered her. I have heard many bitter things she has said of her father, and know she was deeply resentful of her father's maintained stand in this matter."

Harrington's suspicions created a sensation, yet Lizzie's defenders continued to outnumber those who thought her guilty. They would prevail in the court of public opinion. The good citizens of Fall River dismissed the allegations of Harrington, a blacksmith, as those of a jealous working-class relative. He compared unfavorably with Lizzie, an activist and Sunday School teacher in the most prominent church in the city. Lizzie's friends in the Christian Endeavor and the Women's Christian Temperance Union leaped to her defense. Suffragists, fighting hard for the vote in an age when women were denied civil rights, defended Lizzie as a woman unjustly accused by the male power structure.

Unswayed by the rising public defense of Lizzie, the Fall River police homed in on her simply because she was the only logical suspect in the brutal murders. On August 9, District Attorney Hosea M. Knowlton summoned Lizzie to the Fall River jail to testify in an inquest into the death of her parents. Attorney Jennings asked to attend the investigation with Lizzie, but the presiding judge, Josiah C. Blaisdell, denied the request. The judge's decision was his prerogative under the law—it would be more than seventy years before the U.S. Supreme Court granted criminal defendants the right to have an attorney present for questioning. Lizzie could simply have refused to testify, but she did not.

Lizzie's disastrous testimony at the inquest is perhaps the strongest evidence of her culpability in the murders. Knowlton would later refer to her inquest testimony as, in essence, "Lizzie's confession." She offered sharply contradictory and uncredible accounts of her whereabouts and behavior on the morning of the killings. Some of the contradictions may have seemed inconsequential, yet they damaged Lizzie's credibility. For example, she described helping her father remove his Congress boots when he returned from his business in town, yet Andrew Borden's shoes were found firmly on the feet of his dead body.

Under questioning by Knowlton on three separate occasions from August 9 to 11, Lizzie downplayed tensions in the family over the transfer of property to Abby. Lizzie admitted that she and Emma believed that their stepmother had "persuaded father to buy it. At any rate he did buy it, and I am quite sure she did persuade him. I said what he did for her people, he ought to do for his own children. So he gave us grandfather's house. That was all the trouble we ever had." Lizzie insisted that thereafter her relations with her mother were cordial, although she "did not choose to call her mother."

As the inquest continued, Lizzie repeated the story that on the morning of August 4 her mother "told me she had a note, somebody was sick." Lizzie said she did not know who the alleged note was from and never saw it. She added that she "did not hear her go or come back." In actuality Abby rarely left the home, typically only to see her half sister, Mrs. Sarah Whitehead. While now denying that she had heard her mother come home, two witnesses had heard Lizzie state shortly after the murders that she had heard Abby return to the house.

Lizzie also offered contradictory statements on her whereabouts when her father returned home that morning. She testified that she had gone up the front stairs to repair a garment in her room. Lizzie acknowledged being on the stairs, as Maggie had testified, when her father returned. The story then changed and Lizzie insisted, "I was downstairs in the kitchen." Grilled on the matter by Knowlton, Lizzie explained that "I said I thought I was on the stairs; then I remembered I was in the kitchen when he came in." Then Lizzie denied having gone up those front stairs at all while her father was out. She now insisted that she had repaired the garment in her room before her father went out that morning even though she had barely awakened by the time her father had left.

The significance of Knowlton's questioning was obvious. If Lizzie had been up the front stairs, even if not to kill her stepmother, she would likely have observed the body under the high bed. Realizing this, Lizzie backed off her original testimony that she had been up the front stairs at all after her father left the house.

Lizzie's testimony about the time she spent outside the home was even more contradictory. Lizzie faced the challenge of demonstrating not only that she had not committed the murders, but that she had not been in the house when they occurred. Otherwise, she would surely have heard her stepmother's 200-pound-plus body thump to the floor in the old house, and would have encountered her father's killer as well.

At the inquest Lizzie testified that she went out to the barn that Thursday morning to look for sinkers for a fishing trip she planned take on Monday to the Swansea farm. Earlier, Lizzie had told witnesses that she had gone to the barn for a piece of screen to repair an upstairs window, but that story had changed when no window could be found in need of repair. Knowlton pursued Lizzie's fishing story. Asked if there weren't sinkers on the fishing lines at the farm, Lizzie replied "I think there were some. It is so long since I have been there; I think there were some." But Lizzie abruptly reversed herself again, now insisting that she went to the barn because "I thought there were no sinkers at the farm to be had."

Lizzie's story, then, was that she planned to go fishing at the farm for the first time in five years. She had done nothing else to prepare for the trip, but chose that Thursday morning to go look for sinkers in the barn even though at one point she said she thought the lines at the farm already had sinkers on them. She acknowledged, too, that she had not been in the barn in some three months prior to that day.

Even accepting that she had gone to the barn for sinkers, which Knowlton didn't believe for a moment, the district attorney insisted that her search of a box in the barn would only have taken a couple of minutes. Even though Lizzie acknowledged it was "very hot" on the second floor of the barn, and that the window remained shut, she insisted that she remained up there for "fifteen or twenty minutes." Doing what? Knowlton asked. The answer, said Lizzie, was that she stood in the torrid barn loft eating three or four pears that she had picked off the ground from under the back yard pear tree and carried up into the barn to eat while she looked out the closed window.

Turning to the discovery of her murdered father, Lizzie said she had opened the door only enough to see her father's body, but had not even gone in the room to ensure he was dead. Yet she had called to Maggie that her father was in fact dead.

At this point Knowlton appears to have attempted to break Lizzie:
Q: "Did you see the blood on the floor?"
A: "No, sir."
Q: "You saw his face covered with blood?"
A: "No, sir."
Q: "Did you see his eyeball hanging out?"
A: "No, sir."

Q: "See the gashes where his face was laid open?"

A: "No, sir."

Q: "Nothing of that kind?"

A: "No, sir."

Lizzie then covered her face with her hands for a minute or two before the interview resumed. If this account was true, how could Lizzie, denying that she had even seen blood, know that her father was dead?

She went on to deny the statements of both Maggie and Mrs. Churchill that Lizzie had suggested that Abby had returned home from her mission to aid the sick.

"I said, 'I don't know where Mrs. Borden is, that is all I said,'" Lizzie declared.

Q: "Did you not suggest that any search be made for her?

A: "No, sir."

A moment later, however, Lizzie again contradicted her own testimony. "I did not do anything, except what I said to Mrs. Churchill. I said to her: 'I don't know where Mrs. Borden is. I think she is out, but I wish you would look.'"

Q: "You did ask her to look?"

A: "I said that to Mrs. Churchill."

More damning evidence emerged attesting to Lizzie's apparent intent to kill her parents. Once Dr. Bowen had related the vomiting illness that had plagued the family, the police launched an investigation that paid off almost immediately. Eli Bence, a pharmacist at Smith's drugstore in downtown Fall River, offered a statement shattering Lizzie's claim of innocence.

Bence reported that on the day before the murders, between 10 and 11:30 A.M., Miss Borden had appeared at his drugstore and "asked me for ten cents worth of prussic acid," a substance so deadly that a few grains would immediately kill a human being. Lizzie explained that she wanted the acid to clean "a seal skin cape." Bence refused her request, explaining that prussic acid could not be sold over the counter. Lizzie argued that she had purchased the substance on a previous occasion, but Bence remained firm.

Bence was a trusted citizen employed in a profession where trust was important. He had nothing to gain, and indeed, business to lose, by coming forward with evidence damaging to the popular Lizzie. Yet Bence accompanied police to the Borden house and positively identified her. Bence's version of Lizzie's visit was also verified by two eyewitnesses who overheard the discussion at the pharmacy.

How sure was Bence that it was Lizzie Borden who had requested the prussic acid? The pharmacist declared under oath at Lizzie's preliminary hearing that he was "positive" the woman had been Lizzie. He had seen her before on several occasions and knew who she was. Furthermore no one else had ever requested prussic acid and Lizzie had done so in a "tremulous" voice, the pharmacist recalled.

Lizzie knew well that such damning evidence could be used to demonstrate her intent to poison her parents. This was especially true since no one had heard of prussic acid being used to clean a seal skin cape. But Lizzie's flat denial of the visit to the pharmacy, contravening three direct witnesses, was even more damning than the story about wanting to clean a cape. When Knowlton asked simply, "Did you ever go into any drugstore and inquire for prussic acid?" Lizzie responded, "I did not."

Lizzie went on to deny even knowing of the existence of Smith's drugstore, which had been located for fourteen years at a central intersection only a few blocks from the Borden home.

For a veteran prosecutor such as Hosea Knowlton, there was little question as to Lizzie's guilt. She had motive, means, and she virtually alone—with the remote possibility of Maggie, who had no motive—had the opportunity to commit the murders. At the inquest Lizzie had not only contradicted the verifiable testimony of other witnesses, but repeatedly had contradicted herself.

Judge Blaisdell conducted the inquest in complete secrecy, releasing none of the damaging evidence against Lizzie. Although that evidence justified Lizzie's subsequent arrest, the public reaction was sure to be one of outrage.

National news reporters who had descended upon Fall River could not fail to note the widespread support for Lizzie. The bulk of the city's residents were unwilling to embrace the possibility that a young woman could butcher her own parents in the sanctity of the home. "Whatever the police may think of the strength of their clues," a *New York Times* correspondent reported on August 11, "it is certain that the opinions of Miss Borden's many friends are entirely in favor of her innocence. This feeling is gaining more adherents every hour."

That very evening, however, Marshal Rufus B. Hilliard arrested Lizzie Borden and lodged her in the matron's room in the jail. After a week of displaying remarkable calm, including little evidence of mourning, Lizzie broke down now that she had actually been charged with the crime. She sobbed, heaved, and vomited until Dr. Bowen appeared to calm her.

That evening, Lizzie's defenders erupted with howls of protest and street demonstrations. The Revs. W. Walker Jubb and the E. A. Buck, the former only a year removed from his native England and Lizzie's pastor at the Central Congregational Church, pronounced her "innocent and blameless." Most of the public continued to believe that the bludgeonings were so heinous that no woman possibly could have committed them. Others scurried to study the Borden family history for incidents of insanity, which alone might explain such an outburst of female violence. They uncovered nothing of substance, however. Suffragists and clubwomen continued to assume that Lizzie was being falsely accused by the same men that denied women the right to vote and confined their activities to the domestic sphere.

Despite a hard rain in Fall River on August 12, the morning of Lizzie's arraignment, a huge crowd withstood the downpour in hopes of gaining a seat in the Fall River District Court as Lizzie faced formal charges. Compelled to respond to the charges, Lizzie entered a plea of not guilty before being removed to the Taunton Jail, which offered facilities for female prisoners. Judge Blaisdell set a preliminary hearing date of August 22.

The purpose of the preliminary hearing was to determine if sufficient cause existed for the case to be moved from the lower District Court—which typically heard cases involving misdemeanors and a few felony offenses—to the Massachusetts Superior Court. After conferring with Lizzie and Emma, Andrew Jennings, the attorney for the accused, called in a prominent former prosecutor from Boston, Melvin O. Adams, to assist him in the case. A high-powered defense team was in the process of being assembled.

As Lizzie squirmed in her chair and sobbed quietly, Jennings delivered an opening statement in which, after recounting the grisly murders, he declared he could not "imagine that any person could have committed that crime unless his heart was black as hell." Although Lizzie possessed a "character past reproach," Jennings continued, the police had "put her upon the rack . . . and thumbscrews." They grilled her at the inquest despite the fact that "the poor girl was drugged." Here Jennings referred to a light morphine sedation prescribed by Dr.

Bowen in order to help Lizzie sleep in the days following the murders. Knowlton rejected the charge, insisting that throughout the process Lizzie had always been "in full control of all her faculties. . . . It is idle for anyone to say she has been confused or dazed."

Lizzie's attorneys adopted a typical defense strategy, arguing that the police and prosecutors had made a precipitous judgment as to their client's guilt. Jennings's impassioned efforts to depict Lizzie as a defenseless victim of the criminal justice establishment struck an immediate chord with the courtroom gallery, which burst into loud applause when the attorney completed his opening statement. For his part, Knowlton received only a stony silence after laying out the case against Lizzie, and concluded: "Yielding to clamor is not to be compared with the satisfaction of a duty well done."

District Court Judge Blaisdell, a distinguished elderly gentleman who had been one of the first mayors of Fall River and had served in both houses of the Massachusetts legislature, again presided during the preliminary hearing. In so doing Blaisdell rejected Jennings's request that he recuse himself since he had presided over the inquest. The judge's decision rested on firm legal ground, but it fueled the baseless, but no less widespread, charge that Lizzie was being railroaded by a handful of Fall River officials.

Jennings and Adams probably did not expect to gain Lizzie's freedom at the preliminary hearing, but they did force the prosecution to display the main lines of its case against Lizzie. The evidence included the damaging excerpts from the stenographic record of Lizzie's inquest testimony. After hearing the evidence, a teary-eyed Judge Blaisdell, who knew Lizzie personally, concluded sadly that "you are probably guilty." Accordingly, the judge ruled that her case be bound over for consideration by the Bristol County grand jury.

In a tradition dating to English common law, the grand jury, a panel of twenty-one citizens, was to decide whether sufficient evidence existed to indict Lizzie Borden for murder. From November 18 to 21, the Bristol County grand jury heard evidence presented by Knowlton. When the panel of citizens reconvened on December 1, they heard from only one witness, but her testimony provided the latest bombshell in the Borden case.

Alice Russell, the friend of the Borden sisters whom Lizzie had visited the night before the murders, told the grand jurors of an incident that obviously convinced her, an initial supporter, that Lizzie was in fact guilty. The evidence

focused on the dress that in all likelihood Lizzie had worn when she bludgeoned her parents to death. At the inquest Lizzie had admitted that she had
changed after the murders from a blue dress into another dress, a "pink wrapper," because "they" had told her to. Lizzie never did say who "they" were and
"they" were never identified.

Following the murders, Alice Russell stayed in the Borden home to comfort
the bereaved family. Indeed, she slept in the room adjacent to Lizzie, with the
door left open. On August 6, Dr. John W. Coughlin, the mayor of Fall River,
appeared at the Borden home. When he advised that it would be best if no one
left the house until the investigation was complete, Lizzie indignantly demanded to know if anyone in the house was a suspect. The mayor confirmed that in
fact Lizzie herself was suspected.

The next morning, testified Miss Russell, she went into the Borden kitchen
and discovered Lizzie preparing to burn a blue dress in the stove. Mrs. Churchill
had recalled that Lizzie had been wearing a light blue calico dress with a navy
diamond printed on it on the morning of the murders. No one had seen any
blood on Lizzie's dress. While standing over the stove to burn the same dress,
Lizzie explained to Alice Russell that the "old thing" was covered with paint.
Shocked, Miss Russell left the room as Lizzie burned the dress. Alice Russell later spoke with the Pinkerton detective, Hanscom, about the incident. The next
day, Alice confronted Lizzie and said: "I am afraid, Lizzie, the worst thing you
could have done was to burn that dress. I have been asked about your dresses."

"Oh, what made you let me do it?" Lizzie innocently replied. Had they been
informed of this incident, few objective Fall River residents could have believed
that a woman would burn a dress rather than tear it into rags, the common
practice in Victorian households, much less do so in the kitchen stove on the
night after learning she was a murder suspect. Hanscom, the Pinkerton detective, left the Borden sisters' employ immediately after the dress-burning incident.

After hearing Alice Russell's testimony, the grand jury voted twenty to one
for a "true bill"—an indictment. The grand jury vote, which the law mandated
be kept secret, was promptly leaked to the press, though the dress burning incident remained less widely known.

On December 2, Knowlton, armed with the grand jury indictment, formally
charged Lizzie on three counts of murder—of her mother, father, and a charge

for the double murder of both parents. Since Massachusetts law did not provide for the posting of bail in capital cases, Lizzie was returned to the Taunton Jail to await her trial.

From the jail, Lizzie granted an interview which served to keep her legion of defenders thoroughly behind her cause. "I know I am innocent," she insisted, "and I have made up my mind that no matter what comes to me I will try to bear it bravely and make the best of it." Although she would spend nine months in the Taunton Jail, Lizzie, unlike the regular prisoners, received daily open-air exercise privileges, ate food catered by a local hotel, and decorated her surroundings with an impressive array of floral arrangements and other gifts sent almost daily by her myriad admirers.

In the wake of Lizzie's indictment, the Borden murders, initially a local event, had become a national sensation. National newspaper reporters and magazine writers descended upon Fall River en masse.

By the time of the Borden murders American journalism had begun to come of age. Technological innovations—specifically the invention of the Linotype machine in 1886—dramatically speeded up typesetting, production, and circulation of the daily newspaper. Moreover, advertising had become a powerful force in an increasingly urban, consumer-oriented society. Newspapers, subsidized by special interests or political parties earlier in the century, now depended on advertising for profits. In order to generate advertising revenue, newspapers needed to increase circulation.

By the 1890s these developments encouraged the emergence of yellow journalism, particularly in the nation's larger cities. Big city editors sought out stories that might generate mass public interest and spur the sale of newspapers. They readily overplayed stories in competition for readership. A sensational murder and subsequent criminal trial could sell more newspapers than anything but a war. When such cases arose newspapers battled one another to mount the most intense coverage and to uncover any scoops that could be had. Hence reporters descended upon Fall River in search of new angles on the bludgeonings of the elderly couple.

Throughout the nineteenth century the American public had betrayed a particular fascination with crimes involving women, especially when violent or sexual in nature. Women were not part of the Victorian justice system, only objects of its administration. There were few women lawyers and hardly any female judges or jurors before the twentieth century. Women committed far fewer crimes than men—less than 10 percent of the total—and most of these were uniquely female crimes such as prostitution. On the other hand, women quite often became the targets of crime, as they were beaten, raped, and abused daily across the country. The law sanctioned patriarchal authority and often exonerated men from violent crimes against women, including rape and murder. On countless occasions men successfully employed the "she had it coming" defense for beating or killing wives who resisted patriarchal domination.

When a woman challenged the Victorian social order, and met with a violent end, the public could not get enough of the story. One of the most famous cases concerned Helen Jewett, a New York City prostitute murdered by one of her clients in 1836. The attractive, twenty-three-year-old Jewett had been bludgeoned with a hatchet and left smoldering in her burning bed. A ceaseless stream of narratives for years after the murder emphasized that, owing to her moral corruption, the violent end had been an inevitable fate for the beautiful but "fallen" Helen. Popular accounts suggested that by tempting and seducing men, rather than fulfilling woman's assigned role to temper destructive male urges, she had gotten what she deserved. The New York court agreed, taking only fifteen minutes to exonerate the young man, Richard Robinson, who obviously had murdered the "disreputable" young woman.

Similar narratives emerged five years later with the mysterious disappearance and death in 1841 of Mary Cecilia Rogers. Known as the Beautiful Cigar Girl, the twenty-one-year-old Mary worked in a tobacco shop and lived in a boardinghouse in a male-dominated district of modernizing New York. The discovery of her nude body floating in the Hudson River inspired sensational news accounts and reams of narratives, including an Edgar Allan Poe story. Mary, who had defied Victorian mores by being sexually active, appeared to have died after being beaten and raped, or possibly as a result of a botched abortion. In any case, public fascination with her death reflected the powerful appeal of narratives of sex, death, and independent womanhood in the modern urban environment.

The Borden case lacked the salacious sexual angle of the Jewett and Rogers cases earlier in the century. But the major difference in these sensational cases involving women and murder was, of course, that in Lizzie's case a woman—and a Christian woman of the respectable class—was charged as the perpetrator rather than the victim of brutal violence.

Increased literacy and growing public fascination with crime and dime novel detective stories heightened interest in the sensational Borden murders. Public fascination with crime and detection gave rise to a new genre of literature, beginning with Edgar Allan Poe's mystery stories at mid century. By the late 1880s an Englishman, Sir Arthur Conan Doyle, provided millions of readers with the most famous detective hero of all time, Mr. Sherlock Holmes. Holmes's keen intellect was a reflection in the popular culture of the efforts by the late nineteenth century of police and detectives to employ more sophisticated methods to track down criminals. Conan Doyle's detective stories emerged at the same time that London's Scotland Yard searched desperately for the world's first notorious serial killer, Jack the Ripper.

While the reading public craved news about the Borden murders, there were no significant developments to report in the months before Lizzie's trial. As a result, the press sometimes resorted to printing fabrications to satisfy the public craving for new information on the Borden case. Some of the more colorful, albeit baseless, accounts revealed that Lizzie had perpetrated the crime in the nude, thus explaining why the police had found no blood-stained garments.

The low point came on October 11, 1892, when the *Boston Globe* revealed the shocking news that Lizzie had been pregnant when she committed the murders. According to this account, Andrew, having discovered his daughter's condition, ordered her to name the man or leave the house. So Lizzie had murdered him. The *Globe* retracted the baseless story the next day, sheepishly explaining that it had been fed false information. Thereafter, both Boston newspapers, the *Globe* and the *Herald*, treated Lizzie with kid gloves. The spate of wild press accounts had redounded to Lizzie's benefit by reinforcing the argument that the entire case against her rested on prurient and baseless speculation.

Lizzie had some additional luck as well. On May 31, 1893, as she languished in jail awaiting the start of her trial, a woman named Bertha Manchester was killed in her Fall River farmhouse by an axe-wielding murderer who struck her thirty-one times. Newspaper headlines screamed of "startling parallelisms" with the Borden case. Hysteria prevailed in Bristol County, as thousands believed an axe-wielding madman was on the loose.

This event, occurring only days before Lizzie's jury was to be chosen, was incredibly fortuitous for her cause. Lizzie's defenders expressed outrage that the Commonwealth planned to take her case to trial while an axe-wielding serial killer prowled Fall River. The normally taciturn Andrew Jennings seized the opportunity, summoning the press to ask, "Well, are they going to claim that Lizzie Borden did this too?"

On June 4, however, the day before the Borden trial opened, the police arrested Jose Correira, a twenty-two-year-old itinerant farmworker, for the murder of Bertha Manchester. Convicted and sentenced to life imprisonment, Correira received a pardon twenty-six years later on the condition that he return to his native Azores. Correira, who had a grievance with Bertha Manchester, his employer, cannot be considered a suspect in the Borden murders because he did not arrive in the United States from the Azores until April 1893, some eight months after the slaughter on Second Street. But the full story of the Manchester murder had not been revealed at the time of Lizzie's trial. Many continued to believe that an immigrant axe-murdering maniac had committed both sensational murders.

The unsavory nature of the case, as well as the popular perception of Lizzie's innocence, apparently intimidated Massachusetts attorney general Albert E. Pillsbury, who under normal circumstances in the 1890s would have handled a major capital case such as the Borden murders. Pillsbury informed Hosea Knowlton that he was not well, though he probably simply wished to avoid prosecuting a popular defendant.

Knowlton, forty-five, a graduate of Tufts and Harvard and a former state legislator, also lacked enthusiasm for the case. Noting the high level of public support for Lizzie, Knowlton explained in a letter to Pillsbury on April 24, 1893, that because the prosecution's case rested on circumstantial evidence "there is every reasonable expectation of a verdict of not guilty." Knowlton acknowledged that the case might result in a hung jury, but added that "even in my most sanguine moments I have scarcely expected a verdict of guilty." Not surprisingly, Knowlton confessed that he would "very much like to get rid of the trial of the case."

These statements by Pillsbury and Knowlton reflect the extent to which the prosecution team believed that evidence in the case would be overwhelmed by public sentiment. Although Knowlton revealed a defeatist attitude in his private correspondence, he brought in an aggressive legal talent in the person of

William H. Moody, a young district attorney from northeastern Massachusetts. Only thirty-nine at the time of the Borden trial, Moody would go on to a distinguished career in Washington as secretary of the navy, U.S. attorney general, and associate justice of the Supreme Court of the United States.

Knowlton had recognized the need to bolster the prosecution after Lizzie's attorneys, in a brilliant stroke, added former Massachusetts governor George D. Robinson to her legal team. The ruddy-faced popular governor, from Chicopee, had served three terms in Springfield before retiring six years previously. Robinson lacked the technical legal knowledge of the other attorneys in the case, but he had spent his entire career managing public opinion, which would continue to play a decisive role in the Borden case. Robinson also had a soothing effect on Lizzie as she struggled to maintain her composure amid the ordeal of the murder trial. "It's going to be all right, little girl," Robinson assured her at their first meeting. Lizzie believed him.

Following Lizzie Borden's arraignment on May 8, 1893, final preparations were made for the trial set to begin on June 5 in superior court, which was sitting in New Bedford. As stipulated under Massachusetts law at the time, three superior court judges would preside over the capital murder case. The three grey-bearded magistrates were Chief Justice Albert Mason and Associate Justices Caleb Blodgett and Justin Dewey.

With the trial set to begin, the town of New Bedford prepared for the renewed onslaught of nationally known newspaper columnists, reporters, sketch artists, and Lizzie's frenzied defenders. Workers strung wires so that Western Union could report quickly on developments in the case by Teletype. Officials put up fences to seal off the crowds of people, many of them women, who milled outside in hopes of garnering one of the few seats allotted to spectators.

Hot weather prevailed on June 5, 1893, as officials escorted Lizzie to the courthouse. Lizzie appeared resplendent in a new dress and carried a bouquet of pansies. Her striking gray eyes were fixed straight ahead as she and her entourage entered the courtroom. Reporters and spectators crammed into the New Bedford courtroom, their collective body heat making the environment stiflingly hot. Palm-leaf fans waved as the bailiff pounded his gavel and the court crier called the historic trial into session.

The first day ended with the selection of the customary all-male jury, this one comprised overwhelmingly of farmers middle-aged and older. These men, all of whom wore variants of facial hair characteristic of the era, had been selected from a pool of 145. Some prospective jurors had been dismissed for prejudice and others as a result of fifteen challenges by the defense and fourteen by the prosecution.

Although the all-male jury, typical of the era, exemplified the subjugation of women in American society, in reality the New Bedford jurors would prove ideally suited to Lizzie's cause. The farmers had lived a traditional lifestyle and held conventional views, including denial of the notion that a woman, especially a Christian society woman, could possibly have bludgeoned her parents to death in the sanctity of the home.

Several of the jurors admitted after the trial that they opposed capital punishment, another point in Lizzie's favor. Under Massachusetts law at the time, death was the only sentence allowed for the premeditated murders for which Lizzie stood accused. Those Massachusetts farmers did not relish the thought of condemning a woman to the gallows. During jury selection, however, not all of the prospective jurors were asked their views on capital punishment and the prospect of executing a female offender.

On June 6, prosecutor Moody began to display his formidable legal skills by offering a concise, chilling, and persuasive opening argument. He emphasized the estrangement between the defendant and her parents, recalling how Lizzie had interrupted a policeman on the day of the murders when he referred to Abby Borden as Lizzie's mother. "She is not my mother," Lizzie had interjected. "She is my stepmother. My mother is dead."

Tensions and seething resentments inside the Borden home preceded the murders, Moody explained to the jury. "Although they occupied the same household," he intoned, "there was built up between them by locks and bolts and bars, almost an impassable wall."

Moody pledged to present evidence on Lizzie's premeditated plans to kill her parents, including the effort to purchase prussic acid. He informed the jurors that Lizzie had spent the evening before the murders "predicting disaster and cataloging defenses" in the company of Alice Russell. Lizzie's contradictory and incriminating statements, as well as the dress-burning incident, now made public for the first time, would attest to the defendant's guilt, Moody declared.

The prosecutor stressed that nothing had been disturbed in the Borden home and that no stranger could have come and gone undetected by Lizzie, Maggie, and the crowds of people downtown. Lizzie alone could have committed the crimes, a reality that the first witnesses to the scene unwittingly grasped, Moody declaimed. "Instinctively there leaped to the lips of every inquiring person, of the prisoner—'Where were you?'—before a thought of suspicion was over her head."

After press reports on the first day of the trial commented on how cool Lizzie had appeared in the courtroom, her demeanor had now suddenly changed. Dressed in black, on Robinson's advice, and motionless throughout Moody's presentation, Lizzie dramatically fainted when the prosecutor concluded his opening statement. While the jury was excused, she was revived through the administration of smelling salts.

This "ladylike" behavior on Lizzie's part was crucial to her defense, which sought in every way to reinforce the popular view that a woman could not have committed such heinous crimes. Had Lizzie continued to appear cold and unaffected, the prosecution might have been able to make the case that she was in fact a cold-blooded murderer. By appearing to faint Lizzie reinforced Victorian gender mores that resonated with the all-male jury.

When the trial resumed, Bridget "Maggie" Sullivan appeared as a key prosecution witness. Dark haired, solidly built, and attired in a new dress and hat, Maggie took the stand on June 7. Knowlton, who had initially suspected that Maggie might know more than she had told, had kept the Borden maid under the sheriff's supervision since the murders. While the good people of Massachusetts were reluctant to accept the idea that an upstanding Protestant woman such as Lizzie could have committed the crimes, a young Irish Catholic immigrant woman was another matter. Many suspected Maggie, who would, they noted, have had some familiarity with the use of a hatchet in the course of her various duties around the house.

Despite the willingness of many nativists to cast suspicion on the working-class Irish immigrant, Bridget Sullivan's story remained consistent from the inquest through the trial. No one ever suggested a plausible motive for Maggie suddenly and savagely to murder her employers.

Maggie and Lizzie had always been friendly and apparently remained so as they exchanged nervous smiles in the courtroom. The maid testified that the family took its meals separately, but pressured on cross-examination by the defense she offered that "So far as I could see they lived congenially and pleas-antly." When Andrew Borden returned home on the morning of the murders, Maggie testified, Lizzie "spoke very low" but she clearly heard her tell her father that Abby received a note and had gone out to attend to someone who was sick.

Maggie contradicted Lizzie's inquest testimony on the events that followed the discovery of Andrew's body. She stated that when the question of Abby's whereabouts arose, Lizzie had said, "'Oh, Maggie! I'm almost sure I heard her come in; go upstairs and see if she is there.'" At the time, Abby had already been dead more than an hour so Lizzie obviously could not have been "almost sure" she heard her stepmother return. This statement, in fact, offered powerful evi-dence of Lizzie's own culpability in the murders.

According to the *New York Times*, however, Maggie's testimony with respect to family harmony in the Borden home appeared to make the strongest impres-sion on the sympathetic all-male jury. Few noted that Maggie carefully qualified such statements with words such as "so far as I could see" or "in my presence."

Lizzie apparently found it difficult to maintain her "ladylike" weakness while carefully following the proceedings. The *New York Times* reported from the Fall River courtroom that "the weakness of yesterday had vanished, and today her strong will was again in evidence." Lizzie "appeared highly interested in the pro-ceedings and watched the developments closely."

The state's case gained strength on June 8 when Mrs. Churchill, the Bordens' neighbor, corroborated Maggie's testimony by stating that Lizzie said after her father's body was discovered "she wished somebody would try to find Mrs. Bor-den, as she thought she heard her come in." The evidence presented by Maggie and Mrs. Churchill strongly suggested that Lizzie directed others to discover the body that she alone knew lay upstairs in the guestroom.

Also testifying on June 8, Alice Russell described Lizzie's supposed fears for her father's safety on the night before the murders as well as the dress burning incident three days after the crimes. Alice recalled that Lizzie had told her, "I am afraid sometimes that somebody will do something to him; he is so discourte-ous to people." Observers noted that Lizzie appeared tense as Alice Russell recalled finding Lizzie burning her dress in the kitchen stove. "On Sunday I saw Lizzie standing by the stove, Emma by the sink," Alice Russell explained. "Lizzie had a dress skirt, and I asked her what she was going to do with it, and she said she was going to burn it, as it was all covered with paint."

Assistant Marshal John Fleet, the next significant prosecution witness, testified regarding his actions after arriving at the murder scene shortly before noon on August 4. The policeman, sporting a bushy mustache, recalled that Lizzie had been remarkably "cool and collected" on the day of the murders. He informed the jury that Lizzie had made a point of correcting his reference to her mother by interjecting, "She is not my mother, sir. She is my stepmother. My mother died when I was a child." Another witness, Hannah Gifford of Fall River, a dressmaker for the Bordens, also testified that Lizzie once corrected her reference to Abby as her mother, declaring "'Don't say that to me, for she is a mean good-for-nothing.'"

The most significant aspect of Fleet's testimony, however, was his account of finding the alleged murder weapon, a hatchet with its handle broken off, in a box in the cellar. According to Fleet, Maggie escorted the police to the basement, where she pointed out a box on a shelf that contained hatchets. On one of the implements, the handle appeared to have been freshly broken off near the head of the hatchet, which had a blade on one side and a claw on the other. Fleet found the blade of the tool covered in white ash, on both sides, whereas other items in the box were covered with dust only on their exposed sides.

Despite the widespread misperception that the Borden murder weapon was never found, the prosecution argued that the handleless hatchet was the likely murder weapon. This could not be proven, however, and the prosecution case would prove weakest on the handling of the issue of the murder weapon. It appears that the killer had broken the wooden handle during the savage attacks and had tossed the greater part of the handle into the fire to burn away. Lizzie earlier had been seen stoking the fire, ostensibly to warm her irons, and Dr. Bowen, looking into the fire after the murders, recalled seeing an unusual cylindrical form in the embers. After dropping the handle into the fire to burn, Lizzie could have quickly washed off the blade and covered it with ash to make it appear not to have been moved. She could then have placed it back in the toolbox in the cellar.

The prosecution's case with respect to the alleged murder weapon began to break down when another Fall River policeman, Michael Mullaly, contradicted Fleet. Like Fleet, Mullaly testified that a split in one hatchet handle near the clawed blade "looked fresh, as if just broken," but he added that the broken-off piece of wood had been laid out in the basement for examination with the two

This editorial cartoon, typical of the favorable press Lizzie received during the murder trial, depicted her as an innocent victim of the criminal justice establishment. The bearded figure represents chief prosecutor Hosea M. Knowlton. The abundance of hatchets, and hatchet blades, reflects a key issue in the trial, contradictory police testimony about the murder weapon. Courtesy Fall River Historical Society

hatchets and two axes that were also found. Recalled to the stand, Fleet testified that there had been no broken piece of handle and Knowlton acknowledged that this was the first he had heard of such a piece.

The contradiction among the two officers on handling of the murder weapon fueled public perceptions of a police conspiracy to frame poor Lizzie. Mullaly's testimony "created a decided sensation in the courtroom," Fall River reporter Edwin Porter recalled. Defense attorney Robinson exploited to the fullest the contradictory statements of the two officers, underscoring the argument that the Fall River police had bungled, if not stacked, the evidence against

Lizzie. "Here was a break in the prosecution's case," reported the *New York Times* on June 10, "and the attorneys for the defense were greatly elated."

The prosecution had bungled an otherwise strong presentation of the evidence against Lizzie through its own ignorance as to the details to which its witnesses would attest. With two axes and two hatchets having been found and laid out, Mullaly had apparently become confused amid the shock and chaos of the Borden murders and imagined that he saw a broken off piece of wood in the basement which no one else recalled seeing.

From this point forward all the momentum of the trial went the way of the defense. Confusion over the hatchets had made a striking impression in the courtroom. In addition to the questions raised about the murder weapon, the police had also failed to produce virtually any evidence of blood or blood-stained garments. "I searched all the rooms," Fleet explained, "but did not open a trunk; we just looked in, but did not disturb anything. We looked into everything we could look into, but not very closely. We were not there long."

Fleet's testimony suggested that the blue calico dress that Lizzie burned in front of Miss Russell might easily have gone undetected in their search. Lizzie apparently discovered a small amount of blood evidence on the dress and decided she had to burn it after being informed by the mayor that she was a suspect in the case. ·

While the failure of the police to mount a thoroughgoing initial search strikes the modern reader as an example of incompetence, matters were not so simple in Fall River in 1892. It was no routine matter for police to root through the personal belongings of a prominent family such as the Bordens. It would have been considered unseemly in the Victorian era for men to make an exhaustive search of a woman's garments. And once Lizzie had emerged as the primary suspect, the dress went up in flames before a second, more complete search could be undertaken.

In the Borden case, much like the O. J. Simpson case a century later, police errors proved devastating to the prosecution. In reality, the police actions did little to demonstrate the defendants' innocence, yet in both cases alert defense attorneys seized the opportunities offered by the official missteps to advance the prospects of their client's acquittal. With support from the press and public, the inevitable weak links in otherwise compelling prosecution cases became turning points for the defense attorneys in their efforts to exonerate a popular defendant.

With the prosecution's case against Lizzie Borden already reeling, a series of devastating blows, culminating with a knockout punch from the bench, was still to come. A crucial setback came on June 12 when the three judges ruled that Lizzie's highly incriminating inquest testimony could not be admitted into evidence. The defense offered several reasons for exclusion, including the assertion that Lizzie had been rendered confused by sedatives administered by Dr. Bowen in the days after the murders.

While the prosecution insisted that Lizzie had not been under arrest and therefore had testified freely at the inquest, the three-judge panel sided with the defense argument that Lizzie had been in police custody and hence for all practical purposes under arrest. Since Lizzie did not have benefit of counsel at the inquest, and received no warning that her statements could incriminate her, the testimony should not be admitted.

The defense argument anticipated rulings made more than a half century later by the United States Supreme Court led by Earl Warren, which guaranteed defendants the right to counsel and to be warned that their statements could be used against them. These provisions were not, however, the law in Massachusetts in 1892. In fact, Moody cited fourteen precedents in a persuasive case for the testimony being admissible. After all, Moody explained, Lizzie's denial of guilt should not be excluded—if she had admitted guilt, he conceded, that might be another matter.

The court dismissed Moody's arguments in favor of the dubious defense claim that Mayor Coughlin's admission to Lizzie that she was a suspect was tantamount to her arrest. With the jury out of the courtroom, Chief Justice Mason ruled that "it is plain that the prisoner was at the time of the inquest as much a prisoner as she ever has been, and the evidence has been excluded."

"Big Gain for Lizzie Borden," blared the headline in the *New York Times* on June 13. The judges' decision, the *Times* accurately predicted, "will go a long way toward making Lizzie Borden a free woman." She had achieved a "decided advantage" in the proceedings since her statements at the inquest "were of a contradictory character, extremely damaging to her interests, and if they could have been introduced at the present trial might have been hard to dispose of."

On June 13, the prosecution tried to rebuild its case with a presentation of forensic evidence. All medical experts, including the Lizzie partisan, Dr. Bowen, concurred from the evidence of Abby's congealed blood, as well as the condition of the victims' stomachs, that Mrs. Borden had died at least an hour and probably an hour and a half before her husband. Both victims had died of skull fractures and brain injuries. Neither had offered resistance nor had either body been moved.

The prosecution's medical experts agreed that the murderer would have been spattered but not covered with blood since the direction of the spatter in both cases was away from the perpetrator. The only blood found on clothes eventually taken from the Borden home was a spot on Lizzie's underskirt six inches from the hem.

Lizzie Borden's explanation for the blood spot offers insight into Victorian sexual mores. During the inquest Lizzie stated that she had "fleas" at the time of the murders, a Victorian euphemism for menstruation, a subject that was strictly taboo in public discourse. However, since the blood spot was on the outside of the underskirt, rather than the inside, it is unlikely that the blood was menstrual. In this instance, the Victorian aversion to open references to female menstruation worked to Lizzie's advantage. The prosecution simply could not dwell on the matter nor did the all-male jury of rural farmers wish to contemplate the peculiarities of feminine biology.

With the defendant granted a request to be excused from the courtroom, the "ghastly relic" of Andrew Borden's "grinning skull," as the *New York Times* put it, was displayed for all to see. Both corpses had been decapitated to facilitate the murder investigation.

Pointing to the skull, two Harvard Medical School professors testified that the handleless hatchet fit the wounds on Andrew Borden's head. The experts testified that the blows on both victims did not reflect an attacker of overwhelming strength and that they were consistent with blows that could have been made by a woman. Microscopic testing found no evidence of blood on the hatchet, however, meaning that it had been cleaned if it was indeed the murder weapon.

On cross-examination, defense attorney Adams orchestrated an effective maneuver for benefit of the jury. Adams showed a new hatchet of the same make as the handleless hatchet to one of the witnesses, Dr. Frank W. Draper. The witness acknowledged that the blade did not fit the wounds on the victims' skulls. "It was plain that the effect of this demonstration upon the jury was great," reported the next day's *Times*.

The public clamor over this alleged revelation belied a simple explanation.

As Draper demonstrated on redirect testimony, the new hatchet did not fit the wounds precisely because it was new and had never been sharpened. The blade from the handleless hatchet did fit the victims' head wounds.

Although the apparent lack of fit between the head wounds and the new hatchet was easily explained, the facts became increasingly irrelevant as all the momentum headed toward a not guilty verdict. This aspect of the Borden trial nicely parallels the infamous Isotoner glove a century later in the Simpson case. With respect to the new hatchet, the Borden attorneys might well have employed the line used so successfully by Simpson's lead attorney, Johnnie Cochran, in 1995: "If it does not fit, you must acquit."

Following the medical evidence, the prosecution presented testimony by Hannah Reagan, matron of the Fall River police station, who claimed that she overheard a quarrel between Lizzie and Emma in the jail. The argument concluded with Lizzie declaring, "Emma, you have given me away."

This evidence made little impact, however, as Mrs. Reagan, after first reporting it, had later signed a statement under pressure from Lizzie's lawyers and others in the community disavowing her own previous account. Apparently the Irish police matron liked Lizzie well enough during their interactions at the jail, and she may have regretted offering evidence against Lizzie. After finally deciding that Lizzie was guilty, however, Mrs. Reagan reversed herself again and testified in court. But with all her changes of heart, the police matron lacked credibility and her testimony served only to confirm in the minds of many a police conspiracy against Lizzie.

Robinson called witnesses who successfully refuted Hannah Reagan's story, by explaining that the police matron had retracted her own account of having overhead Lizzie chastising Emma for "giving her away." The witnesses, as the *New York Times* put it, "showed that the police matron had made a mass of false statements, and set her testimony entirely at naught."

As the Commonwealth's case foundered, the three-judge panel continued to rule in Lizzie Borden's behalf. On June 14, the prosecution tried to show that on August 3 Lizzie had attempted to purchase the deadly prussic acid at Smith's drugstore. Governor Robinson immediately disputed the relevance of the testimony, sparking another decisive legal wrangle.

The Commonwealth argued the obvious: that Lizzie's attempt to purchase prussic acid the day before the murders evidenced her intent to kill her parents.

Once again outshining his legal brethren, Moody cited nine cases in which evidence of murderous intent by the defendant had been ruled admissible. Robinson insisted, however, that it had not been demonstrated that Lizzie bore her parents any ill will.

The judges had already excluded the testimony of Anna B. Borden, who was not a relative of the defendant but a friend who had accompanied Lizzie abroad on her cruise to Europe in 1890, sharing the same cabin. She offered evidence that Lizzie had declared that she was not looking forward to returning home because her home was such an unhappy one.

As it did throughout the case, the court sided with the defense, paying little heed to Moody's incisive arguments and citation of precedent. After some thirty minutes of off-the-record whispering amongst themselves, the three judges barred the evidence without offering a basis for their decision. Incensed, Moody urged Knowlton to resign the prosecution's case and denounce the proceedings as a farce. But Knowlton, as we have seen, had not anticipated success for the prosecution.

The judges' decision to bar the prussic acid testimony of pharmacist Eli Bence created "a decided sensation in the courtroom," the *New York Times* reported. While the prosecution thus ended its case on a defeatist note, "Miss Borden's friends were, of course, jubilant. Her attorneys profess to be well pleased with the present condition of the case. On every legal point the prosecution has been defeated." Most courtroom observers confidently predicted either an acquittal or, at worst, a hung jury.

Confident of victory, Robinson presented only one day of evidence compared with a week of testimony for the prosecution. After her performance at the inquest, obviously Lizzie would not be taking the stand. The defense summoned two teenage boys in an effort to undermine police testimony that the barn loft had not only been stifling hot on August 4, but that no one appeared to have walked across the dusty floor. The two boys from working-class families, Everett Brown and Thomas Barlow, insisted that after hearing about the murders they had walked throughout the barn—looking for the culprit! The boys could not remember what time they went into the barn, or whether they'd seen police officers on the scene that day, but they did remember that they stayed in the barn "quite a while" because it had been "nice and cool." Even Lizzie had admitted during her inquest testimony that the barn had been "very hot" on the day of the murder.

After the boys' preposterous testimony the defense presented its key witness, saved until the end, the defendant's sister Emma. Years later, Emma would explain that "When my darling mother was on her deathbed she summoned me, and exacted a promise that I would always watch over 'baby Lizzie.'" Emma was now determined to fulfill that deathbed pledge.

Robinson began by having Emma explain that relations in the Borden home were cordial and that Lizzie had no motive to murder her parents. Emma then flatly denied Mrs. Reagan's story, claiming that the alleged argument between Emma and Lizzie at the jail had never occurred. The primary objective of Emma's testimony, however, was to defuse Alice Russell's damaging account of the dress-burning incident. Emma explained that a dressmaker had made Lizzie's blue calico dress in early May, but that it quickly became stained as a result of a painting job being done at the Borden home. The dress, she added, was "not only soiled but badly faded." During what Emma described, in contradiction to Marshal Fleet, as an "extremely thorough" police search of the home, she, Emma, had noticed the stained and faded dress and suggested to Lizzie that she get rid of the garment. Thus, explained Emma, the burning of the dress was a routine housekeeping chore that she herself, rather than Lizzie, had precipitated.

While he had been content to let Moody conduct most of the prosecution's case, Knowlton handled the cross-examination of Emma, whom he had previously questioned during the inquest. He scored a series of direct hits. Hadn't Emma said at the inquest that there were tensions in the home sufficient for Lizzie to cease referring to Abby as "Mother?" Emma could not recall.

Hadn't she explained that the purchase of the home in Abby's name had angered the sisters and that the purchase of a piece of property for them had not mollified their anger? Again, Lizzie's sister could not recall having said that. Hadn't they hired a private detective, Hanscom, who mysteriously dropped the case after the dress-burning incident? Yes, Emma had to admit, they had. How had the dress become faded in only three months' time? Emma could not say. Although Knowlton poked gaping holes in Emma's testimony, the jury apparently paid little attention.

With Emma's testimony the defense rested on Friday, June 16. After Moody presented a handful of rebuttal witnesses, the court adjourned for the weekend. On June 18, the *New York Times* summed up "a week of triumph for the defense and disaster for the prosecution. Blow after blow has fallen on the case of the

Commonwealth." Few courtroom observers thought there would be a guilty verdict.

When court resumed on Monday, Governor Robinson, a veteran of many successful political campaigns, was ready to bring home the voters—or in this case, the jurors. He offered a long, rambling, and down-home closing argument, one that perfectly suited the men on the jury, whose temperament he understood instinctually. Robinson attacked the prosecution's case as weak and circumstantial. Poor Miss Lizzie had no motive to kill her parents—why, hadn't the maid, Bridget Sullivan, testified that relations appeared normal in the household? In an age well before expert courtroom testimony had become a national industry, Robinson assured the hard-working farmers on the jury that they need not believe all the bluster of the prosecution's so-called experts from Harvard, though he did not remind the jury, that he, too, was a Harvard alumnus. Robinson disputed the forensic evidence as well as testimony that the hatchet fit the wounds. Lizzie's attorney concluded by snorting, "So much for the theory of *experts!*"

Citing the confused police testimony, Robinson insisted that no murder weapon had ever been found because the real murderer had carried it away with him. The absence of blood or bloody garments also showed that Lizzie was innocent. Indeed, the defense attorney intoned, "There is absolutely no direct evidence against her. Nobody saw, heard, or experienced anything to connect her with the tragedy. No knowledge of the use of any instrument has been shown, and it is not shown that she ever touched one, knew of one, or bought one."

Robinson emphasized that Lizzie's love of her father made it impossible to consider that she could commit such brutal violence against him. After all, Robinson reminded the jurors, Lizzie's high school ring, a symbol of the father-daughter bond, remained on her father's finger even in death. But Andrew Borden did have potential enemies among his tenants and business associates, Robinson alleged. The note that Abby received might have "been part of the assassin's scheme" to lure her from the house in order to murder Andrew.

As for the fact that no one had come forward to admit sending a note to Abby, despite the offer of a cash reward, Robinson invoked Victorian cultural mores to explain the matter. It was well known, he averred, that people—especially women—are hesitant to become involved in such business as a murder case. Thus, even though no one had come forward, Robinson told the jury, "that a note arrived, you cannot question!"

Robinson told the judge, jury, and the community what most of them wanted to hear. "Miss Lizzie," as he repeatedly referred to her, was a loving daughter, a respected member of the community, and a fine church woman. She embodied feminine virtue, showed no sign of mental illness, and therefore she met none of the criteria of a cold-blooded killer in the nineteenth-century conception of the criminal mind. Absent those characteristics, Robinson emphasized to the jury, Miss Lizzie simply *had* to be innocent.

The veteran politician and country lawyer set himself for the final flourish, emphasizing that an upstanding young woman such as Lizzie could not have committed the crime. Lizzie had been kept "for ten months in irksome and wearisome control." It was time to set her free, he told the jury. Turning to look at Lizzie and then back at the twelve men, Robinson declaimed: "To find her guilty, you must believe her a fiend! Does she look it?"

Lizzie sat quietly, her hair in a bun, with wire rim glasses that offered a schoolmarmish appearance. The governor sat down, well satisfied with his performance, which indeed had been highly effective.

While Robinson had delivered an impassioned closing argument, Knowlton remained uninspired. He failed to drive home the evidence that Moody had outlined so clearly in the prosecution's opening statement.

Short, bearded, and heavy set, Knowlton sounded a defensive note precisely because he knew that, in contrast with Governor Robinson, it was his task to tell people what they did not want to acknowledge: that this otherwise respected Massachusetts woman had savagely murdered her parents. Knowlton allowed that Lizzie had "the strength of good Christian character" and, as a woman, she was "of a sex all high-minded men revere." He even went as far as to declare that he himself "should be slow to believe Lizzie Andrew Borden killed her father." Astonishingly, the prosecutor of the murder case added, "I hope she did not."

Continuing in a defeatist vein, Knowlton averred that it was "scarcely worthwhile to recapitulate the evidence," though he did go on to argue somewhat perfunctorily that the burning of the dress, the fit of the hatchet wounds, and the logic of the evidence demonstrated Lizzie's guilt beyond a reasonable doubt. Knowlton described Lizzie's motive as the belief that Abby stood between her and her father.

Rage and relative weakness explained the repeated blows to the victims. "A great strong man would have taken that hatchet and with one blow only would have made an end of it," Knowlton declared. "The arm that wielded that hatchet was strong only in hatred. When that woman fell under the blows—the 200-pound woman—the fall must have been heard by whoever was in the house at the time. If Lizzie was downstairs she was in the passageway of the assassin; if she was upstairs she was on the same floor, quite near, and she could not have helped hearing it. No matter how craftily murder is planned there is always some point where the plans fail, and they failed her at a critical time." The district attorney insisted that Lizbeth Andrew Borden, as he typically referred to her in contrast with Robinson's more endearing "Miss Lizzie," had fabricated the alleged note to Abby. However, Knowlton risked too much with the jury by declaring that the prosecution would "stake the entire case on your belief" that no note had been delivered.

Knowlton derided the intruder theory as ludicrous. The alleged madman or enemy of Andrew Borden would have had to penetrate a tightly secured home, kill Mrs. Borden, cool his heels for an hour and a half, unseen by Lizzie or Maggie, kill again, and leave without a trace, all while carrying a bloody hatchet around with him. Despite his lack of enthusiasm, the logic of Knowlton's concluding argument was compelling to the relatively few who would still listen.

On June 20, the thirteenth day of the trial, Lizzie Borden herself delivered the coup de grace to the Commonwealth's case. She told the jurors what they wanted to hear. As required by Massachusetts law, Chief Justice Mason offered Lizzie a final opportunity to speak. In yet another parallel with the Simpson case, Lizzie seized the opportunity to declare her innocence while declining to testify and face cross-examination. Looking directly at the twelve men on the jury, she declared in a clear voice. "I am innocent. I leave it to my counsel to speak for me."

Mason then turned to Associate Justice Dewey, the youngest and least experienced of the three justices, for the obligatory charge to jury. For the next hour and a half Dewey instructed the jurors in such a biased manner as to endure as a classic case of sheer judicial incompetence. Dewey's performance eliminated all doubt, had any still existed at this point, that Lizzie Borden would be set free.

Dewey converted the charge—whose purpose, of course, was to instruct jurors on how to make their deliberations consistent with the law—into an argument for the defense. He repeatedly cast doubt on the prosecution's case, while not once calling into question a single defense argument. Dewey, from Springfield, had been given his lifetime appointment to the superior court bench by none other than Governor George Robinson.

Echoing the defense, Dewey stressed that Lizzie's upstanding community reputation, as well as her strength of character, "may raise a reasonable doubt about the defendant's guilt even in the face of strongly incriminating evidence." The associate justice then proceeded systematically to attack the evidence presented by the prosecution.

Dewey well represented Victorian attitudes about gender. The father of three daughters himself, he clearly did not believe a woman capable of committing the Borden murders. Moreover, he asked the jury, was it "reasonable and credible that [Lizzie] could have killed Mrs. Borden at or about the time claimed by the Government, and then with the purpose in her mind to kill her father at a later hour, have gone about her household affairs with no change of manner to excite attention?" No woman could possibly behave in such a cold and unemotional fashion! "As you have the right to reason from what you know of the laws and properties of matter," the judge intoned, "so you have a right to reason and judge from what you know of the laws and properties of human nature and action."

Dewey took it upon himself to impugn on purely gendered grounds testimony that tended to incriminate Lizzie. He advised the jury to keep in "proper proportion" Hannah Gifford's testimony that Lizzie stated she disliked her stepmother, refused to call her "mother," and ate her meals separately. Dewey cautioned the jurors to "remember that it is the language of a young woman and not a philosopher or jurist." As everyone knew, "the habit of young women in the use of language" favored "intense expression" in which words often "go far beyond their real meaning." In fact, there were no contradictions in Miss Gifford's testimony about what Lizzie said, and no reason to doubt her account, which Marshal Fleet and others had corroborated.

Following his political benefactor's lead, Dewey echoed Robinson's attack on "the words of some gentlemen of medical and scientific knowledge who are termed 'experts.'" On matters such as the hatchet, the wounds inflicted, or the circumstances of death, Dewey suggested that the jury of laymen could judge "as well as any 'expert.'" Dewey declared that the indisputable medical fact that

Mrs. Borden died sixty to ninety minutes before her husband remained "to some extent a matter of opinion."

The judge went on to plead the defense case by stating that it would have been foolish for Lizzie to invent the story about a note being sent to get Mrs. Borden out of the house. "What motive had she to invent a story like this? What motive? . . . What motive had she to take upon herself the responsibility of giving utterance to this distinct and independent fact of a letter or a note received with which she might afterwards find it difficult to explain, if she knew that no such thing was true?"

The Commonwealth had argued that the absence of any evidence of a note demonstrated that Lizzie had in fact invented the story to explain her mother's absence to her father when he had returned home. Maggie had overheard the fabrication. Judge Dewey, however, asked the jury to "contemplate the possibility of there being another assassin" who forwarded a note to the Borden home in an effort "to withdraw Mrs. Borden from the house." Once the assassin arrived and found her still there, however, he killed her and took the note with him. Despite a complete absence of evidence to the effect, Dewey urged the jury to believe in the existence of both the note and an anonymous assassin in place of Lizzie Borden.

Dewey explained to the jury that no matter how many facts the Commonwealth produced which tended to reflect Lizzie's guilt, only one fact "which cannot reasonably be reconciled with her guilt" was needed for acquittal. Dewey, of course, proceeded to offer the fact in question, namely that Lizzie had "no blood stains upon her person or clothing" and that she had had "no sufficient opportunity either to remove the stain from her person or clothing, or to change her clothing. If these supposed facts should be found by you to be real facts, you could not say upon the evidence that defendant's guilt was to a moral certainty proved."

Judge Dewey ignored the issue of the dress that Lizzie destroyed in her kitchen stove. Nor did he remind the jury that the defendant had changed from her blue calico dress to a pink wrapper on the day of the murders.

After explaining that Lizzie herself was under no obligation to testify, Dewey offered testimony for her by explaining that her absence from the stand was merely another way of saying that she did not know who killed her parents. Furthermore, had she testified, the poor innocent girl ran the risk of having her words "severely scrutinized and perhaps misjudged!"

Even reporters who had shown favorable treatment to Lizzie throughout the trial found Dewey's charge remarkable. Joseph Howard, who covered the trial for the *Boston Globe*, described Dewey's charge as "a plea for the innocent." When the jury duly returned with its not guilty verdict, Dewey granted a press interview in which he declared he was "perfectly satisfied" with the outcome, adding that he "was satisfied when I made my charge to the jury that the verdict would be not guilty, although one cannot always tell what a jury will do."

In reality, most observers knew what the jury would do, and the Bristol County farmers did not disappoint. Much like the O. J. Simpson jury a century later, their "deliberations" lasted only minutes, though they elected to stay out a full hour for appearances' sake. They examined no exhibits, studied no testimony, and asked no questions. What they did was vote immediately and unanimously to exonerate Lizzie Borden.

When the jury returned, Lizzie stood as the jury rendered its unanimous verdict of not guilty. The defendant collapsed in her chair, covered her face in her hands, and sobbed, her head resting on the railing in front of her. Governor Robinson beamed with approval. According to the *New York Times*, when the jury issued its not guilty verdict, "a cheer went up which might have been heard half a mile away through the open windows." Outside the courtroom Lizzie radiated smiles before the huge public throng, telling a reporter she was "the happiest woman in the world." After making her way to her coach, Lizzie shamelessly shook hands with well-wishers as the carriage slowly made its way through the masses of people. A crowd of 2,000 quickly amassed outside the Borden family home on Second Street, where they remained until late evening. A band played and the crowd sang "Auld Lang Syne." Rather than fight through the crowd, Lizzie stayed the night with friends.

The press, local and national, shared in the public's jubilation and condemned the Fall River police and district attorney for having subjected the "poor innocent girl" to such a public ordeal. Even the *New York Times*, whose coverage of the trial had been the most evenhanded, editorialized on June 21, 1893, that Lizzie had been "cruelly persecuted" and that her acquittal offered "a condemnation of the police authorities of Fall River and of the legal officers who secured the indictment and have conducted the trial."

While Lizzie won her case in the jury box and in the battle for public opinion, the verdict of history is a different matter entirely. Today, we enjoy the advantages of having the ability to consult the full public record, including the inquest and the prussic acid testimony that were denied to the jury. Moreover, today we are free (or at least freer) of the constraints of Victorian attitudes on gender. Nor are we constrained by the provincial insecurities of Fall River society, which desperately sought to prevent the vicious crime from marring an era of prosperous growth.

The evidence strongly suggests that Lizzie Borden was guilty beyond a reasonable doubt. The trial was not merely a perversion of justice. It was a farce. Lizzie alone had the motive, means, and opportunity to commit the murders. Her anger and resentment of her parents, especially her stepmother, were well known. Lizzie was obsessed with the economic and social constraints laid down by her father, but powerless to do anything—short of murder—to change her situation. As her father got on in years, the threat that her detested stepmother would control the estate, and her life, was too much for this brooding, self-righteous, and unstable young woman to bear.

Lizzie Borden may well have been in the grips of some sort of psychological affliction. Modern readers might recognize an obsessive-compulsive or anti-social personality—a person capable of deflecting any feelings of empathy for her victims or of guilt over their deaths. She had revealed a criminal bent through shoplifting, but it was certainly unusual and indicative of a pathological personality for her to deteriorate to the point of exercising the option of a brutal double homicide of her parents.

Having decided initially to poison her parents, Lizzie turned to the hatchet when that first effort failed. She probably reasoned that no one would believe a woman capable of such a heinous act, a faith for which she was richly rewarded. Although she apparently would have preferred poison, Lizzie may have rationalized the choice of the hatchet by recalling her father's own willingness to decapitate pigeons that Lizzie had fed and nurtured in their roosts around the house and barn. Andrew had killed the birds, only weeks before his own murder, despite Lizzie's pleas that they be spared. Lizzie possessed a profound love of small creatures. At her death in 1927, Lizzie Borden left her single largest bequest, $30,000, to the Animal Rights League of Fall River.

Lizzie's actions before the murders, including the attempt to purchase prussic acid and the stories she told Alice Russell of the supposed threats to her father, suggest premeditation. Lizzie's explanation of her activities after the murders, as Knowlton demonstrated at the inquest, was riddled with contradictions. Lizzie was inconsistent about where she had been in the house and she offered divergent accounts to explain her unlikely presence in a hot barn loft for at least twenty crucial minutes.

Nothing better illustrates Lizzie's consciousness of guilt than the dress-burning incident. Only the gullible can accept the notion that Lizzie Borden would decide to thin out her wardrobe by burning a dress, in the kitchen stove no less, in the midst of a murder investigation in which she had just been named as the primary suspect. Alice Russell, a family friend who stayed to comfort Lizzie and Emma in their hour of need, suddenly realized that she had been sleeping in the room next to a murderer. Hanscom, the Pinkerton detective hired by the Bordens, quietly left the case in the wake of the dress-burning incident.

Lizzie probably thought that she would never be a suspect at all. The savagery of the murders, combined with her own good standing in the community and the prevailing Victorian attitudes about womanhood, all worked in her favor. The brilliance of Lizzie Borden's evil was her recognition that committing the murders in such brutal fashion would deflect attention away from her, or any woman. Once she became the only logical suspect, however, she could no longer count on the police to content themselves with a "respectful" search of a woman's garments in the family home. The dress she had worn—containing only a few drops of blood, as the direction of the blood spatter had been away from the killer—had to be destroyed.

Lizzie Borden's handling of the hatchet was also sloppy, but, as it turns out, good enough. Contradictions in the police testimony, as well as Robinson's persistent efforts to obscure the matter, led to the myth that the Borden murder weapon had never been found. The truth was that the hatchet head fit the wounds precisely and that it had recently been broken off from its handle, which Lizzie probably burned in the kitchen stove.

In addition to the compelling evidence of Lizzie's guilt, no one has ever come up with a credible alternative explanation of the Borden murders. Bridget "Maggie" Sullivan alone besides Lizzie had the opportunity to murder the Bordens, but she had no motive—no complaint against her employers and nothing to gain by their murder. As an Irish immigrant, Maggie of course knew that she would be an immediate suspect, as indeed she was in Knowlton's eyes. It was known, however, from the Kelly's maid next door, and Lizzie herself, that Maggie spent time outside washing windows and then resting in her attic room, providing Lizzie alone with the time she needed to commit the two murders.

Other initial suspects included Uncle John Morse, but he was one of the few individuals in the world who actually liked Andrew and Abby Borden. Even if the old man had had a discernible motive, which he did not, his relatives and other witnesses provided an alibi as to his whereabouts away from the Borden home that morning. Emma, of course, was fifteen miles away when the murders were committed (a hard fact that has not, somehow, prevented one author from claiming that she, not Lizzie, was the "real killer").

This leaves only one of Andrew Borden's angry tenants, business associates, or the proverbial deranged axe-wielding madman as suspects. Here the infamous note supposedly delivered to Mrs. Borden comes into play. Both Maggie and Mrs. Churchill heard Lizzie proclaim that Abby had received a note and left the house. This was not true, of course: Abby was dead upstairs on the guest room floor. Governor Robinson and Judge Dewey offered tortured explanations since there was no getting around the fact that Lizzie had claimed that a note had come. The defense and the biased judge both claimed that the "real killer," an enemy of Mr. Borden's, had sent Abby a note to get her out of the way. When she did not take the bait, the killer executed her as well.

How this killer would have encountered Mrs. Borden upstairs in the guestroom and killed her without a struggle was not addressed. But why send a note to a feeble old woman when Maggie and Lizzie, healthy women who might pose a real obstacle to a killer, were also home to impede the murder of Mr. Borden? Why kill him at home at all—why not kill him out on the street as he made his morning rounds rather than force one's way into an occupied home that was routinely kept secure with double and triple-locked doors? And why, finally, were the blows so numerous, classic indications of a crime of rage, especially on Abby, if Andrew Borden was the object of the killer's hatred?

Although the prosecution, William Moody especially, put forward a strong case against Lizzie, the defense, the court itself, and community pressures overwhelmed the Commonwealth's efforts. Governor Robinson was no match for Moody in his understanding of the law, but that mattered little, especially given the biases of the bench. The defense focused on the strengths of Lizzie's case—the absence of eyewitnesses and of blood on the defendant. Where was the evidence, Robinson repeatedly asked, that this Christian young woman had committed such a foul crime? He emphasized the absence of bloodstains on the defendant when witnesses encountered her only moments after the murders.

Although Lizzie and Emma, who shared the costs, later blanched when they received Robinson's bill for $25,000—a massive sum in 1893—he had clearly been worth every cent. Robinson knew that his grasp of the law was not half as important as his handling of the jury. He had spent much of his life mastering the attitudes of men such as those Bristol County farmers who decided Lizzie's fate. He understood them and they reciprocated in full. Robinson appealed to the jurors, not only as a man most of them had voted for, probably more than once, but as a simple country lawyer standing behind a virtuous woman against the evil forces of centralized authority and the Harvard "experts" with all their "theories."

Robinson also gained the support of the three-judge panel, which sided with the defense throughout the trial. The judges' ruling barring the inquest testimony was disastrous. Even worse was the ruling barring testimony that the defendant in a homicide trial had attempted to purchase a deadly poison less than twenty-four hours before a double murder was committed. The judges offered no basis for their decision because none existed. Moody showed that legal precedent rested firmly on the side of the prosecution. The judges ignored the law.

If, as seems obvious, all the evidence points to Lizzie Borden, why then did she go free? The answer is not simply that the case against Lizzie rested on circumstantial evidence. It did, but most homicide cases do insofar as murderers typically avoid being seen when they kill people. Despite the popular prejudice against circumstantial evidence, there is no prejudice under the law against such evidence when that evidence is compelling, as was the case with Lizzie Borden in 1893.

What possessed three superior court justices, twelve jurors, otherwise sober newspaper editors, and masses of law-abiding citizens to side with a woman who murdered her parents with a hatchet? Lizzie clearly won her case in the proverbial court of public opinion. The public cheered her on and, as the judges and jurors must have been aware, would have reacted with outrage to a guilty verdict.

Victorian gender mores, combined with popular anxieties about the reputation of a burgeoning mill town, overshadowed the evidence in the trial. The

Borden case, like those that follow in this study, illustrates that prejudices and community pressures can prove stronger than even the most compelling evidence. When confronted with a choice between the evidence and their own deeply held beliefs, the press, the public, the judges, and the Borden jury chose the latter.

The not-guilty verdict in the Lizzie Borden case can only be explained as a triumph of community pressures heavily influenced by Victorian gender mores over a quest for genuine justice. The Borden case thus illustrates the profound tensions over changing gender roles in modernizing American society.

To have acknowledged Lizzie's guilt would have been to shatter Victorian convictions of female piety. Such a verdict would have done violence to the prevailing myth that the home represented a separate sphere, a sanctuary from the harsh realities of the world, a place where the moral superiority of women held sway. In reality, as this case demonstrated, the Victorian home could also be a place of repression and violence. What made the Borden case so compelling was that a woman rather than a man had perpetrated the incident of domestic violence, and in horrifying fashion.

On a national level the "respectable classes" were probably relieved by the verdict. They did not want to believe that an upstanding Christian woman could have committed such a horrific crime. A guilty verdict in such a high-profile case would have contravened the Victorian image of the middle-class woman as a nurturing force, the vital center of the nuclear family structure. If an apparently loving daughter and good Christian community woman could commit such crimes, no one was safe and the entire social order would be called into question. Better that a guilty woman go free.

An honest assessment of Lizzie's motives for the crimes might have led logically to the reality that there was something terribly wrong with the position of women in American society. Lizzie Borden contributed—albeit unconsciously and grotesquely—to the coming-of-age of American women. Although Lizzie herself lacked any such nobility of purpose, her hatchet blows were struck against patriarchy, denial of female autonomy, and economic inequality between the sexes in Victorian America.

On a local level, the residents of provincial Massachusetts, in Fall River and surrounding communities, had no desire to sully their collective reputations through association with a notorious hatchet murderer. They hoped, with the cooperation of judges and jury, to handle the matter in their own way, to sweep it under the rug with a not guilty verdict, rather than to accept the blot on the community reputation. The matter was theirs to handle. It was, as Victoria Lincoln entitled her book, "a private disgrace."

Despite their best efforts, and the initial wave of jubilation over the jury's verdict, the fate of Fall River was to be exactly what those good citizens feared that it would be: it became a town known primarily for the homicidal violence of an enraged young woman. Long after the mills shut down and the immigrants ceased to arrive, Fall River would be known as place where "Lizzie Borden took an axe."

Finally, the Borden verdict cannot be viewed in isolation from perceptions about the death penalty. Even those who acknowledged (if only in private) that Lizzie was probably guilty had no desire to see her, or any woman, executed. The Commonwealth of Massachusetts had not executed a woman since the hanging of Bathsheba Spooner, who had contracted for her husband's murder in 1778. Mrs. Spooner had begged for her life to be spared, even offering the seemingly desperate plea that she was pregnant. Ignoring her pleas, the authorities carried out the sentence. An autopsy revealed, however, that Mrs. Spooner had been telling the truth: she had gone to her death "with child." She was the first, last, and only woman ever to be executed in Massachusetts.

Newspapers recounted the dreadful story of Bathsheba Spooner following the Borden murders. And, only a few years before the Borden murders, a Massachusetts woman, Sarah Jane Robinson, had been convicted of six murders, but because she was a woman her sentence was commuted to life imprisonment. In the Borden case, however, the law would have required death by hanging since it was obvious, given the time span between the two murders, that the murder of Andrew Borden had been premeditated.

Although the not guilty verdict had been a popular one in Fall River, a substantial number of citizens did take a closer look at the facts and concluded that Lizzie Borden was guilty. Over time, the conviction that Lizzie had gotten away with murder grew stronger among the public. Not long after the trial people began to shun Lizzie, whose behavior quickly alienated many former supporters as well.

Some weeks after her acquittal, Lizzie attempted to return to her regular Pew 21 in the Fall River Central Congregational Church. The pastor welcomed her back, but as she sat through the service, Lizzie felt the bitter sting of a community's ostracism: all around her the pews were empty. No one would be seen sitting close to Fall River's most notorious citizen. As she sat alone in her own private circle in the middle of the congregation, Lizzie had to know what it would be like for her the rest of her life in Fall River.

Ever stubborn and self-righteous, Lizzie Borden refused to leave the city to start anew somewhere else where she would not have been known. In 1893 she did begin to identify herself as "Lizbeth" Borden. And she and Emma, as the sole inheritors since Andrew died intestate, at long last began to enjoy spending some of their dead father's money.

The two sisters left their Second Street home, and all its wrenching memories, to move into a house that Lizzie would have killed for: a stately Victorian home at 7 French Street, on the Hill. The home, reposing on ample grounds, featured large glassed-in porches and a tree-filled garden. Over the years Lizzie accumulated a live-in housekeeper, a maid, a chauffeur, carriages, and, eventually, one of the first automobiles in Fall River. At a sale price of $13,000 the home was far from the most expensive in town, but it was one of the nice ones. Certainly Lizzie was living well on her murdered father's hard-earned money.

Citizens of Fall River did not normally succumb to the pretension of naming their homes, but Lizzie's small-town aspirations continued to overwhelm her. She chose the name "Maplecroft," and had it inscribed on the top concrete stair leading to her front door. "Lizbeth of Maplecroft" was how Lizzie Borden chose to reinvent herself.

In order for Lizbeth to thrive, the old hatchet-wielding Lizzie had to fade away. The prospects for that happening were not good, however. In 1893, Edwin H. Porter, who covered the murder trial for the *Fall River Daily Globe*, published the first, and still classic, history of the Borden case, entitled *The Fall River Tragedy*. Legend has it that Lizzie promptly bought up as many copies as she could, well more than half of the 1,000 put into circulation by the Fall River publisher.

The vast majority of Fall River citizens had come to resent Lizzie by 1897 when she again embarrassed the community by reverting to one of her old habits: shoplifting. Local newspapers broke the story that a Providence, Rhode Island, merchandise store, Tilden-Thurber, had filed charges against Lizzie for the theft of two art works on porcelain, "Love's Dream" and "Love's Awaken-

The home that Lizzie would have killed for, located on French Street in the fashionable Hill district of Fall River. Lizzie and her sister Emma purchased the home, and named it Maplecroft, with the money they inherited from their father's estate. Emma later moved out, scandalized by the goings-on at parties hosted by her younger sister. Courtesy Fall River Historical Society

ing," jointly valued at $100. She had given one of the plates to a friend, who had taken it back to the store for repairs after accidentally breaking it. At that point the merchants demanded to know how Lizzie's friend had gotten the plate, explaining that it had been stolen. As her father had done for her years before, Lizzie went to the store, made restitution, and went on as if the incident had never occurred.

The people of Fall River, however, had once again been reminded of the true character of Lizbeth of Maplecroft. By now Lizzie had her groceries delivered. If she left Maplecroft at all it was usually for a private carriage ride along the river. In this way she could avoid the stares, taunts, and jeers of her fellow citizens. It was about this time that the cruel, but no less delightful, children's rhyme became popular on the streets of Fall River:

> Lizzie Borden took an axe,
> And gave her mother forty whacks.
> When she saw what she had done,
> She gave her father forty-one.

We can assume that Lizzie was not amused, and not only because it more than doubled the number of "whacks"—somewhere between twenty-nine and thirty-one—that the murderer actually delivered.

Even more aggravating than the children's rhyme, the *Fall River Globe* began the practice of marking the annual anniversary of the Borden murders with bitter sarcasm. On August 4, 1904, for example, the *Globe* noted that Lizzie and Emma had not yet had "to pay out that $5,000 reward for the detection of the murderer . . . who robbed them of their father and mother—no, stepmother, please!"

The local newspaper condemned not only Lizzie, but the superior court as well. "What a lonely, uninhabited, and inexpensive institution the state prison in Charlestown would be if it was as difficult to get straightforward, common sense evidence before the courts of the Commonwealth, in all criminal cases, and capital crimes as it was once upon a time, say about twelve years ago?"

Although protests from the clergy eventually put a stop to the *Globe's* annual ritual, it is no wonder that Lizzie frequently felt the need to get away from Fall River society. Fulfilling her lifelong dream to be a cosmopolitan and cultured woman, Lizbeth traveled regularly to Boston, New York, and Washington to shop and patronize the theater.

In the course of her trips to Boston, Lizzie went backstage to make the acquaintance of the actress Nance O'Neil. Miss O'Neil had seen better days on the stage, but the tragic roles she typically played struck a chord with Lizzie. After they met backstage, Lizzie invited Nance O'Neil, and some others of the theater set, to Maplecroft for a catered party, complete with live music and drinks all around.

Poor Emma, ever the prim and proper elder sister, could no longer abide Lizbeth's behavior. She was consorting with an immoral lot and showing no shame about it. Emma moved out in 1905. Though they had been through a great deal together, to say the least, the two sisters never spoke again. The old Women's Christian Temperance Union and churchgoing set, once Lizzie's staunchest defenders, now joined Emma in their embarrassment over Lizzie. Some of the Puritan gossip centered on Lizzie's sex life, including the theory that she and Miss O'Neil were more than mere friends.

Emma would never speak of such matters, but the people were wrong if they thought her departure from Maplecroft constituted an admission that Lizzie had committed the terrible murders of 1892. Emma granted a single interview, published in the *Boston Sunday Post* on April 13, 1913, to clarify the matter. "No—emphatically," Emma declared. "No—Time and again [Lizzie] has avowed her innocence to me, and I believe her."

If Emma was sincere in her defense of Lizzie, it was because she had drunken as deeply of Governor Robinson's courtroom rhetoric as had the jury of Bristol County farmers. "The authorities never found the axe or whatever implement it was that figured in the killing," Emma explained in justifying her faith in Lizzie's innocence.

We will never know whether Emma really believed in Lizzie—one does wonder why Lizzie had to avow her innocence "time and again"—or whether the elder sister was simply engaged in denial over the truth about "baby Lizzie," for whom she had, after all, pledged to be responsible. Emma must have been coping with some guilt of her own, for she too was living a comfortable life on her murdered father's money.

Lizzie soon gave up the wild parties and spent more and more of her time alone being catered to by her servants. She became heavy and jowly as she aged. She was friendly toward the neighbors, especially children, when they encountered her in the yard or on the street. The people and the newspapers ceased complaining about her. Fall River tried to forget.

In 1926 Lizzie underwent gall bladder surgery, checking into the hospital under an assumed name. Never fully recovering, she died on June 2, 1927, of complications from pneumonia. As far as anyone knows, she never spoke about the murders or the trial and left no documents to posterity. Her estate was valued at $265,000.

Lizzie was buried under the cover of darkness, to avoid a public scene, at Oak Grove Cemetery. In compliance with her wishes, she was interred next to her father.

By this time Emma was living under an assumed name in Newmarket, New Hampshire. Finally freed of any lasting concern for "baby Lizzie," Emma died only a few weeks after Lizzie's passing.

Only Bridget Sullivan outlived her former employers. Shortly after the trial Maggie abandoned the notoriety of Fall River, eventually settling in Anaconda, Montana, where she continued to work as a domestic. She married in 1905 and reportedly bore children. Bridget Sullivan died on March 25, 1948, in Butte, Montana, without ever having made any public statement about the murders.

Fall River no longer avoids its inevitably perpetual association with Lizzie Borden, although the citizenry still would like to be known for something other than a sensational parricide in 1892. Yet the narrow home on Second Street, Maplecroft, and the Borden burial site just inside Oak Grove Cemetery are impeccably maintained. One can take a tour of all of the major Borden sites and, if your pockets are deep enough, spend a night at the crime scene or at Maplecroft, both of which have been preserved as trendy bed-and-breakfast establishments.

The sites endure as memorials to a time when an angry young woman hacked her way to freedom in a provincial Massachusetts town.

II VENGEANCE: BRUNO RICHARD HAUPTMANN AND THE LINDBERGH BABY KIDNAPPING

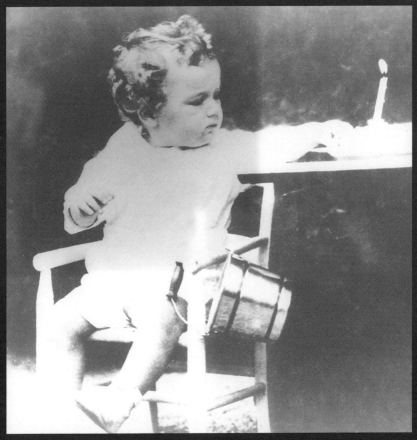

The Lindbergh baby, Charles Augustus Lindbergh Jr. The dimpled, curly haired son of a popular American hero was born on his mother's birthday, June 22, 1930. The kidnapping on March 1, 1932, shocked the nation and precipitated an arduous criminal investigation. The baby's body was not discovered in its shallow grave until more than two months after the kidnapping and murder. Courtesy New Jersey State Police Museum

II VENGEANCE: BRUNO RICHARD HAUPTMANN AND THE LINDBERGH BABY KIDNAPPING

Despite the bitter cold wind and the weight on his back, the thin man moved steadily through the woods. Sweat trickled down his back as he entered a clearing and made his way toward the big stone house.

The sound of the wind, he realized, was a blessing—it would cover any noise he made traversing the frosty ground with the clumsy implement he carried in his arms.

Breathing hard now, the man carefully unfolded the ladder he had designed solely for the purpose for which it was now to be used. He placed it against the house and slowly pushed it upward until it was balanced below the window into the child's nursery.

A deep breath. He knew he had the courage, the sheer daring, that even the great American hero inside would soon be forced to acknowledge. He would show Lindy that he wasn't the only man who could defy the odds and shock the world!

The ladder settled nicely as he put all his weight on the first rung. He ascended step by step, reaching into his pocket for the chisel as he reached the middle rungs. He discovered that the shutters did not need to be pried open, however, and the window lifted up without a sound.

The intruder stepped into the French window, placing his foot on a suitcase that lay under the sill. He walked noiselessly across the room and peered into the crib. There he was, the curly-haired baby, looking just like his picture in the newspapers. The child began to stir as the cold wind enveloped the nursery.

Trying to control his own nervous excitement, the intruder reached down into the crib, clamped his hand harshly over the baby's mouth, and yanked the helpless child from beneath its blankets. He stuffed a handkerchief into the baby's mouth to stifle its desperate cries and tumbled the little boy into a burlap sack. Quickly now, he balanced himself while holding the sack and used his other hand to place the envelope that he had brought with him on the window sill.

The kidnapper pushed the window shut and began to descend as fast as he could. In a few seconds he would be back to his car and safely on the road to New York.

Then it happened. The horrible crackling sound followed by the plunge to the ground. The baby fell from his arms and landed with a thud against the base of the house. Momentarily stunned, the intruder didn't notice that he had turned his ankle. Fighting off a wave of panic, he scrambled to his feet, grabbed the burlap sack and collected the sections of the ladder under his arms.

The ladder was heavy and cumbersome, however, and the kidnapper feared that he might have been heard. Dropping sections of the ladder as he ran, the intruder reached the clearing and then the trees to Featherbed Lane. He now felt the pain shooting up his leg. The kidnapper placed the burlap bag on the seat and started his car. He drove as fast as he dared to cover the less than four miles back to Hopewell. He turned right, heading east, into town, then left, heading north, back in the direction from which he had come.

His mind raced. Had the family or the servants heard the noise of the ladder breaking? Were the police even now converging upon the isolated home? Would they set up roadblocks? Determined, he vowed that he would not go to prison again. Never!

Just over a mile outside of Hopewell, on the road to Princeton, the kidnapper abruptly veered to the side of the road. He had decided to dispose of the evidence linking him with the crime. The kidnapper ran some seventy-five yards into the woods. Pulling the baby from the burlap sack, he saw that the child had been injured in the fall.

The man was unmoved—he had smelled and seen death before—many, many times before. Regardless of what his plans might have been, there was only one thing to do now. Picking up a stone, the killer delivered a lethal blow that shattered the baby's soft skull.

He removed the child's sleeping suit and placed the tiny corpse face down on the cold ground. Grabbing a stick, sweating furiously now, he dug the shallowest of graves, rolled the little body into the hole, and hastily threw the loose dirt, sticks, and leaves back on top.

The killer fled back to the safety of his car and, none too soon, found himself

back on the open highway en route to New York. Things had not gone smoothly,
but at least he had escaped.
    And, he thought with a smile, I can still collect the ransom!

A merica's first couple, Charles and Anne Morrow Lindbergh, sat before the
fireplace in their living room as the cold winter wind whipped through
the thick forest outside their secluded New Jersey estate.

It was late in the evening on March 1, 1932, and both Charles and Anne were
tired. Lindbergh had not returned home from his work at the airline offices in
New York, followed by a trip to the dentist, until 8:30 P.M.

After a late dinner, the couple now sat, reading the newspaper and chatting.
Suddenly, amid the tranquility of their home, Charles heard a distinctive crack-
ing sound over the wind. "What's that?" he asked Anne. Unable to identify the
sound, Lindbergh assumed it had come from inside the home, probably one of
the servants breaking something in the kitchen.

Only later did it become clear that what they had heard was the sound of one
of the most notorious crimes in American history—the kidnapping of their
twenty-month-old son, Charles Augustus Lindbergh Jr.

Before long Anne went up to her bedroom and Charles continued his reading in the library. Betty Gow, the baby's devoted nursemaid, went up to the
nursery to make a last check on the baby before settling in for the night.

Opening the door into the room, Betty left the light off so as not to disturb
young Charlie. "I crossed the room, closed the French windows, and plugged in
the electric heater," the nursemaid recalled." I crossed to the baby's cot and discovered that I couldn't hear the baby breathing. . . . In the half light I saw he
wasn't there."

Shocked at first, Betty experienced a quick flood of relief when she realized
that Anne must have come in and taken her firstborn child into her own bedroom for some good-night cuddling. But when Betty Gow found Mrs. Lindbergh the latter declared, "Why, no, I haven't had him." The two women could
only assume that Charles had taken the baby downstairs, but when Betty burst
into the library and asked the famous aviator if he had the child, Lindbergh
responded, "No. Isn't he in his crib?"

Bolting up to the bedroom, Lindbergh found that the blankets, pinned to the mattress by safety pins, had been jostled and the baby had vanished. "I went in to the nursery," Lindbergh later recalled, "and from the appearance of the bed clothes I felt sure something was wrong." What combination of fear, of violation, and then anger Lindbergh must have felt when his eyes moved from the empty crib to a plain white envelope lying on the sill of the southeast window.

Lindbergh stopped for a moment to look into the eyes of his despairing wife, pregnant with their second child. "Anne," he said, "they've stolen our baby!"

"Oh, God," was all Anne Lindbergh could breathe in response. Lindbergh ordered the butler, Oliver Whateley, to call the local police.

Lindbergh deferred reading the note, racing instead into his bedroom to take his Springfield rifle from the closet. The servants looked in closets, the cellar, the attic, and even opened drawers in a desperate search for the missing child.

Outside the night was windy, cold, and black as coal. Lindbergh had no visibility and could hear nothing but the wind. Concluding after several minutes that his efforts were futile, Lindbergh returned inside to telephone his attorney and confidant, Henry C. Breckinridge. He then awaited the arrival of the police from Hopewell and from New Jersey State Police headquarters down in Trenton.

At midnight the man who would lead the investigation of the Lindbergh baby kidnapping, H. Norman Schwarzkopf, arrived at the Hopewell estate. Schwarzkopf—whose son would become an army general and the leader of U.S. forces in the 1991 Persian Gulf War—was himself a West Point graduate. The senior Schwarzkopf was a second-generation German American who had fought in France as an artillery officer during World War I. Schwarzkopf was the superintendent of the New Jersey State Police, an organization he had served for ten years. Lean and erect with a small mustache and chiseled features, Schwarzkopf radiated military discipline.

Entering the baby's room, a state police officer opened the white envelope on the windowsill to reveal a crudely written note from the kidnapper. It demanded "50000$" and warned against "making anyding public or for notify the police. The child is in gut [good] care" The barely literate note—the first of fifteen the kidnapper would send—displayed a symbol of two interlocking circles outlined in blue. A large red dot appeared in the center of the inner oval formed by the linking of the two circles. The kidnapper advised Lindbergh to respond only to notes containing this "singnature."

Having summoned the police before reading the note, Lindbergh realized that it was already too late to follow the kidnapper's instruction against informing the authorities. Determined to try to save his child's life, Lindbergh made the decision that from that point forward he would cooperate in every conceivable way with the kidnapper as the best means of getting his son returned safely. Lindbergh never deviated from this path.

Modern readers might have difficulty imagining the control that Lindbergh would exercise over the ensuing investigation. Lindbergh's own tremendous prestige, as well as the weakness of police agencies and the absence of federal jurisdiction in the case, allowed the aviation hero to take personal charge of the kidnapping probe. The Lindbergh case thus was distinguished by the unusual degree of authority over the criminal investigation held by the family of the victim. Lindbergh's personal involvement in the investigation was another example of the complications inherent in celebrity murder cases.

Since May 1927, when he had become the first man to fly solo across the Atlantic from New York to Paris, Charles "Slim" Lindbergh had achieved the status of an icon. Ticker tape parades, prizes, awards dinners, and even the Congressional Medal of Honor had been bestowed upon the daring young aviator.

The frenzied acclaim for the Lone Eagle reflected Americans' reverence for individual achievement. Lindbergh had bucked the odds, taking off on a wet field and enduring sleeplessness and menacing weather to conquer the Atlantic in his tiny, specially constructed aircraft, the *Spirit of St. Louis.* Lindbergh's heroics aroused Americans from their sense of complacency in the materially successful but spiritually vacuous 1920s. Tall, handsome, and shy, but possessing a winning smile, the Minnesota farmboy turned aviation hero embodied the image of the all-American boy.

Lindbergh, twenty-five years old at the time of his historic flight, quickly became the country's most eligible bachelor. Although notoriously girl shy, and previously interested only in his work as an aviation pioneer, Lindbergh decided to seek a wife. In the fall of 1928 he telephoned the estate of Dwight Morrow at Englewood, New Jersey, and invited the financier's youngest daughter, Anne, to go flying with him over Long Island. Lindbergh had become acquainted with the Morrow family when they entertained him after a celebrated flight to Mexico City, where Morrow had served as the American ambassador. While the press had focused on rumors of Lindbergh's attraction to Morrow's older daughter, Elisabeth, actually it was Anne who commanded the aviator's attention.

Dark haired, petite, and athletic, Anne was a graduate of Smith College and an aspiring writer. She had been immediately attracted to Lindbergh upon meeting him in Mexico City. By February 1929, with rumors swirling about Lindbergh and one of the Morrow daughters, the Morrows released a public statement announcing the engagement of Anne and Charles.

The story was an instant sensation. Both were young, attractive, and adventurous. The glamorous and wealthy couple was as close to regal as was possible in a country without royalty. The couple was married in a private ceremony at the Morrow estate, called Next Day Hill, in Englewood, New Jersey, on May 27, 1929.

Showing that she was as courageous as her husband, Anne joined Charles on myriad national and international tours designed to promote aviation as a safe and efficient form of travel. On July 27, 1929, Lindbergh, joined by Anne as copilot, flew from Los Angeles to Winslow, Arizona, the first leg of the first transcontinental air route. The Lindberghs promoted Pan American Airways as well as Trans World Airlines, which became known as the "Lindbergh Line."

While Lindbergh willingly capitalized on his fame to promote aviation and his own commercial ventures, he resented the constant intrusions of the press and public into his private life. When they were not crisscrossing the country on a survey or expedition, the Lindberghs secluded themselves in the Morrows' New York apartment or at Next Day Hill, the fifty-six-acre Englewood estate.

Public demand for interviews and photographs of America's first couple only increased with the birth of their son, Charles Augustus Jr., on June 22, 1930. The birth of the namesake of an American hero was front-page news across the country. "**IT'S A BOY—LINDY**" screamed the *New York Daily News*. Born on his mother's birthday, the dimpled, curly-haired "Eaglet" was adopted as America's first child in the midst of an otherwise bleak era of the Great Depression.

With the desire for privacy paramount in their minds, the Lindberghs purchased a 400-acre site in the Sourland Mountain area near Hopewell in southern New Jersey, and commissioned construction of a whitewashed stone, two-and-a-half-story home under a slate roof. Beyond the clearing for the house, thick woods covered the area. Lindbergh planned to construct a private runway near the home to enable him to fly to New York in twenty minutes and return to seclusion the same day. The estate provided the Lindberghs the privacy they craved. They had few neighbors and theirs was the only house in the area that had even been hooked up for electricity.

At the time of the kidnapping, the Lindberghs had not moved into their new home on a full-time basis. The family typically spent the workweek at the Morrow estate in Englewood, but passed virtually every weekend at the house near Hopewell. Indeed, the family's presence at the Hopewell estate at the time of the kidnapping, on a Tuesday, was unusual and an immediate focus of the inquiry.

Early in the investigation the state police jumped to the conclusion, as the first crime report put it, that "The kidnappers consisted apparently of a party of at least two or more persons." The initial investigators believed they could discern two sets of footprints below the crime scene.

Schwarzkopf suspected that the kidnapping might have been, at least in part, an inside job involving some of the Morrow family servants. How else had the kidnapper known that the family had remained at the home near Hopewell until Tuesday when they normally returned to Englewood after the weekend? And how had the kidnapper known which window to enter to seize the baby from his crib?

Such questions soon became paramount, but in the immediate aftermath of the kidnapping confusion reigned. After a sleepless night, the Lindberghs found their estate inundated the next day by an estimated 400 reporters and photographers. It seemed that every newspaper and picture man in New York and Philadelphia had descended upon the Lindbergh property. Reporters booked all of the available rooms in the local hotel while others paid local residents to room in their houses while they covered the story.

The Lindbergh crime was a sensational news story. The emergence of modern media technology made the Lindbergh crime, the investigation, and the subsequent criminal trial a more compelling national drama than the Lizzie Borden murder case forty years previously.

The advent of radio in the 1920s revolutionized communications and linked the United States in a single national media culture. Events such as World War I, the Scopes "monkey trial," Lindbergh's solo flight, and the Great Depression all commanded national media attention. The country was far more literate and urbanized than at the time of the Lizzie Borden murders. News of the Lindbergh crime spellbound newspaper, radio, and newsreel audiences. Newspaper circulation shot up more than 300 percent, as the public could not get too much coverage of the wrenching family tragedy.

The motion picture, flourishing in the 1920s, encouraged an emerging American obsession with visual imagery that television would take a step further in the post–World War II years. Newsreels updated millions of Americans on the Lindbergh crime in movie theaters across the country. Until the assassination of President John F. Kennedy in 1963, the Lindbergh baby kidnapping was the most sensational crime in the United States in the twentieth century.

By the time of the kidnapping, Americans had become attuned to crime as a national cultural phenomenon. The 1906 murder of New York architect Stanford White in a love triangle involving actress Evelyn Nesbitt had been the most sensational celebrity murder case of the new century. An even more shocking homicide occurred in 1924 when Bobby Franks, a Chicago schoolboy, was murdered by two privileged and well-educated young men who lived in his neighborhood. Nathan Leopold and Richard Loeb confessed to the apparently senseless crime, which occurred as a result of the complex psychology of the two young men. Following a riveting trial and a defense anchored by the nation's preeminent defense attorney, Clarence Darrow, Leopold and Loeb were spared the death penalty, although Loeb was later murdered in prison.

A few years later another sensational case had a different outcome when Nicola Sacco and Bartolomeo Vanzetti, avowed anarchists, were executed for a robbery-murder that had occurred in South Braintree, Massachusetts, in 1920. Evidence against the two was dubious. Antiforeign and antiradical sentiment, particularly virulent in the United States in the years after the Bolshevik Revolution in Russia and World War I, overshadowed the trial and the unsuccessful appeals on the part of the two Italian immigrants. Their execution shortly after midnight on August 23, 1927, was an international cause célèbre.

Finally, the Prohibition (Eighteenth) Amendment, outlawing sale and distribution of alcoholic beverages, spurred growth of both crime and law enforcement. Gangsters trafficked in liquor, as well as drugs, gambling, and prostitution, all of which focused national attention on crime and punishment in the new age of radio and newsreels.

The Lindbergh kidnapping, shocking in its audacity and targeted against a popular national hero, riveted a mass public now long conditioned to receptivity to sensational crime stories. Though a terrible tragedy, the sensational crime

New Jersey State Police recreated the "crime of the century," placing the homemade ladder against the side of the Lindberghs' whitewashed stone home in the Southland Mountain area near Hopewell, New Jersey. The baby was taken from the window, open in the photograph, on the second floor. The kidnap ladder became crucial evidence in the subsequent trial of Bruno Richard Hauptmann. Courtesy New Jersey State Police Museum

also offered a welcome diversion from the Depression, the most severe economic crisis in American history.

Under intense public pressure to solve the "crime of the century," the New Jersey State Police began slowly to uncover the evidence of the criminal's modus operandi. Investigators found a three-quarter-inch chisel, which the kidnapper had brought in the event that he needed help opening the window. Police theorized that the intruder had dropped the chisel when the ladder broke.

The home-built ladder was clearly the most intriguing remnant of the sensational crime. Crude but ingenious, the ladder was eighteen and a half feet long. Dowel pins held together three sections of the ladder, which could be folded to a third of its size for transporting. Eighteen inches, rather than the standard foot, separated the rungs of the specially constructed ladder. As it turned out, two sections of the ladder proved long enough for the killer to reach the baby's room. Investigators immediately noticed the shattered section, about five feet from the base, where the ladder had broken upon the kidnapper's descent.

Footprints appeared below the window but the state police failed to make a cast of the impressions. It was a crucial crime scene blunder, one that would complicate efforts to identify a perpetrator or to determine whether more than a single individual had been involved. Instead of carefully preserving the crime scene, an army of cops, reporters, and cameramen obliterated the prints, destroying key evidence in the case.

Schwarzkopf did order the ladder and the windowsill dusted for finger-prints. The absence of any identifiable impressions suggested that the kidnap-per had taken the elementary precaution of wearing gloves. The state police searched across a radius of about five miles, discovering nothing, in the woods surrounding the crime scene.

While Schwarzkopf set up a communications center in Lindbergh's three-car garage, the aviator and his wife worried that the presence of the police and the rampant publicity, in defiance of the kidnapper's demands, would lead to the child being harmed. Schwarzkopf already feared the worst. With the pins still fastened to the baby's blankets in the crib, it was apparent that the child had been pulled out from under the covers, probably feet first. It seemed likely that the child had been roughly treated and, though there was no sign of violence, for all the police commander knew the baby might have been strangled or suffocated on the spot.

Relief, of sorts, at least for the Lindberghs, came in the form of a second ran-som note, delivered on March 4. The note scolded Lindbergh for contacting the police, but assured him the child was safe. The kidnapper upped the ransom demand from $50,000 to $70,000, explaining that because of the police and publicity the process would now require more time. "We will form you later were to deliver the mony," the note said. "But we will note do so until the Police is out of the cace and the pappers are quite."

Getting the "pappers" to be "quite" was impossible, of course. Sensational coverage of the case would not abate for weeks. Lindbergh, who had grown more than weary of reporters and photographers since his emergence as a national icon, now resolved to use the press to reassure the kidnapper of his intention to cooperate to gain his son's release. Their only concern was the safe return of their child, Lindbergh emphasized to the mass of reporters who followed his every move. He added that he would not seek "to injure in any way those concerned with the return of the child."

Lindbergh, like much of the national press, assumed that the crime must have been committed by organized crime gangs which dominated the news in the last year of Prohibition. In New York a hood named Vincent "Mad Dog" Coll had challenged the supremacy of the Dutch Schultz gang, using kidnapping and ransom against Schultz and his allies. Kidnapping and occasional shoot-outs followed as the "snatch racket" gained notoriety. Contributing to the theory that gangs had kidnapped the Lindbergh baby was a pledge by gangster Al Capone, lodged in Chicago's Cook County Jail on charges of income tax evasion, that he could obtain the child's freedom, if only he were released.

Schwarzkopf rejected the theory of organized crime being responsible for the kidnapping. The crudely written notes, the relatively small ransom demand, and the sloppiness on the part of the kidnapper suggested otherwise. Organized criminals would have demanded more than a mere $50,000 to $70,000, especially since the Morrow family was worth millions. The barely literate notes and the home-built ladder suggested a small-time operation.

Despite the logic of these arguments, Lindbergh responded positively to an offer of help from the well-known organized crime figure Morris Rosner, who operated in New York and New Jersey. Schwarzkopf strenuously opposed the decision of Lindbergh and Breckinridge to show Rosner the ransom note and provide him with $2,500 spending money to seek out the kidnapper in organized crime circles.

Although he soon proclaimed that he knew which criminals had abducted the child, Rosner in reality knew nothing about the crime. Nevertheless, Schwarzkopf could not dissuade Lindbergh from supporting Rosner nor could he get the aviation hero to agree to allow police to tap his telephone. Lindbergh insisted that he had to win the kidnapper's trust in order to secure his child's freedom. In an NBC radio message, the Lindberghs pledged to keep secret the kidnapper's identity and pay the ransom demand in return for the child's safe return.

Both Lindbergh and Schwarzkopf refused J. Edgar Hoover's efforts to intrude the Bureau of Investigation—precursor to the FBI—into the sensational kidnap case. As part of his unrelenting efforts to gain recognition and respect for the federal crime-fighting agency, Hoover appeared personally in Hopewell three days after the kidnapping. The Lindberghs refused to see him, however, and Schwarzkopf insisted that the New Jersey State Police, despite their limited resources and absence even of a crime lab, could do the job without federal help.

Meanwhile, blanket radio and press coverage prompted an outpouring of national and international sympathy for Lindbergh and his wife. Hundreds of thousands of citizens spewed their contempt for anyone who would perpetrate such a cruel crime against America's first couple. Thousands more called in tips, fingered alleged suspects, and offered their advice on how to catch the kidnapper.

Few of these citizens were more upset by the crime than John F. Condon, a retired schoolteacher from the Bronx, New York. The sentimental Condon worshipped "Colonel" Lindbergh, who had been commissioned as an officer in the U.S. Army Air Corps, as the ultimate all-American boy and national hero. Condon viewed the kidnapping of the Lindbergh baby as not only a crime against the family, but an attack on America itself. In an offer published in the *Bronx Home-News*, Condon pledged to donate his life savings of $1,000 and act as a go-between for the kidnapper, if only the culprit would return the child to its parents. On March 9—much to his own astonishment—Condon received a note from the kidnapper accepting the public offer to serve as an intermediary.

Condon promptly telephoned Lindbergh, who assumed the call was another in an endless series of false leads, cranks, and hoaxes. However, when Condon described the symbol of interlocking circles, the kidnapper's "singnature," Lindbergh bolted out of his chair. The aviation hero realized that Condon's description matched the design on the original ransom note, information that had not been made public. Lindbergh immediately urged Condon to drive the sixty miles from New York to Hopewell. After the retired school teacher arrived, it was readily apparent that the note he had received from the kidnapper was authentic. In addition to the matching symbols, both the note sent to Condon and the ransom notes to Lindbergh contained similar misspellings and the dollar signs placed on the right rather than the left of the figures cited.

It would take a long time for Schwarzkopf to trust Condon, but Lindbergh continued to call the shots in the investigation of his son's kidnapping. Condon, who invariably dressed in three-piece suits and a dark hat, was a respected member of his Bronx community. He had received a master's degree from Fordham University, where he lectured part-time in the education department. Although he did not hold a Ph. D., the educator liked to be known as "Doctor" Condon. Now seventy-one years old, Condon was active in community affairs in the Bronx neighborhood where he lived with his wife. He did have a richly earned reputation as an eccentric and, as all concerned would come to realize, Condon could be contradictory and overbearing. But by all appearances he was what he appeared to be, an honest citizen who had been deeply moved by a genuine American tragedy.

Lindbergh authorized Condon to act as his go-between with the kidnapper. He endorsed the elderly man's suggestion that his initials, J. F. C., be merged together into the code name "Jafsie" which would be employed in communications with the kidnapper. On Saturday evening, March 12, as Henry Breckinridge sat with Condon in his Bronx living room, the kidnapper delivered a note through a taxicab driver, Joseph Perrone, informing Jafsie where to meet and to bring the money.

Although Condon considered that he might be risking his own life, especially since they had not yet raised the ransom money, he followed the kidnapper's directions to Woodlawn Cemetery in the Bronx. Condon then followed the man down the street to Van Cortlandt Park. As he approached, Condon found the man, who identified himself only as John, holding his coat collar up around his chin. Beneath the upturned collar Condon saw a man with deep-set eyes and a triangular face. He estimated the man to be in his mid-thirties. Condon recounted that he tried to win the man's confidence by asking him to sit "as my guest" on a park bench. As the two men talked, Condon pulled out a handful of four-inch safety pins, which John identified as those which had fastened the baby's blankets to the mattress in the crib.

Satisfied that he was in the presence of the real kidnapper, Condon informed John that he had not brought the ransom money and would only do so when assured that the baby would be returned safely. They agreed that John would send the baby's sleeping suit to confirm that he was indeed the real kidnapper.

Condon asked the heavily accented man, "Are you German?" but John replied, "No, Scandinavian." Condon tried to get the kidnapper to soften, asking him what his mother would think of his crime. John admitted his mother would "cry" if she knew, but insisted that he was only a messenger for a larger gang. John then stunned Condon by asking nervously, "Would I burn if the baby is dead?" Condon responded sharply, asking about the baby's condition, but John replied hastily that there was no doubt that the baby was alive and in good health.

News of the meeting encouraged the Lindberghs, whose only thought was the safe return of their son. Determined to handle the ransom by his own means, rather than tapping the vast wealth of his in-laws, Lindbergh sold stock and amassed numbered gold certificates from the Morgan banking house. He believed, based on Condon's account, that the kidnappers were keeping their side of the bargain and could be counted on to release Charles Jr. once the ransom had been paid.

Accordingly, Lindbergh refused the requests of both the New Jersey State Police and New York City Police to follow Condon to the next rendezvous with "John." He wanted nothing to interfere with the transfer of the money and the return of his child. What motive would the kidnappers have to harm the child as long as they were being paid?

Even though Lindbergh believed that John was the real kidnapper, he continued to pursue other possibilities on the outside chance that they might be authentic or related to Condon's man. John Hughes Curtis, a fifty-two-year-old Norfolk, Virginia, businessman and socialite, insisted that he had been contacted by organized crime figures who had the Lindbergh baby in their possession. A close friend of Lindbergh's, a Navy admiral, vouched for the character of Curtis, who had no apparent reason to invent such a tale.

While Lindbergh pursued all avenues of investigation, "John" became impatient. On Monday, March 28, Condon received a letter in which the kidnapper chided Lindbergh for pursuing false leads and threatened to increase the ransom demand. The kidnapper continued to insist "there is absolute no fear aboud the child it is well."

Finally, on Saturday, April 2, Jafsie and the kidnapper had concluded arrangements for their final meeting that evening. Lindbergh himself had decided to accompany Jafsie, after first insisting that Schwarzkopf give his word that he would not attempt to follow them to the ransom meeting. Feeling he had no choice, Schwarzkopf reluctantly agreed.

After arriving on the periphery of St. Raymond's Cemetery in the Bronx, both Lindbergh and Condon heard the heavily accented voice call out from the darkness, "Ay, Doctor. Over here." "I could hear the voice distinctly," Lindbergh told police later, "and the 'Doctor' was pronounced with a definite accent."

Upon calling out, John rose from behind a gravestone. Based on their earlier meeting, Condon had decided that the kidnapper would be content with $50,000 of Lindbergh's money rather than the second demand of $70,000. After a brief argument, Condon handed over the $50,000 ransom, although, had John insisted, Condon was ready to give him the additional $20,000. It occurred to neither Condon nor Lindbergh at the time that John's willingness to settle on the spot for a smaller ransom suggested that he was more than merely the gang messenger that he claimed to be. Otherwise, John presumably would not have been able to accept $20,000 less than demanded without consulting his superiors.

With Lindbergh observing from the nearby shadows, John congratulated Condon on handling his intermediary role. He then handed Condon a note that purported to explain where the baby could be picked up. After issuing a final warning that the note should not be opened for eight hours, John slid off into the darkness.

Condon then rejoined Lindbergh at the cemetery's edge. After a short time they decided to disregard John's orders and open the note, which stated that the baby could be found on a "boad" (boat) named "Nelly" near Elizabeth Island in the Rhode Island Sound off Martha's Vineyard. Ecstatic in the belief that his child would be freed as promised, Lindbergh prepared to fly out the next morning in search of the boat. Back home in Hopewell, Anne placed fresh blankets in little Charlie's crib.

After two days of relentless aerial reconnaissance, however, it was obvious that there was no "boad" named Nelly on the Rhode Island Sound. Jafsie placed frantic ads in the Bronx newspaper, but this time John ignored him. Desperate, Lindbergh continued to follow up on John Hughes Curtis's alleged contact with a different gang of kidnappers. On May 12 he boarded a launch in the Chesapeake Bay to search for his son on a tip from Curtis. But Curtis was about to be revealed as a cruel hoaxster.

At 3:15 in the afternoon, on the same day that Lindbergh boarded the launch in the Chesapeake, and seventy-two days after the kidnapping, a forty-three-year-old truck driver named William Allen got out of the vehicle in which he was riding with another man on the Princeton-Hopewell Road. "I was taken up short and had to go into the woods to answer a call to nature," Allen explained later to the state police. "As I got into the woods I ducked my head to go under a bush and when I raised up I seen this skeleton or something . . . and it had a person's foot at it."

The child's head, still covered with his distinctive wispy blond hair, was face down in the mud. The little body, blackened from decomposition, had been in the same spot since the night of the kidnapping. Both hands were gone and the child's right leg was missing from the knee down, the work of scavenging animals.

While officials radioed messages to Lindbergh, Schwarzkopf took it upon himself to inform Anne Morrow Lindbergh and her mother, who was staying with her daughter in Hopewell. He stressed that the head wound indicated that the baby appeared to have been killed almost immediately and that there had been little time for pain and suffering.

Anne received the news with remarkable stoicism. Schwarzkopf then read a statement to the press explaining that "the body of the Lindbergh baby was found at 3:15 P.M. today by William Allen, Negro, of Trenton, who was riding on the Mount Rose Road toward Hopewell." Within minutes a carnival scene materialized, as cars filled with sightseers, reporters, and photographers jammed the highway. Petty entrepreneurs set up stands along the way selling peanuts, popcorn, and photographs.

Meanwhile, Walter H. Swayze, the Mercer County coroner, performed the autopsy on the badly decomposed body. "Diagnosis of the cause of death is a fractured skull due to external violence," he recorded. Police theorized that the remnants of a burlap bag found at the scene had been used by the killer to transport the child. The grave had obviously been quick work, involving only a shallow covering of dirt, sticks, and leaves.

Already stunned by the discovery of their murdered child, the Lindbergh family endured one final indignity. In an act that confirmed Lindbergh's contempt for American journalism, photographers broke into the morgue and snapped pictures of the dead child.

Lindbergh himself went to the morgue to confirm that the baby's body was that of his firstborn and namesake. Without hesitation, he asked the attendant to remove the cover that had been placed over the tiny corpse. Despite the advanced decomposition, the child's face had been preserved by lying in the dirt rather than being exposed to the open air. Lindbergh observed the familiar dimpled chin before reaching into the child's mouth and counting his teeth. The aviation hero also looked carefully at the distinctive, upturned toes on the child's one remaining foot. Asked if he could confirm the baby's identity, Lindbergh replied "I am perfectly satisfied that it is my child." Lindbergh would receive the ashes of the child's cremated body to scatter from the air, together with his wife, over the Atlantic.

The discovery of the child's body stunned and angered the nation. Revealed as a cruel liar, John Hughes Curtis confessed that he had perpetuated the hoax about organized crime figures kidnapping the child because he was in a condition of emotional and financial instability. He would serve a brief prison term for obstruction of justice.

Meanwhile, Schwarzkopf and the New Jersey State Police were justifiably criticized for their less-than-thorough search of the area around the Lindbergh home. For weeks the Lindberghs had been tracking the kidnapper in hopes of their child being returned alive, when a more intensive search of the entire area would have revealed that he had been dead all along.

It would become clear, however, that the police lapse was a proverbial blessing in disguise. Without the payoff to "Graveyard John," as events would unfold, the kidnapper probably never would have been apprehended.

In the wake of the discovery of the child's body, President Herbert Hoover ordered J. Edgar Hoover to coordinate a federal effort to aid Schwarzkopf and the New Jersey State Police in solving what the press had long since dubbed the "crime of the century." Because kidnapping was not then a federal offense, J. Edgar Hoover, though he was anxious to become as involved as possible, legally could play only a supporting role.

Congress soon remedied the problem, however, by passing the so-called Lindbergh Law on June 22, 1932. The measure provided for federal criminal jurisdiction in cases involving kidnapping and ransom notes. The Lindbergh case thus became a significant landmark in the evolution of American criminal justice. However, as the new law was not retroactive, any perpetrator who would be charged in the Lindbergh case would be called to account under state rather than federal law.

President Hoover expressed some reluctance about expanding federal authority but, perhaps in part because of his friendship with Lindbergh, he signed the measure into law. The next president, Democrat Franklin Roosevelt, architect of the New Deal, possessed far less reluctance about extending federal jurisdiction. He proposed additional steps to bring "the Federal Government's anti-crime machinery up to date." J. Edgar Hoover's Bureau of Investigation was strengthened and renamed the Federal Bureau of Investigation. These changes in federal law enforcement emerged from a climate of concern generated by the growth of organized crime during Prohibition and capped by the sensational Lindbergh case.

The public not only supported stronger federal authority to combat crime, but looked for scapegoats to explain the failure to capture the kidnapper. Rumors, speculation, and wild charges abounded. Some insisted that Lindbergh's servants had plotted the kidnapping. Irresponsible press accounts fingered Betty Gow, the child's nursemaid, or Oliver Whateley, the butler in Hopewell on the night of the kidnapping, and his wife, Elsie. Other accounts suggested that Dr. Condon had been behind the incident from the outset. Lindbergh came to Condon's defense by publicly thanking the Bronx schoolteacher for his courage and assistance.

Though Schwarzkopf had opened his files to federal investigators, the New Jersey State Police maintained primary jurisdiction over the case. Schwarzkopf received intense criticism, however. More of a quasi-military organization than a modern law enforcement agency, the state police at the time lacked adequate funding and the trained personnel needed for a first-rate criminal investigation. Moreover, the only real opportunity to identify and arrest the kidnapper—during the exchange of money—had now come and gone. Despite their disagreements, Lindbergh and Schwarzkopf continued to respect and trust one another. Aware that he had been duped by the kidnapper into impeding the investigation, Lindbergh publicly defended Schwarzkopf for his efforts.

Privately, however, despite their mutual respect, Lindbergh and Schwarzkopf continued to disagree about key elements of the investigation. Schwarzkopf focused his investigation on the Lindbergh and Morrow family servants. The servants had known of the Lindberghs' intention to deviate from their normal schedule by remaining at the home near Hopewell after the weekend. Anne had called the Morrow home in Englewood to explain that they would stay at Hopewell because the baby was suffering from a cold. She summoned Betty Gow, the child's nursemaid, who came under suspicion as a result.

Police questioned and then arrested Henry "Red" Johnson, Betty Gow's boyfriend, whom she had told of her plans to travel to Hopewell. Although he was jailed for several days, and later deported as an illegal alien, Johnson spoke freely about his activities at the time of the kidnapping. Schwarzkopf ultimately concluded that Johnson had no connection with the crime. He reached the same conclusion about Charles Henry Ellerson, the Morrow family assistant chauffeur, who had driven Betty Gow to Hopewell on the day of the kidnapping.

Schwarzkopf was far more suspicious of Violet Sharpe, a twenty-eight-year-old English maid who worked for Mrs. Morrow at the Englewood estate. All of the staff at the Morrow home had been told that the Lindberghs would be staying in Hopewell because of the baby's cold. While any one of them presumably could have passed that information on to the kidnapper, only Violet offered contradictory testimony and failed to satisfactorily account for her whereabouts on the night of the kidnapping. She admitted, too, that she had gone out with men whom she barely knew at the time of the kidnapping and that she may have told one of them about the Lindberghs remaining in Hopewell.

Violet, thin with short dark hair and brown eyes, virtually broke down under questioning. She lost weight and battled illnesses. After having her tonsils removed, she checked out of the hospital prematurely on May 14. The state police interviewed her again, in Lindbergh's presence, on May 23. Violet continued to display raw nerves and offered no explanation as to why she had been going out with strange men, especially as she was engaged to the Morrow butler, Septimus Banks. During questioning at the Englewood estate on June 9, Violet became hysterical and a physician was summoned to treat her.

The next day, after contemplating Violet's "contradictory and evasive" statements, Schwarzkopf ordered investigators to telephone the Morrow estate to inform Violet that she would be picked up and taken in for further questioning. Violet could no longer bear the ordeal. The young British maid took a can of cyanide-based crystals designed to clean silver, mixed the powder with water, and drank the poison.

By the time the police arrived, Violet was dead. Mrs. Dwight Morrow, Anne's mother, and others insisted Violet had been "frightened to death," but the police interpreted her death as an indication she had been part of a plot, or at least knew more than she had told. Noting that she had become morose after the baby's death, some theorized that she had been part of the conspiracy but had expected the child to be returned safely once the ransom had been paid.

But no one had more than speculation to draw upon. Contrary to the charges of Mrs. Morrow and the London newspapers—inflamed over the alleged harassment of a British subject—Schwarzkopf denied the police had badgered Violet. Although Violet had fainted once during questioning, Schwarzkopf insisted that she was "always treated gently, never roughly."

Anne and Charles Lindbergh did not believe Violet knew anything about the kidnapping and murder of their son. Lindbergh's explanation was apparently the accurate one. The aviator believed that the anxiety-ridden young woman, who had been having affairs with as many as five men, was embarrassed over being grilled about her personal life, especially given her engagement to Banks, who himself had a drinking problem. Violet felt disgraced, feared that she would be fired by Mrs. Morrow, and ultimately deported back to England. "Life is getting so sad I really don't think there is much to live for anymore," she wrote to her sister in the days before her suicide. Lindbergh, who never believed any of the servants had a connection with the crime, now stymied all of Schwarzkopf's efforts to question them or subject them to polygraph examinations. Lindbergh's actions frustrated Schwarzkopf at the time, but no evidence ever surfaced linking the Morrow family servants to the crime.

Determined to investigate every individual connected with the case, Schwarzkopf now focused his attention on Dr. Condon's version of events. Some press accounts had suggested that Condon's actions were suspicious and that he ought to be a suspect himself. After all, was it not a bit too much of a coincidence that Condon just happened to advertise an offer to serve as a go-between in a newspaper that the kidnapper just happened to read? Was the dramatic story the elderly man told of his conversation with the kidnapper in the cemetery really credible? Lindbergh, who had seen and heard Graveyard John, told the press that he "had faith in Doctor Condon then and I have faith in him

now." Schwarzkopf remained suspicious, however. The police and FBI grilled
the old gentleman repeatedly, tapped his telephone, and intercepted his mail,
but never found any incriminating evidence. After the most intense scrutiny,
nothing could be produced to indicate that Condon was anything other than
what he said he was: an outraged citizen who had wanted to help a celebrated
American family.

With no evidence of involvement by the servants or Condon, and with
Graveyard John having long since disappeared, the investigation of the crime of
the century was stymied. The Lindberghs went on with their lives, but Charles
remained obsessed with the case. He slept and ate little, losing as much as thirty pounds from an already lanky frame. Anne preserved her health and gave
birth to a second son, Jon, in August 1932. The kidnap investigation continued
throughout 1933 and into 1934, but consisted mostly of a series of false leads and
hoaxes that left Lindbergh and Schwarzkopf frustrated.

After starting all over again, investigators slowly began to mark progress.
The police reassembled and tested the kidnap ladder at the crime scene. A
trooper climbed the ladder and took on the approximate added weight of the
baby before descending. As he did so, the ladder broke at the same the rail,
alongside the fourth rung from the bottom, where it had shattered before.
Police theorized that the kidnapper may have dropped the child at that point.
Ominously, when the ladder split during the test, Schwarzkopf dropped a bag of
sand simulating the baby. It struck a windowsill and bounced to the ground.
Such a blow might have been sufficient to account for the fatal head injury sustained by the baby.

Even more significantly, the police began to learn vital information about
the origin of the wood in the ladder. Schwarzkopf solicited the assistance of
Arthur Koehler, chief wood technologist at the U.S. Department of Agriculture
Forest Service Laboratory in Madison, Wisconsin. One of the foremost experts
on wood products in the world, Koehler would play a key role in the Lindbergh
case. After painstaking efforts, he succeeded in tracing the wood used to make
the kidnap ladder to a lumberyard in the Bronx.

Schwarzkopf also employed handwriting experts as part of an effort to construct a profile of the kidnapper. These efforts paid off, as the experts agreed
that the similarity of misspellings suggested a single writer of the ransom notes.
They also concluded that the various spellings and word constructions clearly

demonstrated that the writer was German. When translated from English into German, the grammar and syntax of the ransom notes flowed logically.

Constructing a profile of the kidnapper was one thing; apprehending him was quite another. Once Graveyard John had disappeared into the night, Schwarzkopf and FBI officials knew that the marked Lindbergh ransom bills might represent their last hope of solving the case. Lindbergh had insisted on paying the ransom with his own money. After at first balking, the aviation hero finally did agree to a Treasury Department request to include gold certificates whose numbers were recorded so that the money could be identified later. Marked gold certificates made up two-thirds of the $50,000 cash paid to the kidnapper.

The break in the Lindbergh case came as a result of one of the financial reforms of President Roosevelt's Depression-fighting New Deal. On April 5, 1933, the president signed the Banking Relief Act mandating that all persons possessing gold bullion, gold coins, or gold certificates—paper currency redeemable in gold—valued at more than $100 immediately turn them in to a Federal Reserve bank. On May 1—the last day for such exchanges—an individual, using a false name as it turned out, exchanged $2,980, all Lindbergh ransom bills, at the Federal Reserve Bank in New York. By this time both Lindbergh and the New York City Police were offering small cash rewards for each ransom bill that could be identified and turned in.

Over the course of the next year, Lindbergh bills turned up with regularity at Federal Reserve depositories. On occasion eyewitnesses described receiving a bill from a white male with a German accent, blue eyes, and a pointed chin, a description which matched the profile of Graveyard John as provided by Condon and cabdriver Joseph Perrone. In September 1934, for example, a grocer remembered that a man matching Condon's description of the kidnapper had cashed a ten-dollar gold certificate for a six-cent purchase.

By this time the Bureau of Investigation, sure that Graveyard John drove a car, had sent a circular to New York service stations advising attendants to record the license numbers of autos whose drivers paid with the now illegal gold certificates. The newspapers cooperated by withholding this information from the public.

The breakthrough came on September 18, 1934, when a banker in the Bronx, long the center of the investigation, received a bill with a license number written on it. The service station attendant who had jotted down the license number—4U-13-14 N.Y—-recalled that the automobile had been a 1930 blue four-door Dodge. The driver, he recalled, had paid for a dollar's worth of gas with a ten-dollar gold certificate that, under the new law, should already have been turned in. He had spoken with a German accent. A check of the New York State Motor Vehicles Bureau provided the name and address of the car's owner.

The man's name was Bruno Richard Hauptmann. The German immigrant lived at 1279 East 222nd Street in the Bronx—ten blocks from the lumberyard where the wood had originated and one mile from Van Cortlandt Park where the ransom had been negotiated with Dr. Condon.

Early on the morning of September 19, 1934, the day after the license plate had been identified, a stream of New York, New Jersey, and federal officials patrolled Hauptmann's neighborhood. New Jersey state police, New York City police, and FBI officials competed with one another for authority in the case. Several residents observed the squadron of sedans cruising the neighborhood.

Hauptmann came down from his apartment and pulled away in his Dodge sedan shortly after 9 A.M. The plan had been "to follow Hauptmann with a view to detecting him in the act of passing some of the ransom money," according to FBI reports. "However, the speed at which he was driving and his actions in constantly looking in his rear vision mirror convinced the officers that Hauptmann was aware of the surveillance and was attempting to elude pursuit."

After forcing Hauptmann to pull over, Arthur T. Keaten, Schwarzkopf's chief lieutenant, pulled the suspect from his car, whereupon representatives of all three law enforcement agencies, guns drawn, insisted on frisking him. They found a twenty-dollar bill from the Lindbergh ransom in Hauptmann's wallet. Police slapped Hauptmann in handcuffs. After some debate, they determined that they had to await the arrival of the New York City police inspector before proceeding to the apartment that Hauptmann shared with his wife, Anna, also a German immigrant, who worked as a waitress.

While the officials drove Hauptmann around the city for an hour and a half, Bureau of Investigation officials summoned J. Edgar Hoover, who would claim public credit for the arrest of the alleged kidnapper and murderer of the Lindbergh baby in order to enhance the prestige of the FBI.

A carpenter by trade, Hauptmann was thirty-five years old and spoke with a decided German accent. He was a well-built man, five feet and nine inches tall,

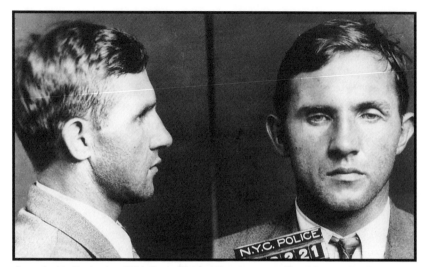

Arrested in September 1934, Bruno Richard Hauptmann, an illegal German immigrant, was eventually tried, convicted, and executed for the kidnapping and murder of the Lindbergh baby. During and after the trial, and to this day, many refused to believe that the handsome young carpenter could have perpetrated the "crime of the century," but the evidence against Hauptmann was overwhelming. Courtesy New Jersey State Police Museum

weighing about 180 pounds, with brown hair, high cheekbones, a small mouth, a slightly pointed chin, and almond-shaped, deep-set blue eyes. Hauptmann's physical appearance matched the descriptions offered by Condon and witnesses who had exchanged money with the German immigrant.

Looking into his background, police found that the native of Kamenz, Saxony, had attended school through the eighth grade and been drafted into the German army in 1914, as a teenager, to fight in World War I. After being wounded at the front, Hauptmann left the service in 1917. He had arrived in the United States in 1923 and married Anna in 1925. They had a son, Manfred, nicknamed "Bubi," in October of that year.

With the arrival of the New York police inspector, the FBI took Hauptmann back to his five-room, second-floor apartment, which they noticed contained brand new furniture. Anna, still in her robe and slippers, appeared shocked and repeatedly asked her husband if he had done anything wrong. Downstairs, the Hauptmanns' landlady—who let the officials know that she did not particularly care for her male tenant—produced two ten-dollar notes from the ransom money that Hauptmann had used in partial payment of the month's rent.

While searching the apartment, investigators found a notebook of sketches, including one of a homemade ladder. They found Hauptmann's tool chest, which was missing the standard three-quarter-inch chisel, the size of the tool found on the ground below the kidnap window. They found maps of New Jersey and of the Massachusetts coastal waters where the "boad" Nelly was supposed to have been moored with the baby safely on board. Several days later, and more compelling still, police found John Condon's name, address, and telephone number scrawled on the door trim inside the closet in the Hauptmanns' nursery. The information had been secreted inside the closet and required some effort to be seen.

The most damning evidence of all, however, lay outside, hidden in the walls of Hauptmann's garage. While searching the apartment and questioning Hauptmann, an FBI man noticed the carpenter repeatedly looking out the window at the garage. The small one-car garage was tightly padlocked. Hauptmann had also run a line from his bedroom to the garage that allowed him to switch on a light and illuminate the structure. Investigators proceeded to the garage and began searching. Removing a board from the wall behind a workbench, they discovered packages wrapped in newspaper. The first one they opened contained a stack of ten-dollar notes from the ransom money.

Whooping with excitement, the investigators realized they had found the smoking gun in the Lindbergh kidnap case. By the time they had finished dismantling the garage, they had found $14,600 of the Lindbergh banknotes and a small loaded pistol. Officials placed Hauptmann under arrest and transported him to police headquarters on Manhattan's lower west side. The suspect was fingerprinted, photographed, and then subjected to a grueling interrogation.

Hauptmann remained calm throughout the ordeal, never losing his temper and continuing to insist upon his innocence. Having initially denied knowledge of possession of any of the Lindbergh ransom money, Hauptmann now changed his story in the face of the highly incriminating evidence uncovered in his own garage. He now explained that he knew nothing about where the cash had come from, but that he had merely been given charge of the money for safekeeping by a friend of his, another German, Isidor Fisch. Conveniently for Hauptmann, Fisch had returned to Germany and died from tuberculosis.

While officials failed to wrench a confession from Hauptmann, they were more convinced than ever of his guilt as a result of writing tests the German immigrant performed during the interrogation. A handwriting expert dictated passages, which Hauptmann was compelled to write down. This exercise, carried out for more than four hours, produced several examples of spelling, grammar, and construction that matched the Lindbergh ransom notes. Police also noticed that Hauptmann began to make a concerted effort to alter his writing style, which they interpreted as an indication of guilt.

The arrest, after months of frustration, of the accused murderer of the Lindbergh baby spurred frenzied media coverage. Police and FBI assured reporters that they had the uncovered the guilty man in Hauptmann. Banner headlines blazed across the front pages of newspapers throughout the country. The *New York Daily News* devoted its entire front page on September 21, 1934, to the headlines alone. The presumption of guilt was manifest in the massive boldfaced *Daily News* headline:

LINDBERGH KIDNAPPER JAILED

The Hearst chain, which had covered the Lindbergh case intensively, offered a series of articles leaving no doubt as to Hauptmann's guilt. The evidence was indeed compelling, but the Hearst *New York Journal* embellished it with misinformation, such as the false report that police had found detailed maps in Hauptmann's apartment of the roads around Lindbergh's estate. Another *Journal* article revealed that a shoe of Hauptmann's matched a footprint below the nursery window, when in reality the state police had taken no casts and the footprints had been obliterated the morning after the kidnapping.

With the FBI claiming credit for capturing the culprit—and press, radio, and newsreel reports embellishing the evidence and leaving little question as to Hauptmann's guilt—it would prove impossible for the German immigrant to receive a fair trial from an impartial jury. The American public spewed venom at the mention of Hauptmann's name. The brutal murder of the innocent child of an American hero struck a chord in a nation whose own remaining innocence had been shattered by the seemingly insoluble economic collapse.

The presumption of Hauptmann's guilt was so widespread that even the nation's chief law enforcement officer, U.S. Attorney General Homer S. Cum-

mings, when asked if he thought the evidence against Hauptmann was compelling, replied: "I didn't know that anyone doubted it." Presumed guilty,
Hauptmann also did not enjoy the benefit of the guarantees of rights accorded
to criminal suspects in more recent times. By the time J. Edgar Hoover arrived
in New York to claim public credit for the arrest, Hauptmann had been kept in
jail for thirty-two hours without food, sleep, or the presence of an attorney. But
that was not the worst of the treatment that Hauptmann received.

Failing to induce the suspect to confess on his own volition, police tried to
beat an admission of guilt out of him. A physician later confirmed that Hauptmann "had been subjected recently to a severe beating, all or mostly with blunt
instruments." Hauptmann himself said he had been strapped into a chair in the
dark, beaten with a hammer, and kicked in the chest and stomach.

The treatment of Hauptmann reflects the vulnerability of criminal suspects
under U.S. law until the reforms of the Supreme Court led by Earl Warren some
three decades after the Lindbergh case. High court decisions in *Gideon* (1963),
Escobedo (1965), and *Miranda* (1966), guaranteed accused criminals the right to
an attorney, to remain silent, and to receive a warning from police that anything
they did say could be used against them in court.

In 1934, however, police were not about to accord such rights to the accused
kidnapper and murderer of the Lindbergh baby. Unfortunately, the violent
third degree to which police subjected Hauptmann was not only crude but
counterproductive as well. Hauptmann's life experiences had shown that he was
nothing if not resilient, stubborn, and determined to defy authority. The beatings merely reinforced his determination to refuse to cooperate with the
authorities.

Had the police assembled a more sophisticated psychological profile of the
defendant, a common practice of the FBI today, they would have had a much
better idea of how to approach the accused kidnapper. Physical violence and
intimidation only ensured that Hauptmann would clam up and that his natural
resentment of authority and determination to weather any ordeal would triumph.

Born on November 20, 1899, Hauptmann had become the proverbial black
sheep of an otherwise respectable middle-class family in Kamenz. As a machine
gunner during the war, he had belonged to an elite unit and had been responsible for a number of successful actions. Gassed and shot in the leg, Hauptmann

had been hardened by his bitter experiences in the Great War, during which two of his brothers had been killed. Only nineteen when the war ended, Hauptmann, like many Germans, faced a grim existence marked by high unemployment and food shortages. Together with another war veteran, he turned to crime.

Two examples of Hauptmann's criminal past in Germany immediately stood out to investigators in the Lindbergh case. On one occasion Hauptmann used a ladder to gain entry to a second-story window in order to steal 300 marks and a silver watch. The victim had been a prominent public figure, the mayor of the city. In another incident Hauptmann robbed women pushing strollers full of food, waving a gun and threatening to shoot. Apprehended on March 6, 1919, and convicted of grand larceny, theft, and armed robbery, Hauptmann received a sentence of two and half years imprisonment before gaining parole.

Accused once again of theft in 1923 and lodged in a local jail, Hauptmann escaped, leaving a taunting note in defiance of the authorities. A wanted man in Germany, Hauptmann attempted to stow away on ships bound for New York. Twice he failed, once having to jump overboard and swim ashore to avoid arrest in a German port. On July 13, 1923, Hauptmann arrived in New York, identifying himself as Karl Pellmeier, after stowing away on the SS *Hanover*. Apprehended, he was deported the next day.

Finally, on his third try Hauptmann succeeded, but only by lying in the coal bin in the hold of the SS *George Washington* all the way to New York. He slipped on board carrying only two loaves of bread and a jug of water. At night he scavenged the deck, battling rats for scraps of food during the ten-day voyage. When the ship arrived in New York, Hauptmann walked ashore carrying a stolen landing card. Speaking no English, he met a German on the street and secured his first job as a dishwasher. He eventually found work as a mechanic, a machinist, and finally as a carpenter.

Hauptmann's record thus revealed a criminal past marked by boldness, determination, and a modus operandi strikingly similar to that employed in the Lindbergh case. Hauptmann had shown himself to be patient, hardened, and resourceful. Hauptmann revealed some of the characteristics of a classic sociopath, or antisocial personality. Handsome and determined to maintain an appearance of innocence, Hauptmann often made a favorable impression on observers. Lindbergh himself captured Hauptmann's dualistic character, later describing him as "a magnificent-looking man, splendidly built," but with eyes "like the eyes of a wild boar—mean, shifty, small, and cruel."

The subsequent investigation into Hauptmann's finances produced still more compelling evidence of his guilt. Officials found that Hauptmann had quit his work as a carpenter the very month that the ransom was paid. He explained to his wife, Anna, that he had invested so well in the stock market that he no longer needed to work. In fact, Hauptmann had practically no cash assets as of April 1, 1932, yet he soon embarked on a spending spree in the midst of the Great Depression. He sent his wife on a trip to Germany, where she investigated the statute of limitations on the crimes for which Hauptmann was still wanted, finding that he would still have been subject to arrest in 1932. Meanwhile, Hauptmann himself had enjoyed a Florida vacation and a hunting trip to Maine. He bought himself a new hunting rifle, a top-of-the-line radio set, a canoe, German field glasses, and other items. He spent $190 a year for a Wall Street newsletter.

Finally, eyewitnesses identified Hauptmann as the kidnapper. Cabdriver Joseph Perrone, whom Hauptmann had hired to deliver a note to Condon's home, offered a positive identification. Two gas station attendants selected Hauptmann from a police lineup as the man who had passed a ten-dollar ransom note. A cashier in a New York theater identified Hauptmann for passing another ten-dollar banknote from the ransom money. An elderly New Jersey man, Amandus Hochmuth, a neighbor of the Lindberghs, identified Hauptmann as the man he saw driving a vehicle, which nearly went off the road and which contained a ladder, on the day of the crime. A Princeton University student also reported seeing a dark-colored Dodge with an extension ladder in the back. Months later another man, Millard Whited, identified Hauptmann as the man he had seen on the Hopewell estate in February 1932.

In subsequent years, conspiracy theorists in the Lindbergh case have cast doubt on many of the eyewitness identifications of Hauptmann. Some of their suspicion is warranted. A secret Bureau of Investigation report, for example, described Whited as "a confirmed liar and totally unreliable." Even more disturbing, years later newly released documents on the case revealed that police and prosecutors had withheld eyewitness accounts and other information that might have been used to contradict the evidence of Hauptmann's guilt. Had such evidence been turned over to the defense, as required by modern discovery laws, Hauptmann's attorneys might have been able to construct a plausible alibi for the defendant or call attention to other potential suspects.

Bolstered by press and popular sentiment against the defendant, the men who operated the justice system were determined to garner a conviction and the death penalty against the German immigrant. In the Lizzie Borden case, officials had ignored the law to prevent damaging evidence against a society woman from being admitted in the murder trial. In the Hauptmann case, by contrast, investigators and prosecutors deliberately withheld information that might have been used to cast doubt on their case against an immigrant with a criminal past.

Had the full investigatory record come to light it would have revealed that John Condon initially stopped short of identifying Hauptmann as Graveyard John. Although officials kept the information secret for almost the next half century, Condon at first declared that "I would not say he is the man. . . . I am not positive." Nonetheless, Condon would later testify that he knew from the moment he saw him that Hauptmann was John. When first brought before a police lineup that included Hauptmann, Condon initially indicated that Hauptmann was one of three men that he would eliminate as suspects. Rethinking the matter, Condon looked more closely and then subjected Hauptmann to a series of questions and had him repeat the words he had heard in the cemetery. "He is the one who would come nearer to answering the description than anybody I saw," Condon now told police. "You gave me no hint but I picked him out. He is a little heavier . . . "Condon declined to make a positive identification. "I have to be very careful. The man's life is in jeopardy." The eccentric schoolteacher, who possessed a flair for the melodramatic, insisted to dismayed New Jersey officials that he would wait for the trial to make a positive identification. "I am holding my identification in abeyance for the present!" he declared.

Lindbergh himself offered a positive identification of Hauptmann. Relieved by the news of John's capture, the aviation hero arranged to have a look at the alleged kidnapper while he underwent questioning. Disguising himself in a hat and dark glasses, Lindbergh sat in on an interview with detectives, who compelled Hauptmann to say, "Ay, Doctor, over here," the same words that Lindbergh had heard when he had accompanied Condon with the ransom money.

Lindbergh declared that he was "sure" that Hauptmann's was "the voice I heard that night."

Other eyewitnesses included a New York City physician who, after treating Hauptmann early in 1933, recalled that the German immigrant had a chronic leg injury as a result of an ankle and leg sprain suffered sometime in the previous year. Officials theorized that the injury stemmed from Hauptmann's fall from the fourth rung during the kidnapping. In addition, a car dealership employee recalled seeing Hauptmann's left foot in bandages when he brought in his Dodge for repairs in March 1932.

In assessing the eyewitness evidence as a whole, it is clear that while some of the accounts were reliable, others were contradictory and more unreliable than officials would admit in their public statements or in Hauptmann's subsequent murder trial. In this respect the Lindbergh case was not atypical: criminal investigators recognize that eyewitness identifications are notoriously divergent and unreliable.

While questions about the identifications have provided fodder for conspiracy theorists, eyewitness accounts represented only part of the evidence against Hauptmann. Abundant circumstantial evidence continued to bolster the case against the German carpenter.

As the evidence mounted against Hauptmann, he remained in jail in New York, charged with extortion, while New Jersey officials developed the case for extradition on charges of kidnapping and murder. New Jersey Attorney General David T. Wilentz, thirty-eight, a prominent Democrat from Perth Amboy, seized the opportunity to prosecute the case, although he had never prosecuted a defendant in his life. Appearing before the Hunterdon County grand jury, Wilentz presented testimony by handwriting experts, Koehler (the Wisconsin wood expert), police and FBI officials, and Lindbergh himself.

On October 8, 1934, the grand jury, meeting in the tiny Hunterdon County, New Jersey, burg of Flemington, took less than a half hour to indict Hauptmann for murder by a ballot of twenty-three to zero. The New York Supreme Court granted extradition of Hauptmann to New Jersey. After being transported to Flemington, Hauptmann was lodged in a seven-by-nine-foot cell in an annex behind the courthouse where he would be tried. Officials took no chances after discovering new evidence of Hauptmann's resourcefulness. During his imprisonment in New York, the carpenter had hidden away a spoon, out of which he attempted to fashion a crude key as well as a knifelike weapon. In Flemington, however, a guard occupied the cell next to Hauptmann and maintained constant surveillance of the prisoner.

The media frenzy in anticipation of the trial had now mushroomed to levels unprecedented in American history. Day after day front-page headlines and breathless radio accounts presented the leaked evidence against Hauptmann.

Under this barrage of hostile publicity and public outrage over the victimization of an American icon, Hauptmann could not hope to receive a fair trial. The public wanted retribution after waiting in frustration almost three years since the brutal crime had been committed. Although millions of German immigrants lived in the United States, they were vastly outnumbered by those who harbored lingering resentment of German aggression in World War I. With Adolf Hitler and the Nazis having come to power, anti-German sentiment became increasingly palpable across the United States. Hauptmann was a convenient target for popular resentments in an age of economic depression and international insecurity.

Newspapers and radio reporters, in relentless pursuit of scoops on the Lindbergh case, displayed virtually no sensitivity to the issue of conflicts between a free press and a fair trial, which would preoccupy subsequent generations. Nothing better illustrated the intrusiveness of the press in the Lindbergh case than an offer by Hearst's *New York Journal* to pay for Hauptmann's defense in return for exclusive rights to the inside story both before and after trial.

The man hired under this arrangement, Edward J. Reilly, was a well-known New York criminal defense attorney. Agreeing to the deal, Hauptmann and his wife fired the defendant's original attorney, James Fawcett of Brooklyn, and replaced him with Reilly in November 1934. The fifty-two-year-old Reilly was known for his bombast as well as his slick black hair and cutaway suits, spats, and the ever present carnation on his lapel.

Nothing better illustrated media intrusion into the criminal justice system than the hiring of a defense attorney by a newspaper. Not surprisingly, Reilly displayed more enthusiasm for the media attention than he did for the hard work that would be required to mount an effective defense. Reilly had only a few weeks to prepare for the "trial of the century," slated to begin on January 2, 1935. The New York defense attorney would head a team of four, including

Flemington attorney C. Lloyd Fisher, who knew the background of the investigation as a result of having defended John Hughes Curtis, the Norfolk hoaxer, in his trial for fraud.

On the prosecution side, Wilentz marshaled the evidence against Hauptmann with the clear intention of securing a death penalty against the defendant—inflamed public opinion would settle for nothing less. Wilentz, aggressive and determined, headed a prosecution team of six. The FBI, New Jersey State Police, and New York police, as well as myriad technical experts summoned from across the nation, would buttress the prosecution's case.

Judge Thomas W. Trenchard, a seventy-one-year-old, white-haired jurist from Trenton, presided as the trial opened on a clear and cold winter day. Inside, the courtroom was dimly lit, poorly ventilated, and hopelessly overcrowded. Witnesses would sit alone in a plain wooden chair on a raised platform just a few feet away from the opposing attorneys and the pressing crowd.

Hauptmann himself sat quietly during jury selection, but his deep-set eyes probed the 150 potential Hunterdon County jurors as the process began. The Hauptmann prosecution exercised its prerogative by dismissing potential jurors who opposed or appeared to have reservations about the death penalty. For its part, the defense dismissed several jury candidates who appeared to have followed the case especially closely in the news media, which had long since condemned Hauptmann.

Finally, a jury of eight men and four women, ranging in ages from twenty-five to sixty, was chosen. They included a machinist, a farmer, two housewives, a teacher, an insurance man—a white, middle-class jury that well represented Hunterdon County. At the end of the day Judge Trenchard ordered deputies to accompany the jurors to their new temporary home, across the street on the third floor of the Union Hotel, where they would be sequestered. He instructed the jurors to avoid reading or listening to news accounts or discussing the case with any individuals that they might encounter.

The jurors could hardly ignore the mob scene outside, however. The throng that assembled daily outside the courtroom regularly shouted its opinions and encouragement to convict and execute the defendant. With some 700 reporters in attendance, media representatives alone overwhelmed the tiny New Jersey town.

The nation's most renowned journalists attended the "trial of the century."

Masses of people descended on the courthouse in the tiny burg of Flemington, New Jersey, in hopes of obtaining a seat in the Lindbergh baby trial. Unprecedented media coverage accompanied the trial. Outside the courthouse vendors hawked souvenir models of the kidnap ladder and "genuine" wisps of the dead baby's hair. The carnival atmosphere in Flemington complicated the prospect of Bruno Richard Hautpmann receiving a fair trial. Courtesy New Jersey State Police Museum

They included Damon Runyon, normally a sports and fiction writer; writers Edna Ferber and Dorothy Kilgallen; broadcasters Heywood Broun, Boake Carter, and Walter Winchell. The most popular radio reporter of the era, Winchell had long since repeatedly pronounced Hauptmann guilty over the airwaves. Abandoning all pretenses of journalistic objectivity, Winchell offered his advice to the prosecution during the trial.

Celebrities, too, descended on Flemington, which reporters now invariably described as "sleepy." Humorist Jack Benny, commentator Lowell Thomas, and Robert Ripley of *Believe It or Not!* fame were among those captivated by the drama of the historic trial. The audience included a smattering of Europeans, who crossed the Atlantic to witness the memorable events.

A committee of the American Bar Association later noted disapprovingly that the trial attracted "more correspondents, sob-sisters, sportswriters, psychiatrists, cameramen, etc. . . . than represented American papers in France in World War I." When the doors opened in court on the morning of January 3, hundreds of spectators poured across the threshold, as sheriff's deputies proved unable to restrain the frenzied throng. The people crammed together on the benches, in the aisles, balconies—any cubbyhole they could find. Altogether, more than 600 persons jammed into the county seat courtroom.

Outside, a carnival atmosphere prevailed throughout the trial. A string of automobiles jammed the roads leading into Flemington. Thousands of people milled about. Families ate picnic lunches while vendors hawked souvenirs and hot dogs. Lunch counters offered daily specials named for the key figures in the trial. An enterprising New Jersey youth capitalized on the idea of constructing small wooden ladders, which he sold in great quantity outside the courtroom. Other hucksters offered "genuine" locks of the dead baby's hair. Taking note of the hullabaloo, the acerbic journalist H. L. Mencken quipped that the trial was "the most important event since the Resurrection." Echoing Mencken, Norman Levy wrote in the *American Mercury* that "All sense of proportion and much of decency was lost." Edna Ferber was even more blunt, observing that the circus atmosphere surrounding the Hauptmann trial "made you want to resign as a member of the human race."

When Trenchard finally summoned the buzzing mass of humanity to order, Wilentz delivered an opening statement charging that Hauptmann was a heinous killer who deserved to be put to death for the brutal murder of a helpless child. The prosecutor brought "Baby Charlie" to life by describing the child's appearance, good humor, and endearing physical characteristics, such as his wispy blond hair and cleft chin. Wilentz made sure to link the Little Eagle with his heroic father, the Lone Eagle, conqueror of the Atlantic, who had inspired the pride of his country and of the world.

Clapping and waving his hands for emphasis in front of the jury box, Wilentz had gotten the prosecution case off to an effective start. He had played to the public desire to vilify Hauptmann and to avenge the brutal kidnapping and murder of the Lindbergh baby. When Wilentz had finished, Reilly bolted to his feet and demanded a mistrial. He declared that Wilentz's "impassioned appeal" was inimical to his client's ability to receive a fair trial. Judge Trenchard rejected the motion, but both lead attorneys had shown that there would be no shortage of passion and theatrics in the courtroom.

The trial, with its attendant mass publicity, was a wrenching ordeal for the camera-shy Lindberghs. Anne Morrow Lindbergh appeared only twice: on the first day of the proceedings and later to testify about the scene at home on the night of the kidnapping. Lindbergh himself attended every day, however, filing through the crowds of reporters and photographers, armed with a pistol, rumor had it, that he now carried for protection in the wake of crank callers making death threats. He appeared grim but focused upon the proceedings, studiously ignoring the press and the crush of people around him.

Testifying himself on the second and third days of the trial, Lindbergh proved to be an effective prosecution witness. The aviation hero made a pronounced impact on the gallery, and on the jury as well, when he explained in response to Wilentz's questions that he had clearly recognized Hauptmann's voice during the police interrogation as the one he had heard in the cemetery as the ransom money changed hands. "That was Hauptmann's voice," Lindbergh firmly declared.

Newspaper headlines exploded with the damning identification of the Lindbergh kidnapper by the popular American hero himself. "**LINDY: IT WAS HAUPTMANN!**," screamed the *New York Daily News*. Some trial observers later declared that from the moment Lindbergh, calm and dignified, identified Hauptmann from the stand, the German was a condemned man.

While many at the time and in subsequent years wondered how Lindbergh possibly could have remembered Hauptmann's voice after so many months, the

Newspaper readers and radio audiences across the nation riveted their attention on the events in New Jersey when Charles A. Lindbergh testified on the second and third days of the 1934 trial in the kidnap and murder of his infant son. Striding into the courthouse with Lindbergh, on the far left, was H. Norman Schwarzkopf, captain of the New Jersey State Police. When Lindbergh, a revered national hero, positively identified Hauptmann's as the voice he had heard during an exchange of ransom money, the German defendant's fate was all but sealed. Courtesy New Jersey State Police Museum aviator insisted that he had listened intently and consciously strove to remember the voice of the man who, after all, he presumed to be his son's kidnapper. Moreover, Hauptmann possessed a distinctive voice—somewhat shrill, with the words seemingly constricted in his throat as he forced them out.

Although he had told reporters he intended to take apart Lindbergh's testimony, Reilly made no headway in his efforts to undermine the famed aviator's credibility. Failing to sway Lindbergh from his identification of Hauptmann, Reilly made equally little progress in trying to suggest that one or more of Lindbergh's servants or neighbors had kidnapped the child—the latter supposedly out of their resentment over his purchase of land that cut them off from their habitual hunting grounds.

The same pattern that manifested itself in Lindbergh's testimony was repeated throughout the trial. The grandstanding Reilly repeatedly told reporters outside of court that he would produce evidence damning to the prosecution's case. When he consistently failed to deliver on those promises, instead coming up with an increasingly absurd array of alternative and contradictory theories of the crime, the case for the defense was left badly deflated. Despite his inexperience as a prosecutor, Wilentz beautifully marshaled the evidence, maintaining the momentum that the prosecution claimed at the outset.

Following Lindbergh's testimony, a series of witnesses offered positive identifications linking Hauptmann to the crime. Those witnesses included the New York cabdriver, Joseph Perrone, who identified Hauptmann as the man who gave him a dollar to deliver a note on March 12, 1932, to Condon's address. Like Lindbergh, Perrone described "the voice and manner of [Hauptmann's] speech" as distinctive. When he heard Hauptmann speak at the police lineup, Perrone explained, "It was exactly as he spoke to me that night."

Amandus Hochmuth, Lindbergh's eight-seven-year-old neighbor, identified Hauptmann as the red-faced man in a "dirty green car" who had nearly run his car into a ditch in front of Hochmuth's home or near the Lindbergh estate on the day of the kidnapping. Critics pointed out that Hochmuth, suffering from cataracts, had very poor vision late in his life. Hochmuth could still see in 1932, however, and there were few enough visitors to the remote area around Lindbergh's estate that it was logical to assume he might have remembered a strange car containing a ladder and being driven erratically.

The most anticipated prosecution witness, after the Lindberghs themselves, was the highly publicized Jafsie. Wilentz, like the New York officials before him, had been frustrated by Condon's insistence on holding his identification of the kidnapper "in abeyance." But the old gentleman had made it clear in their discussions that he would identify the kidnapper in the courtroom, and he proved as good as his word.

Displaying none of the reluctance and uncertainty he had shown after the police lineup, Condon positively identified John, the man he had met in the cemetery, spoken with over the telephone, and to whom he delivered the Lindbergh ransom. "John," Condon pronounced dramatically on the sixth day of the trial, "is Bruno Richard Hauptmann." Newspaper headlines and radio reports blared Condon's positive identification of the graveyard kidnapper.

The prosecution feared that Reilly would score points with Condon by calling attention to his eccentricities and taking advantage of his penchant for garrulousness. Would the seventy-four-year-old retired schoolteacher become confused, hesitant, and ineffective under an onslaught of defense questioning? They need not have worried—Condon was more than a match for Reilly. The old gentleman won the upper hand at the outset of his cross-examination by eliciting laughter in the courtroom with clever responses to light-hearted opening questions that backfired on the defense. From that point forward Condon dominated the seventh day of the trial. He resonated credibility, leaving the apparently truthful impression that he was an old-fashioned patriotic citizen whose actions had stemmed from his outrage over the Lindbergh crime. Reilly's unsuccessful assault on Condon's credibility contributed to the rapid deterioration of the defense effort.

In addition to the positive identifications by Lindbergh, Condon, and those who had seen Hauptmann around Hopewell, eight handwriting experts testified that the same person had written all fourteen ransom notes. One after another the specialists testified to devastating effect that the same spelling errors, as in "mony" for "money," and transposition of letters, as in "singnature," appeared in several of the notes. One of the experts declared that the conclusion that one man had written all of them was "irresistible, unanswerable, and overwhelming."

As always, Hauptmann stood condemned in the next day's newspaper headlines, which read: "**BRUNO WROTE ALL RANSOM LETTERS**" and "**HAND-**

WRITING EXPERTS ACCUSE BRUNO." Although Hauptmann's friends called him Richard, the press invariably employed the more foreign first name of "Bruno" in references to the defendant.

Typically, Reilly promised reporters that he would take apart the testimony of the government's leading handwriting experts, but the defense attorney again failed to deliver. The trial of the century was fast becoming a fiasco for the defense. Growing distraught, Hauptmann and his wife occasionally interrupted the proceedings, charging aloud that prosecution witnesses were lying. Trenchard firmly but tactfully reined in the defendant and persuaded both Richard and Anna to agree not to speak out of place again.

As the trial continued through its second week, additional witnesses testified to sightings of Hauptmann "casing" the Lindbergh estate in New Jersey in the weeks before the kidnapping. Still others identified him as the man with whom they exchanged ransom bills for various services in New York City. Also indicative of Hauptmann's guilt was testimony that no new ransom bills had surfaced since the carpenter's arrest.

On the sixteenth day of the trial the prosecution presented its last, but arguably most compelling witness, Arthur Koehler, the wood expert from Wisconsin. The authoritative Koehler possessed impeccable credentials as one of the world's top experts on wood. For twenty-nine years he had served as the federal government's foremost authority on the subject. He was the author of fifty-two publications, including a text, *The Properties and Uses of Wood*. Koehler had testified previously in myriad court cases. The state, having already presented testimony from the witnesses who had seen the device folded up in the back seat of Hauptmann's car, now entered the kidnap ladder into evidence. Koehler's testimony would leave little doubt that Hauptmann had manufactured the ladder himself.

Under direction from Wilentz, Koehler explained how he traced the North Carolina pine used to make the kidnap ladder from the original milling site in the South to the lumberyard in the Bronx where Hauptmann had presumably purchased the wood. Even more compelling, however, was Koehler's testimony revealing that the carpenter had run out of wood needed to construct the third tier of the fold-up ladder—ironically, an extension that Hauptmann had not needed to use to reach the second-floor bedroom.

Koehler testified that his analysis of the size, grain, and angle of cutting revealed that the wood used on the third tier of the ladder clearly matched the wood in Hauptmann's attic. Koehler found that on rail nineteen of the kidnap ladder the nail holes "correspond exactly with four nail holes in the joists in that attic and the grain of the wood in that rail corresponds exactly with the grain of the wood of the board next to it." Koehler went on to explain that tests had demonstrated conclusively that a plane found in Hauptmann's garage had been used to file down the board from the attic floor before it had been attached to the kidnap ladder. Finally, Koehler's analysis showed that the three-quarter-inch chisel found on the ground outside the kidnap window and missing from Hauptmann's toolbox had been used in the making the recesses for the rungs in the ladder.

With his calm demeanor, an air of dispassionate scientific detachment, and devastating expert testimony, Koehler made a decided impression on the jury. In the by now familiar pattern, the defense team utterly failed to shake the prosecution witness on cross-examination. At the conclusion of Koehler's testimony on the seventeenth day, Wilentz could declare with confidence and satisfaction, "The State rests."

In his opening statement, Flemington attorney Lloyd Fisher asserted that defense would produce eyewitnesses and expert testimony that would shatter the prosecution case and reveal how police had bungled the investigation in a rush to judgment at Hauptmann's expense. He declared that defense handwriting experts would refute the prosecution testimony "to a point where there can't be a doubt in any of your minds that that is not the handwriting of Bruno Richard Hauptmann." In reality, several handwriting experts sought out by the defense concluded, like the prosecution experts, that Hauptmann was the author of the kidnap notes. The defense, of course, dropped these prospective witnesses and failed to produce compelling replacements.

The first witness for the defense, however, was Hauptmann himself. Despite the defendant's many vulnerabilities, including his halting command of English, Reilly put his client on the stand. Hauptmann himself somehow seemed convinced that he could persuade the Hunterdon County jurors of his innocence. In response to Reilly's questions, Hauptmann, speaking deliberately, denied any connection with the kidnapping or murder of the Lindbergh baby. His eyes never settled on the dead child's father, who sat quietly in the courtroom but focused intently on the defendant.

A series of ransom notes offered damning evidence against Bruno Richard Hauptmann. The German immigrant consistently misspelled words such as "singnature" (bottom), mistakes which the prosecution successfully linked with other examples of Hauptmann's prose. Handwriting experts testified that Hauptmann wrote the ransom notes. The first note advised Lindbergh to look for the interlocking circles (bottom right) to authenticate the ransom notes. Courtesy New Jersey State Police Museum

Looking over the ransom notes, Hauptmann denied writing them. He added that he had spelled words the way police told him to during the relentless interrogation in New York. In other words, the defense argued that police framed Hauptmann by creating a match between his written tests and the ransom notes. Hauptmann went on to explain that when his friend and occasional business partner, Isidor Fisch, returned to Germany he left Hauptmann in possession of a small tin box. The carpenter declared that initially he did not even examine the contents of the box, which he placed on a shelf in a kitchen closet. Only after Fisch's death did Hauptmann discover thousands of dollars in the box. He then relocated the money into hiding places in his garage and began to spend some of it because, he explained, Fisch had owed him money from investments Hauptmann had made in Fisch's fur business.

Hauptmann's defense testimony was not only ineffective but undramatic. The fireworks emerged, however, on cross-examination, as Wilentz could hardly contain his eagerness to tear apart the German carpenter's version of events.

Under New Jersey law at the time, Hauptmann's previous criminal record was admissible as evidence in the kidnapping and murder case. Wilentz began by establishing Hauptmann's criminal record in Germany, including the second-floor ladder job at the mayor's home as well as the armed robbery of the women pushing baby carriages. Wilentz forced Hauptmann to acknowledge that he was a criminal who had escaped from prison, was a fugitive from German justice, and had entered the United States illegally. Wilentz compelled Hauptmann to admit that he had lied initially about being in possession of the ransom money. "'I LIED,' CRIES BRUNO," screamed the next day's headlines.

After attacking Hauptmann's credibility, Wilentz confronted the carpenter with the misspelling of "boad" (boat) in both a personal notebook and in the ransom notes. The prosecutor followed up that evidence by prompting Hauptmann to make similar misspellings and transposition of letters on the witness stand.

On January 28, 1935, the nineteenth day of the trial, Wilentz subjected Hauptmann to a devastating review of his finances, all meticulously recorded by the carpenter in his personal notebooks. A special agent from the Treasury Department intelligence unit had carefully analyzed Hauptmann's expenditures, investments, and accounting. The prosecution destroyed Hauptmann's claim to gains in stock investments by demonstrating that he had actually lost $9,132.29.

Wilentz exploited the opportunity provided by Hauptmann's admission that he had never told his wife about the money he allegedly received from Fisch to emphasize the defendant's secretive and deceitful behavior. "You were hiding a lot of things on your wife, weren't you?" Wilentz asked, shifting the discussion to Hauptmann's relationship with another German woman, a Mrs. Gerta Henkel. Hauptmann may have had an affair with the woman during Anna's trip to Germany, an irrelevant point but one that Wilentz nonetheless succeeded in impressing upon the jury. The intimation of adultery would further prejudice the jury and the public against the defendant.

More substantively, the prosecution cast grave doubt on Hauptmann's "Fisch story." Wilentz emphasized that Hauptmann only met Isidor Fisch in July 1932, by which time he had already begun to spend some of the ransom money. Although Fisch induced Hauptmann to invest in his fur-trading business—which turned out to be bogus—it hardly seemed likely that Fisch would have handed over thousands of dollars to Hauptmann for safekeeping after making his acquaintance only a few months before. Moreover, Fisch's brother had reported that Fisch, who lived a spartan existence, had been substantially indebted at the time of his death.

Wilentz produced correspondence sent by Hauptmann to Fisch's family after his death. He informed relatives that he had two trunks of Fisch's things in his possession, adding that "There are no important things in them."

The prosecution capitalized on myriad opportunities to pinpoint contradictions between Hauptmann's previous statements to police and his current version of events. For example, when confronted with the evidence of Condon's telephone number and address scrawled on the wall of his attic closet, Hauptmann had told police in New York that he had written the information down simply because of his interest in the sensational kidnapping case. Now, with the defense strategy, such as it was, focusing on an alleged official conspiracy to frame Hauptmann, he denied ever having written the address and phone number in the closet, suggesting that the police themselves had done so.

The cumulative effect of Wilentz's eleven-hour cross-examination of the defendant was devastating. Hauptmann had shown himself to be a liar and a criminal. Hauptmann had lied when he claimed to have been on parole for his criminal activity in Germany; he lied when he declared that officials had read out the word "singnature," forcing him to misspell the word; he lied about turning a profit on the stock market; and, though it was irrelevant to the kidnap and murder charges, Wilentz impressed upon the jury that the defendant had apparently lied to his wife about an affair with Gerta Henkel.

Given Hauptmann's record of deceit, none of the jurors was inclined to believe the biggest lie of all, the defendant's "Fisch story." Moreover, Hauptmann's demeanor elicited no sympathy from the jury. Often expressionless, but just as often smiling, Hauptmann appeared defiant, and strangely arrogant. At one point he dismissed efforts to link him with the kidnap ladder by condemning its construction as inferior. "I am a carpenter!" the defendant declared.

While Hauptmann had utterly failed to present himself as a sympathetic or convincing witness, his strong will remained impervious to Wilentz's efforts to break him on the stand. Near the end of his cross-examination, the prosecutor tried but failed to induce Hauptmann to confess. Tension over the acrimonious exchange of questions and answers filled the courtroom, with both Wilentz and Hauptmann raising their voices.

Angered by one of Hauptmann's smiles as he sat in the witness chair, Wilentz challenged him. "This is funny to you, isn't it? . . . You think you are a big shot, don't you?"

"No, should I cry?" Hauptmann responded.

At one point, the bailiff standing behind Hauptmann stirred uneasily as the defendant responded to Wilentz's grilling by pointing his finger at the prosecutor and shouting, "Stop that! Stop that!"

The exchange culminated with Wilentz shouting, "You wouldn't tell [confess] if they murdered you, would you?"

In a flash Hauptmann shot back, "No!"

The defense finally objected to the exchange, though Wilentz clearly had been badgering the defendant for some time. Trenchard called a recess to restore calm in the courtroom. Taken as a whole, Hauptmann's testimony had been a disaster for the defendant.

Following Hauptmann, the additional defense witnesses were not only anticlimactic but ineffectual. None, aside from his wife, could swear that the defendant had been anywhere else on the evening of March 1. Mrs. Hauptmann was supposed to have evoked sympathy for her supposedly unjustly accused husband, but Wilentz instead scored points for the prosecution through his incisive cross-examination. Anna claimed that for nine months she had failed to notice the shoebox full of money which Hauptmann had testified he had placed on the top shelf of a closet in the kitchen before relocating its contents to the walls of his garage.

Wilentz demonstrated that the shoebox would have been in plain sight on the eye-level shelf of the closet in the tiny kitchen that Anna had used daily. He demonstrated with photographs that Anna daily hung her apron on a hook adjacent to the shelf. The prosecutor also elicited that when it rained the shelf became wet and frequently had to be wiped dry. Overall, Wilentz convincingly demonstrated that a traditional German hausfrau such as Anna, who worked as a domestic, could not have failed to notice the box of money had it been where Hauptmann had said it was, rather than secretly lodged in the walls of his garage all along.

Reilly produced a pathetic pair of "wood experts," who were in reality simply lumbermen who lacked both the expertise and the authority of Koehler. These witnesses did nothing to help the defendant's cause. Other defense witnesses were not merely ineffectual, but farcical. With typical bombast, Reilly had told the press he would present surprise witnesses who would "blow the roof off the courthouse." He even set up chairs with labels reserving them for defense witnesses, who then never appeared. Meanwhile, the defense broadcast desperate radio appeals inviting anyone who had knowledge that might be useful to come forward. Not surprisingly, some of the witnesses who appeared were not credible.

One man, later convicted of perjury, testified that he saw Isidor Fisch jump over a wall at St. Raymond's Cemetery on the night of the ransom payoff. Police records introduced by the prosecution revealed, however, that the witness himself had been involved in an automobile accident several miles away from the cemetery at the time that he had claimed to see Fisch.

Another defense witness claimed to have seen a car with a ladder in it near the Lindbergh estate, driven by someone other than Hauptmann. The witness lost all credibility with the jury, however, when he admitted under cross-examination to previous criminal convictions of assault and battery as well as "carnal abuse." Another defense witness had been repeatedly institutionalized in a mental hospital.

After this litany Hauptmann was left shaking his head over the weakness of his own defense. By this time Hauptmann and Reilly barely spoke to one another and the defendant and his wife had developed a much closer relationship with the Flemington attorney Lloyd Fisher. Fisher, who apparently believed in Hauptmann's innocence, would stand by Hauptmann until the day of his execution.

On the twenty-sixth day of the trial Reilly summoned Gerta Henkel to the stand, which succeeded only in reminding the jury of Hauptmann's frequent visits to her home for "coffee" and his alleged lack of fidelity to his own wife. Sarcastic during cross-examination, Mrs. Henkel was an unappealing witness who did nothing to aid what for Hauptmann was already a lost cause.

Finally, after thirty days of court testimony, the defense rested with a perfunctory motion for a directed verdict of acquittal, which Trenchard summarily rejected. Final arguments in the trial began on February 11, 1935. Reilly's closing argument, halting and disorganized, sought to shift suspicion away from Hauptmann and onto other individuals, including Condon, organized crime gangs, and the Lindbergh family servants. Reilly sketched the vague outlines of a dark conspiracy involving Condon, Betty Gow and her boyfriend Red Johnson, and Violet Sharpe. At one point Reilly offered a venerable solution to the murder mystery by charging that the butler, gentle old Oliver Whateley, had done it.

These unsubstantiated theories were, of course, no match for the prosecution's evidence, which Reilly vainly sought to counter. He dismissed the abundant handwriting evidence by simply insisting that Hauptmann had written none of the ransom notes. The kidnap ladder, he declared, had been nothing more than a plant designed to deflect attention from the inside job perpetuated by the conspiracy of family servants. Reilly's closing argument demonstrated anew what Hauptmann himself had come to realize: the defendant had been poorly represented. The Bull of Brooklyn had failed to mount a credible defense. It was now clear why Hauptmann's attorney had been given another nickname as well: Deathhouse Reilly.

It was true that even the most skilled defense attorney, however, would have faced an insurmountable challenge in the face of the evidence, as well as the public perceptions, arrayed against Hauptmann. Yet Reilly offered melodrama rather than a coherent strategy and a plausible alternative explanation for the kidnap and murder of the Lindbergh baby. He produced weak witnesses and often appeared ill-prepared for cross-examination—especially during afternoon sessions when he returned from lunchtime recesses spiked with cocktails.

Once a top-flight defense attorney, Reilly had shown himself to be past his prime. His bullying of witnesses failed to erode their credibility and alienated the jury. By contrast, the jurors did not seem to hold the bullying of the accented defendant against the prosecution. Overall, Wilentz made a far more favorable impression than Reilly. The jury disliked the flashy New York lawyer, especially as tales of his drinking and womanizing filtered through the courtroom. One juror explained that the Bull of Brooklyn had "showed his contempt for us from the start." Another concurred: "Reilly came down from Broadway to us hicks to show off his tricks. We all thought he was a big bluff, all dressed up like a clothing model."

Reilly's strategy—although it hardly amounted to as much—of vilifying the "hometown" New Jersey State Police was not well calculated to appeal to the Hunterdon County jury. It was true, as Reilly charged, that the state police had jealously guarded their control of a case that they sometimes appeared poorly equipped to handle alone. By the time federal authorities began to play a role, the state police had already obliterated the crime scene below the kidnap window and had allowed Lindbergh too much control over the criminal investigation. Despite these salient points offered by the defense, the prosecution's evidence appeared overwhelming. The contrast between the state's powerful case and the weak defense effort was obvious to the jury.

With Hauptmann's conviction virtually assured, securing the death penalty was all that remained for prosecutor Wilentz to accomplish in his closing argument. Proving himself to be a first-rate courtroom talent, Wilentz had clearly outshone Reilly in both preparation and performance in the trial. Few believed the jurors would render a verdict other than guilty. But would they allow Hauptmann to live?

On February 12, 1935, the thirty-first day of the longest criminal trial in U.S. history at that time, people crowded the aisles to hear Wilentz's closing remarks. "The courtroom is manifestly overcrowded, there is no question about that," an irritated Judge Trenchard observed. He warned the spectators to avoid any outbursts or displays of emotion before turning matters over to the New Jersey prosecutor. Wilentz proceeded to recount in meticulous detail the evidence against the defendant, but marred his own performance in the closing statement by playing to the baser emotions of the jury and the public. In order to secure the death penalty, Wilentz changed the version of events that he had laid out in his opening argument. At that time, Wilentz had left open the possibility that Hauptmann may have dropped the Lindbergh baby when the kidnap ladder shattered during his descent. Such a version of events would suggest an accidental death, when the baby's head struck the windowsill below, albeit a death during the course of a kidnapping.

In his closing argument, however, Wilentz now insisted that Hauptmann had brutally murdered the child in his crib. "This fellow took no chance on the child awakening. He crushed that child right in that room into insensibility. He smothered and choked that child right in that room." The fractured skull which had been the cause of Charles Jr.'s death was a result of being bludgeoned with the chisel that Hauptmann had brought to the crime scene, Wilentz now argued. The prosecutor had no evidence, such as blood in the baby's crib, to support his charge.

Wilentz's version of the murder was important, however, to counter the defense argument that Flemington was an illegitimate venue for the trial because there was no evidence that the baby had been killed in Hunterdon County. Although the baby's body had been found only some five miles from the Lindbergh estate, the killer had crossed the line into Mercer County to dispose of the body. Wilentz dreaded the prospect that he might lose the case on such a technicality and therefore emphasized to the jury the theory that the child had been killed in his crib in Hunterdon County.

Playing to the worst of public instincts, Wilentz attempted to dehumanize Hauptmann for the jury in order to make their task of condemning him to death all the more attractive. Waving his arms and pounding his fist for emphasis, the prosecutor described Hauptmann as not only an "egomaniac" but "the filthiest, vilest snake that ever crawled through the grass." The defendant was nothing more than "an animal lower than the lowest form in the animal kingdom, Public Enemy Number One of this world—Bruno Richard Hauptmann." Wilentz explained that he preferred not to breathe the same air as Hauptmann for fear of being "contaminated." He added, "I feel itchy, I feel oozy, I just couldn't stand being anywhere near him."

With a huge American flag overshadowing the courtroom decor, Wilentz tapped into the xenophobic inclinations of the rural New Jersey jurors with a direct appeal to their antiforeign sentiment. "What type of man would murder the child of Charles and Anne Lindbergh? He wouldn't be an American." Countering defense theories of a gang perpetrating the crime, Wilentz insisted that "No American gangster and no American racketeer ever sank to the level of killing babies." The prosecutor pleaded with the jury to reject "a recommendation of mercy," to eschew "a wishy-washy decision." Wilentz's impassioned appeal kept the jury spellbound. In a fitting end to the trial, the strong conclusion of the prosecution's case offered a stark contrast to Reilly's weak and disjointed summation.

On February 13, the thirty-second day of the trial, Judge Trenchard, calm and firmly in control throughout, delivered his charge to the jury. Although Trenchard counseled the jury to maintain impartiality and to be guided by the evidence, the judge left little doubt that he expected the jurors to do their duty by returning with a verdict of guilty.

While his charge to the jury was not as flagrant as Justice Dewey's in the Massachusetts Superior Court trial of Lizzie Borden, Trenchard took full advantage of New Jersey law, which allowed judges ample leeway in commenting on the credibility of witnesses. In essence, the judge spoke favorably of the prosecution's witnesses while casting doubt on the testimony of those called by the defense, including Hauptmann himself.

Supporting the prosecution argument on the venue of the case, Trenchard instructed the jury that it was a "reasonable inference" to conclude that the killer's "felonious stroke" had been delivered on the Lindbergh estate in Hunterdon County. The judge then cast doubt on the defense theory that criminal gangs in collusion with the Lindbergh servants at the Morrow estate had orchestrated the kidnapping and murder. "The argument was to the effect that it was done by a gang, with the help of some one or more servants of the Lindbergh or Morrow households." Then, in a tone that made no effort to mask his own disbelief, Trenchard added: "Now do you believe that? Is there any evidence in this case whatsoever to support this conclusion?"

Trenchard employed the same rhetorical formula in casting a dubious eye on Hauptmann's "Fisch story," as well as his denial of responsibility for the ransom notes and the kidnap ladder. "The defendant says that these ransom bills, moneys, were left with him by one Fisch, a man now dead," Trenchard told the jury. "Do you believe that?"

"Do you believe his testimony that the money was left with him in a shoe box, and that it rested on the top shelf in his closet for several months?" the judge continued. "His wife, as I recall it, said that she never saw the box; and I do not recall that any witness excepting the defendant testified that they ever saw the shoe box there." While calling attention to Hauptmann's unlikely explanations, Trenchard reminded the jurors that they could consider Hauptmann's criminal record insofar as it pertained to his credibility as a witness.

While clearly revealing his own skepticism about the defense case, Judge Trenchard emphasized the compelling prosecution evidence, particularly the testimony of the handwriting and wood experts. "Does not the evidence satisfy you that at least part of the wood from which the ladder was built came out of the flooring of the attic of the defendant?"

Recalling the strong impression left by Condon's account of events, Trenchard challenged the jurors as to whether there could be "any doubt in your mind[s] as to the reliability of Dr. Condon's testimony?" Turning to Amandus Hochmuth's recollection of seeing the strange car with a ladder in it, Trenchard asked, "Do you think there is any reason, upon the whole, to doubt the truth of the old man's testimony? May he not have well and easily remembered the circumstance, in view of the fact that that very night the child was carried away?"

When Trenchard completed his loaded charge, the jury went out for deliberations at 11:23 A.M. After 32 days, 162 witnesses, and 381 exhibits, the longest and most sensational criminal trial in American history was left in the hands of the eight men and four women of the Hunterdon County jury.

As the day progressed they asked only for a magnifying glass to study maps and documents. The jurors stopped twice for meals. By late evening on February 13, after eleven hours and fourteen minutes, their deliberations were complete.

When the jury returned to the courtroom at 10:44 P.M., Hauptmann appeared before them now manacled for the first time, his right wrist connected with the wrist of a state trooper. Trenchard summoned the assembled throng into silence before turning his attention to the jury box.

Rising to speak in a shaky voice, the foreman read the verdict: "We, the jury, find the defendant, Bruno Richard Hauptmann, guilty of murder in the first degree." Each of the other eleven jurors repeated the verdict in turn.

Hauptmann stiffened, but otherwise showed little reaction as he heard the verdict. Asking Hauptmann to stand, Trenchard gazed down on the defendant and declared: "Bruno Richard Hauptmann, you have been convicted of murder in the first degree. The sentence of the court is that you suffer death at the time and place, and in the manner provided by law." Trenchard set the week of March 18 as the time in which the sentence would be carried out. Hauptmann stumbled out of the courtroom, seemingly in a daze, not even looking up at his ashen-faced wife. Once back in his jail cell, the condemned man collapsed on his cot and began to cry.

The jurors later explained that while they had readily agreed on Hauptmann's guilt, their deliberations focused on whether or not to condemn the carpenter to death. On the first ballot only seven had advocated murder in the first degree, but after discussions and four additional ballots, the decision was unanimous. By making no specific recommendation for life imprisonment, the conviction for first-degree murder meant that Hauptmann would face the electric chair.

At the Morrow family home in Englewood, New Jersey, on the evening of February 13, Charles and Anne Lindbergh and their relatives heard the verdict over the radio. Lindbergh was relieved. He had no doubts himself, having long described the evidence against Hauptmann as "overwhelming."

Following the broadcast, as family friend Harold Nicolson recalled, Lindbergh "very quietly, very simply went through the case point by point." The famous aviator assured his family that "there is no doubt at all that Hauptmann did the thing." Lindbergh added that he had dreaded the possibility "that they would get hold of someone as a victim about whom I wasn't sure. I am sure about this—quite sure." As Nicolson recalled, Lindbergh's recapitulation of the facts of the case "seemed to relieve all of them."

Most Americans applauded the verdict, although many who judged Hauptmann guilty still sympathized with the handsome German immigrant, seeing him as a victim of World War I, in which—while still just a teenager—he had been compelled to serve.

The German-American community, especially in New York, expressed outrage over the guilty verdict and death penalty. German Americans charged that

Hauptmann's foreign birth and imperfect grasp of English had worked against **121**
him in the trial. Public cries for vengeance and Wilentz's xenophobic summation only served to fuel the German-American perception that Hauptmann was
a sacrificial lamb.

The media-driven presumption of guilt was so pervasive that many German
Americans concluded that the opposite must be true: that Hauptmann was an
innocent man being railroaded into the electric chair as a scapegoat. Sixty years
later, a majority of African Americans would arrive at similar conclusions about
the O. J. Simpson case, namely that police authorities were so racist and corrupt
that Simpson must have been innocent.

In the wake of the Hauptmann conviction, German Americans held rallies
and raised money for the appeals process as well as for a speaking tour featuring
the defendant's wife. Crowds cheered Anna in New York, New Jersey, Chicago,
and across the Midwest.

While there seems little doubt that Hauptmann's foreign birth spurred popular prejudice against him, the case against the German was much stronger
than the evidence arrayed against the Italian radicals Sacco and Vanzetti in the
1920s. Their execution in 1927 stemmed at least as much from xenophobia as
from the evidence in the case.

Neither was Hauptmann railroaded as badly as the Scottsboro Boys—young
black men repeatedly convicted in trials throughout the 1930s for an Alabama
rape that in reality had never even occurred. The difference was that while the
Alabama judges and juries convicted the Scottsboro boys almost solely on the
basis of race, in this case abundant evidence existed of Hauptmann's guilt.

Nevertheless, there is no question that the notoriety of the celebrity murder
case complicated the administration of justice. Massive pretrial publicity, virtually all of which pointed to Hauptmann's guilt, undermined the effort to mount
a credible defense. The New York newspapers had given heavy play to the handwriting and wood-matching evidence, reporting that they proved Hauptmann's
guilt beyond a reasonable doubt. In addition to reporting extensively on the
damning evidence, the press frequently printed rumors, no matter how wild or
unconfirmed, throughout the investigation and trial.

Hauptmann's trial unfolded in a circus atmosphere. Tiny Flemington could
not cope with the 70,000 to 100,000 people who descended upon it. During the
weekend recess, tens of thousands of tourists teemed through Flemington.

Nothing precluded them from going inside the courtroom to pose for pictures sitting in the defendant's chair.

Spectators, writers, and photographers sometimes literally fought their way into the courtroom. Court sessions were nightmarishly hot, a result of the over-crowded conditions and the hissing output of the steam radiators.

The six-week trial featured tears and outbursts from the defendant and the gallery, grandstanding by the attorneys, a power outage, and even a confession from a member of the audience. People regularly murmured, gasped, and laughed aloud. Newspaper correspondents compared notes and sent message boys running out when they thought key testimony had been offered, thus lending significance to testimony that the jury may otherwise not have deemed important. Theaters soon began to feature newsreel footage captured by a motion picture camera and microphone hidden in the balcony, yet tacitly toler-ated by Trenchard.

In the wake of the Hauptmann trial, the American Bar Association issued a special report condemning "the commercialization of the administration of justice." The committee urged that cameras and sound equipment be barred from American courtrooms. As a result of the sensational case, states began to pass and strengthen laws against the use of photographic and recording devices during courtroom proceedings.

The jury itself, while sequestered in the Union Hotel, could scarcely avoid contact with the press, celebrities, and onlookers who shared the crowded cen-tral hotel with them. Jurors routinely overheard discussions and comments as they took their meals with only a thin screen placed between them and the crowds of people. When the time came to deliberate, demonstrators outside the courthouse chanted "Kill Hauptmann! Kill Hauptmann!" Lindbergh himself described the throng as a "lynching crowd."

In June 1935, citing the carnival atmosphere that had prevailed in Fleming-ton, Lloyd Fisher filed an appeal before the New Jersey Court of Errors and Appeals. Two months earlier Anna Hauptmann had fired Reilly, who had been briefly hospitalized with "exhaustion," in the midst of a dispute over his fee. In addition to citing the circus atmosphere in and around the Flemington court-room, Fisher argued that Wilentz's summation and Trenchard's biased charge also contributed to Hauptmann's failure to receive a fair trial.

His execution having been stayed pending outcome of the appeal, Hauptmann passed the time under a twenty-four-hour guard at his new home, the state penitentiary in Trenton. Some 600 inmates greeted Hauptmann with a chorus of boos upon his relocation there shortly after the trial. He was one of five New Jersey inmates scheduled for death in the electric chair.

On October 10, 1935, the fourteen justices of the New Jersey Court of Errors and Appeals unanimously upheld Hauptmann's conviction. In a forty-five-page opinion, Justice Charles W. Parker ignored the circus atmosphere in deference to the massive evidence against Hauptmann. "Our conclusion," he wrote, "is that the verdict is not only not contrary to the weight of the evidence, but one to which the evidence inescapably led."

On December 9, 1935, the U.S. Supreme Court declined to hear Hauptmann's appeal. With the final obstacle to carrying out the sentence seemingly removed, Judge Trenchard set an execution date of January 17, 1936. The State of New Jersey had even arranged for the nationally known executioner who had put the electric charge into Sacco and Vanzetti in 1927 to perform Hauptmann's execution.

At this time, however, New Jersey governor Harold Hoffman intervened in the Lindbergh case in spectacular fashion. Hoffman, a former two-term congressional representative and a popular politician, had become enamored with the various conspiracy theories concerning the Lindbergh case. The governor believed that Schwarzkopf had bungled the investigation, that Condon was a fraud, and that the wood and handwriting evidence was bogus.

Sensational headlines blared the reopening of the Lindbergh case when Hoffman delivered a bombshell to reporters by confirming that he had met secretly with Hauptmann in his prison cell and harbored grave doubts as to the carpenter's guilt.

Lloyd Fisher seized the opportunity offered by the governor's sympathy to request a pardon for Hauptmann from the New Jersey Court of Pardons. However, on January 11, only five days before the scheduled execution, the Court of Pardons voted seven to one—with only Hoffman dissenting—against granting a reprieve to the condemned man.

Hoffman then exercised his prerogative to grant Hauptmann a thirty-day stay of execution. The governor failed to realize that he was making the blunder of his political career. Newspaper editorials across the state condemned Hoffman and called for his resignation or impeachment. (Years later they would learn that Hoffman had regularly been bilking the state of monies in order to live a life of luxury. Hoffman would write out a confession to his own crimes, which were publicized only after his death from a heart attack in 1954.)

Hauptmann, Anna, and Fisher had their hopes buoyed by Hoffman's sensational intervention. Ironically, these events may have cost Hauptmann his only chance at life. In the midst of the controversy, Wilentz offered to join with Hoffman in support of a commutation of Hauptmann's sentence to life in prison on the condition that the carpenter would confess to killing the Lindbergh baby.

Still appearing at times strangely confident, Hauptmann preferred to believe that the governor's intervention suggested that he eventually would be freed. He would never confess to the crime as long as he thought he might yet go free.

While Lloyd Fisher apparently encouraged Hauptmann's false optimism, Samuel Leibowitz, a renowned New York defense attorney who had defended clients ranging from Al Capone to the Scottsboro boys, interjected himself into the case in an effort to save the condemned man's life. Gaining an audience with Hauptmann, Leibowitz tried to convince him and his wife that his only chance for life was to confess.

Leibowitz told Hauptmann point-blank that the evidence against him was overwhelming, but that he would arrange for a commutation to life in prison if only Hauptmann would admit his guilt. Hauptmann refused. Wilentz later averred that Hauptmann would never confess because he would not subject Anna to a life as the wife of an admitted kidnapper and murderer of an innocent child. Indeed, Anna would spend the rest of her life insisting that her husband was innocent.

One final obstacle—yet another bogus confession from a publicity seeker—stood between Hauptmann and the executioner's chair. On March 31, 1936, Hauptmann, crying and praying aloud, had his head and leg shaved in preparation for electrocution. At the last moment, however, prison officials delayed the execution while a Mercer County grand jury thoroughly investigated the latest false confession, which was repudiated by its own author. A crowd of 8,000 outside the state penitentiary in Trenton went home disappointed.

With so many reprieves Hauptmann, Anna, and Fisher still hoped the execution could be put off indefinitely. But Governor Hoffman, finally sobered by the landslide of criticism, no longer had the stomach to intervene. At last nothing stood in the way of Hauptmann's execution, now scheduled for April 3.

After the intense public controversy the actual event was somber and anticlimactic. A much smaller crowd than before gathered outside the prison and offered only a halfhearted cheer when news of the execution came. Hauptmann had spent his last moments crying together with Lloyd Fisher. Wearing slippers, Hauptmann was taken from his cell shortly after 8:30 P.M. He had already heard the machine tested in the sterile, white-walled death room into which he was now escorted.

Hauptmann appeared dazed as his spiritual advisers read aloud from the Bible. Officials fastened one damp electrode to his calf and another to his shaved head. At 8:44 P.M. the executioner turned the wheel on the control panel and pumped 2,000 volts of electricity into the killer of the Lindbergh baby. Sixty seconds later, another 1,000 volts were sent to make sure the grim task was complete.

Among the officials looking on was H. Norman Schwarzkopf. By this time Lindbergh and his family, hounded by the press, had moved to England. Columnist Walter Lippmann described them as "refugees from the tyranny of yellow journalism," a family which had been denied its "inalienable right to privacy."

Also denied privacy was Anna Hauptmann. Reporters and photographers barged through a crack in the door at her Trenton hotel room and inundated the grieving widow with questions. Flashbulbs popped as she lay on the bed, dressed in black and crying hysterically, before Fisher cleared the press from the room. Bruno Richard Hauptmann was cremated in a private ceremony the next day.

As with any famous—indeed infamous—crime, controversy was, and remains, inevitable. Hauptmann's widow continued to insist on her husband's innocence until her death in 1994. Authors weighed in with books such as Anthony Scaduto's Scapegoat (1976), which attempted to exonerate Hauptmann despite the evidence against him. Scaduto insisted that the Lindbergh baby was alive and well, living in Connecticut! A few years later microscopic analysis of the baby's hair proved conclusively that the dead child had been Charles A. Lindbergh Jr.

Other wild theories found their way into print. One holds that Anne's older sister Elisabeth, insanely jealous over Charles's selection of Anne instead of her to be his wife, orchestrated the kidnap and murder of the Lindbergh baby. Another theory asserts that Lindbergh, a notorious practical joker, killed his own child—accidentally—during a bungled prank as he attempted to remove the baby from the house by using the folding ladder.

Such accounts, however baseless, are inevitable in a tabloid culture. The evidence against Hauptmann is nonetheless overwhelming. A slight possibility remains that Hauptmann did not act alone. Some analysts of the Lindbergh case believe that he benefited from an accomplice to ascertain the family's whereabouts on March 1 and to identify the window that led into the nursery.

It seems more likely, however, that Hauptmann obtained this information by casing the Lindbergh estate. As the Lindberghs had not moved completely into their new home, there were no curtains over the windows and Hauptmann might easily have identified which room was the child's nursery. The presence of the three-quarter-inch chisel suggests Hauptmann did not know that the warped shutters on the kidnap window did not latch, information that an insider could have provided.

It seems likely that Hauptmann was a classic, and lone, sociopathic criminal. Scarred by his life experiences and incapable of accepting his position in society, Hauptmann targeted the family of a beloved American hero as a means of elevating his own sense of self-worth. He would outsmart the great Lindbergh, accomplish a feat as daring as Lindy's solo flight across the Atlantic, and thus establish his superiority over Lindbergh, a man about his own age, who had obtained the wealth, power, and popularity that Hauptmann craved.

Incapable of confronting his own personality disorders, Hauptmann went to his death without confessing to the crime. Indeed, he insisted on his innocence to the end, claiming that he was a victim of the public's desire for vengeance.

While abundant evidence suggests that Hauptmann kidnapped and murdered the Lindbergh baby, it is equally clear that the German immigrant did not receive a fair trial. In the best legal analysis of the case, Lewis M. Seidman concluded that overzealous New Jersey and federal officials "may have withheld exculpatory evidence, utilized testimony that may have been perjured, and doctored or manufactured evidence used at the trial."

Documents made public some forty years after the trial of the century reveal that the FBI, New Jersey state police, and prosecutors conspired to prevent exculpatory evidence from being presented at Hauptmann's trial. FBI documents show that state and federal officials had grilled several other suspects, many of them also German immigrants, who at one time appeared to have plausible links to the crime. After the arrest of Hauptmann, however, the authorities suppressed that information, thus denying the defense access to material that might have been used to construct an alternative theory as to perpetrators of the crime.

Prosecutors also withheld from the defense and the public contradictory and potentially exculpatory evidence casting doubt on some of the positive identifications of Hauptmann. These actions, which would clearly constitute prosecutorial misconduct today, would sully the outcome of the Hauptmann trial.

Had the defense had access to some of this information, as it would have under discovery rules today, a competent defense attorney would have been able to offer a much stronger defense on Hauptmann's behalf. Today, evidence of the state's actions would almost certainly result in Hauptmann's conviction being overturned and the defendant receiving a new trial. As Seidman's analysis shows, the deck was stacked against the hapless German immigrant. Laudably, however, Seidman does not embrace the syllogism that because Hauptmann failed to receive a fair trial he was therefore innocent of the crime.

While New Jersey officials succeeded in their goal of obtaining Hauptmann's conviction and execution, their handling of the case was unjust and led to distortions of the historical record. Numerous chroniclers of the Lindbergh case have concluded on the basis of the official misconduct that Hauptmann was an innocent man.

As we have seen, however, the evidence against Hauptmann is so overwhelming as virtually to rule out the possibility of his innocence. Yet proper administration of justice is characterized by more than its outcome—it is also a *process* that must be respected.

When officials manipulate and withhold evidence, as they did in the Hauptmann case, their actions call into question the ultimate outcome of the entire judicial proceeding. Once it is clear that the state has manipulated *some* of the evidence, and has lied and cheated, it is but a short step for some to conclude that *all* of the evidence is tainted and the verdict itself in doubt. It was precisely this line of reasoning that O. J. Simpson's attorneys pursued more than sixty years after the Hauptmann trial in convincing a Los Angeles jury that the official version of events could not be trusted and therefore reasonable doubt existed as to Simpson's guilt. Denied access to exculpatory evidence, Hauptmann's defense never had the same opportunity. The prosecution "needed a murder conviction and they were not going to be stopped," Harvard law professor Alan Dershowitz declared after his analysis of the Lindbergh trial.

Hauptmann had indeed been railroaded. Official misconduct, a lynch mob atmosphere, and poor defense representation combined to deny Hauptmann a fair trial. No defendant should be convicted, much less executed, on the basis of manipulated and incomplete evidence. In the Hauptmann case, the actions of the New Jersey officials were not only unprofessional, but ultimately unnecessary. Taken as an unadulterated whole, the evidence against the German carpenter would have been more than sufficient to condemn him.

The longest and most sensational criminal trial in American history revealed the helplessness of a poorly represented defendant confronted with the full panoply of state power and already condemned by the public and the national news media. Although a guilty man died in the electric chair, resolution of the Lindbergh kidnapping cannot be accounted as a triumph of American justice.

III VENDETTA: SAM SHEPPARD AND THE NORTH SHORE NIGHTMARE

High school sweethearts Marilyn Reese and Sam Sheppard married in Hollywood in 1945 while Sam attended the Los Angeles College of Osteopathic Physicians. Returning to Cleveland, where his father had staked out a thriving practice of osteopathic medicine, Sam purchased a white Dutch colonial home on the lakefront in the elite western suburb of Bay Village. It was there that Marilyn Sheppard was bludgeoned to death in the early morning hours of July 4, 1954. Courtesy of Cleveland State University Archives

He would show her, the sexy rich doctor's wife who thought she had everything. Let's see how superior they think they are after I'm done with her!

The big man crept through the kitchen and onto the landing that divided the downstairs kitchen from the living room of the lakeshore home.

A volatile combustion of anger and sexual arousal propelled him up the stairs and into the bedroom, where the woman slept on the nearest of two twin beds. The intruder clapped his hand over the sleeping woman's mouth and began to rip at her cotton pajamas. He must have been a horrifying sight to wake up to, a large man wearing makeup and a bushy wig to conceal his identity.

He had not expected that the woman could put up such a fight, but she was not one to endure the savage indignity of rape without a struggle.

While holding his victim down he struck out with his left hand, in which he held a screwdriver. His rage ignited by her continuing resistance, he slammed the butt of the tool into her head again and again.

Downstairs, the woman's husband lurched himself out of a typically deep slumber on the living-room couch, where he had fallen asleep watching television. Something was wrong with his wife, he suddenly realized, as he tumbled off the couch and ran for the stairs.

Upon entering the room, the husband encountered, as he later explained to the police, "a form in a light garment" standing next to his wife's bed. After grappling with his wife's attacker, he received a stunning blow to the back of his neck and collapsed to the floor.

As he lay unconscious on the floor, his wife's life ebbed away in an immense pool of blood. For her, the horror was at an end. For the husband, the nightmare had just begun.

Cleveland, Ohio, was one of America's big cities in 1954. While not a New York, Chicago, or Los Angeles, it was in the top ten in size and national prominence. Industry flourished during those boom years at the confluence of the Cuyahoga River and Lake Erie, on the "north coast" of the United States. Symbolic of the feel-good era in Cleveland, the Indians baseball team would achieve a rare feat by conquering their perennial oppressors, the New York Yankees, in winning a record 109 games en route to the 1954 World Series.

The Sheppards, a family of osteopathic physicians, prospered along with the city in which they lived. The patriarch, Richard A. Sheppard, and his three sons—Richard, Stephen, and, the youngest, Samuel Holmes Sheppard—worked together and made a handsome living at Bay View Hospital, the osteopathic facility opened by their father in the elite lakefront suburb on Cleveland's west side.

Sam had first met his wife, the former Marilyn Reese, in junior high school. She told another boy, a friend of Sam's, that she wanted to meet the tall, brown-eyed youth who starred on the eighth-grade basketball team.

Sam and Marilyn became sweethearts at Cleveland Heights High School, where both were extremely popular. Named the top athlete at the school, Sam, six feet tall and well built, was a multisport star as well as class president in 1942. Marilyn, dark haired, slim, and attractive, was a year older than Sam. She went off to Skidmore College in New York during Sam's senior year. Sam enrolled in Hanover College in southern Indiana the next year, but the high school sweethearts remained committed to one another.

Marilyn confessed her love for Sam, wrote to him almost every day, and refused all entreaties from the college boys. Sam, one of two freshmen to make the varsity football team, played basketball as well, pledged a fraternity, and studied four to five hours every night to ensure a strong academic performance, which he achieved in his premed regimen of courses.

Following United States entry in World War II after the Japanese attack on Pearl Harbor on December 7, 1941, Sam tried to join the Army Air Reserve. "I received notification that I was 'frozen' where I was and I would not be allowed to quit [college] and join one of the armed services" while continuing medical studies. Sheppard explained that premedical students in osteopathy were not being allowed to join the army and navy and to continue their studies in uniform, whereas other premed students did enjoy that privilege. The example of unequal treatment for osteopathic medical students grated on Sam. While their training was similar to that of M.D.'s, osteopaths emphasized body manipulation as well as conventional medicine. In the 1940s and 1950s, far more so than today, rivalry and resentment prevailed between M.D.s and osteopaths.

Marilyn and her family raised questions, typical of the era, as to why Sam was not in uniform, but they soon accepted his explanation. When Sam followed in his brothers' footsteps, enrolling at the Los Angeles College of Osteopathic Physicians, he asked Marilyn to join him in California. She agreed.

Marilyn and Sam were married in 1945 in a small ceremony in the chapel of a Methodist church in Hollywood. Marilyn, in the manner typical of female deference to her husband, typed Sam's papers and quizzed him as he prepared for his exams. She expressed loneliness—and some jealousy—about the long hours, sometimes all night, that Sam spent at the hospital, where attractive nurses abounded.

Apparently some of the young couple's tensions came to the attention of Sam's parents, who suggested that perhaps it would be a good time for Sam and Marilyn to start a family. Sam's father offered an increased allowance as an incentive. The couple took the advice and their son, Sam Reese Sheppard, was born in 1947.

After receiving his medical degree, Sam continued in the family tradition by moving back to Cleveland to join his father and brothers in practicing osteopathic medicine. By 1954 Sam was earning $33,000 a year, a handsome salary for the era, the equivalent of some $200,000 in 1999 dollars. And the young physician was on the brink of much greater earnings that would guarantee his family financial comfort for life.

Taking a loan from his father, Sam purchased a sixty-year-old white Dutch colonial home, which rose a hundred feet above the Lake Erie shore in Bay Village. The property was two lots to the west of a park and boat launch. Steps led down to the Sheppards' private beach, where Sam swam regularly in the summer. In the driveway Sam, a car buff, parked a Lincoln convertible, a Jaguar, and a jeep. He played basketball in the same driveway with the neighborhood kids, who idolized him.

A close friend and neighbor recalled that Sam was "easily the most popular person" in Bay Village, "well known and well liked through his various activities." A big sports fan, Sam was close personal friends with Otto Graham, the star quarterback of the Cleveland Browns football team. Sheppard often sat on the bench as one of the team doctors during home games.

On the holiday eve of July 3, 1954, the Sheppards entertained their neighbors, Donald and Nancy Ahern. Marilyn baked Sam's favorite blueberry pie and prepared dinner while Sam sipped a martini at the Aherns' down the street. Sam appreciated the drink, as it had been a particularly trying day. He had tried desperately, but ultimately to no avail, to save the life of a young boy, about the age of his own son, who had been struck by a telephone company truck. After opening the boy's chest and trying to massage his heart back to life, Sam finally had been forced to give up.

Before the young surgeon could finish his martini that evening, he received yet another emergency call to tend to a man whose leg had been fractured in an accident. Sighing deeply, Sheppard popped a clove into his mouth to mask the smell of alcohol and drove to the hospital to set the man's leg. By the time he returned, close to 9 P.M., dinner was ready to be served on the lakefront porch.

The Aherns' two young sons and Sam Jr. finished their dinners in the kitchen. Sam turned on the radio to listen to the Indians-White Sox baseball game. The two couples talked about golf. Sam, an avid player, was "quite proud to hear about" Marilyn's rapid progress as a beginner, Nancy Ahern recalled.

After the Aherns walked their boys back to their nearby home, and Marilyn put Sam Jr.—called "Chip"—to bed, the adults settled down to watch the late movie on television. Its title, *Strange Holiday*, was eerily apropos.

Marilyn cuddled affectionately in Sam's lap in a big chair for a time, but as the movie went on he began to nod off. Marilyn nudged him and Sam got up, flopped onto his stomach with a pillow on the couch by the wall near the base of the stairwell, and went to sleep almost immediately. By the time the Aherns left shortly after midnight, Sam was snoring on the couch. "Just before we left," Don Ahern recalled, "it was quite obvious that Sam was sleeping very soundly and did not know that we were leaving."

The Aherns chuckled with Marilyn over this typical behavior—Sam was notorious for fading out in the evening, even when a guest at other people's homes. But they all knew he had had a particularly draining day.

After saying good night to the Aherns, Marilyn sat next to Sam and asked him if he wanted to come up to bed. The exhausted physician grunted and his wife let him be. Marilyn left the upstairs light on in case Sam decided to come up to bed later in the night.

Marilyn went upstairs, put on her white two-piece pajamas patterned with red diamonds, and settled into the twin bed nearest the bedroom door. She needed to get some sleep, as she planned to rise early and begin preparations for the July 4 beach party and wienie roast, with eighteen guests, which the Sheppards were hosting the next day.

The savage attack occurred some four hours after Marilyn went to bed. When Sam heard Marilyn cry out, "Sam! Sam!" his first thought was that his wife, pregnant with their second child, "might be having a reaction similar to convulsions that she had had in the early days of her pregnancy."

After rushing upstairs, Sheppard "charged into the room and saw a form with a light garment." The physician grappled with the intruder as Marilyn lay moaning on the bed. The killer struck Sheppard on the back of the neck and, as he later reported, "I was apparently knocked out."

When Sheppard came to on the bedroom floor, he was groggy with pain and shock. Looking up, he faced the almost surreal vision of his wife, motionless on the bed in a pool of blood, "making little gurgling noises"—sounds characteristic of the human "death rattle." Sheppard's wallet, ripped from his pocket in the struggle, lay on the floor next to him. After putting his wallet back in his pocket, Sam checked his wife's pulse and confirmed that she was dead. He rushed into Sam Jr.'s room where the boy slept undisturbed. Suddenly Sheppard realized that he heard noises coming from downstairs. Through his confusion another emotion emerged—anger—at the realization that the perpetrator of this horrible crime remained in his home.

Sheppard lurched downstairs in time to see the man fleeing the house from the door heading down to the lake. The young physician chased what he later described as a large, well-built man with a "good sized head and bushy hair" down the steps to the shore of the lake. The intruder turned to face Sam, who plunged into the fight "with intentions of really letting him have it." But Sheppard, already seriously injured from the blow to his neck in the bedroom, found himself being choked, punched, and knocked unconscious for a second time.

Some time later—he was never sure how long—Sam Sheppard regained consciousness for the second time that morning. His head and torso were on the shore when he came to, but the waves from the cold lake pushed his legs back and forth in the surf.

Dazed and in shock, Sam stumbled back to his home and up once again to the bedroom to confirm the incomprehensible reality of his wife's lifeless body. She lay face up on the bed in an immense pool of blood, her head battered with deep gashes, breasts exposed, and legs apart, dangling off the end of the bed. After checking her pulse yet again, Sheppard pulled the sheet over her waist. Wandering around the house in confusion, the young physician finally reached for the phone and called the first person he thought of, his close friend and neighbor, who also happened to be the mayor of Bay Village, Spencer Houk.

"Spen, my God, get over here quick!" Sheppard exclaimed. "I think they've killed Marilyn!"

Spen Houk and his wife, Esther, arrived several minutes later, between 5:30 and 6 A.M., and entered the house through the unlocked lakefront door. They found Sam bare-chested, his hair and trousers wet, slumped in a chair in the den. "He appeared dazed," Spen Houk told the police, "was holding the back of his neck. He said 'I think my neck's broken.'"

The house appeared "disorderly," Spen reported. Desk drawers were open and, in the downstairs hallway, Sam's black physician's bag was flung open and askew.

Esther Houk recounted to police that "Sam kept saying, mumbling over and over, 'I heard a scream and I dashed upstairs and somebody clobbered me.'" Looking up at Esther, Sam said, "Somebody should do something about Marilyn."

Taking her cue, Esther mounted the stairs and discovered the grotesque murder scene. After staring a few moments in shock, Esther recalled, "I felt her pulse, and I recall thinking how stupid that was." Moments later Esther was back in the den, ashen faced, exclaiming to her husband, "Call the police. Call an ambulance . . . Call everybody!"

Spen Houk did so, placing a call to Sam's eldest brother, Richard, as well. The first two police officers arrived at 5:57 A.M. After arming himself with a .38 revolver, Richard Sheppard rushed to the scene as well. He examined Marilyn as the police stood by and pronounced her dead at 6:12 A.M.

Sam remained slumped in the chair, holding his neck with both hands. Richard found his brother "sluggish, incoherent," and complaining of his neck injury and "a pounding headache." Bay Village police officer Fred Drenkhan reported that Sam's face "appeared to have been struck on the right side." Sheppard repeated his account of what happened, concluding with his having come to for a second time, with his legs in the cold lake water, before returning to the house to check Marilyn once again and then call the Houks.

The Bay Village police officers, accustomed to responding to boating or swimming accidents, were as stunned as anyone by the gruesome July 4 homicide in the home of one of the community's most respected families. They decided with Mayor Houk to summon the Cuyahoga County coroner and Cleveland police.

Richard Sheppard awoke young Chip, who mercifully had slumbered through the entire ordeal, and took him from the scene to his own home. Sam's other older brother, Stephen, arrived at the home. Aided by an intern, he transported Sam to Bay View Hospital for an examination of his painful neck injury.

Thus by 8 A.M., when the key figure in the subsequent investigation, Cuyahoga County Coroner Sam Gerber, arrived, the man with whom he most wanted to speak was no longer present. Gerber and the Cleveland homicide detectives who arrived after him viewed Sam's absence with deep suspicion. By midafternoon one of the detectives would accuse Sam to his face of murdering his wife.

Gerber, a graduate of Cincinnati Eclectic Medical College and also trained as an attorney, enjoyed enormous power and prestige. A small white-haired man, fifty-six years old at the time of the murder, he would serve as Cuyahoga County coroner for fifty years, until his retirement in 1987. Gerber quickly surveyed the murder scene, ordered Marilyn's body removed for an autopsy, and proceeded to Bay View Hospital to question Sam, whom he had already decided was the prime suspect.

Among those examining Sheppard at the hospital was Dr. Charles Elkins, an eminent neurologist. Elkins found that Sam had suffered facial bruising and "an injury to the spinal column" in the back of his neck. The patient "could not use [his] left hand or arm freely and there was [a] definite lack of reflexes on that side of his body."

By the time Gerber arrived Sam Sheppard was fully coherent, though still in pain. He related the same account to Gerber that he had told to the others. The coroner smiled, saying little, but already convinced that the man who lay before him had murdered his wife and was being shielded by the osteopaths at his father's Bay View Hospital. Gerber left, packing Sheppard's trousers, shoes, and other personal items as evidence.

Back at the crime scene, police found drawers askew, the physician's bag rifled, and Sam's and Marilyn's athletic trophies broken on the floor. A cursory check revealed no fingerprints, encouraging their quick conclusion that Sheppard had perpetrated the crime and arranged evidence of a burglary as a cover-up.

Having concluded that Sheppard was the guilty party, the police failed to conduct a thorough and open-minded investigation. They dismissed the report of a Bay Village couple who saw a bushy-haired man on the road between 3:30 and 4 A.M. as they returned to their Lake Road home near the Sheppards'.

Police questioned the Aherns about the time they spent with the Sheppards the evening before, but gleaned no evidence of tensions between the couple. Sam was "not of the emotional makeup to even make it possible for him to do what was done to Marilyn," Don Ahern told police. "He was certainly very fond of Marilyn, his wife, and I am quite sure proud of the fact that she was an expectant mother."

Knowing that seemingly loving husbands did sometimes kill their wives, the police paid little attention to such accounts that were sympathetic to Sam Sheppard. A more serious blunder was a lack of security at the crime scene. Police allowed journalists and neighbors to enter the home and yard. The lack of police control over the crime scene at the Sheppard home was reminiscent of the Lindbergh case, in which the kidnapper's footprints had been obliterated by cops and reporters.

While searching the Sheppard home and grounds themselves, police encouraged a group of neighborhood teenagers to search for whatever weapon had been used to bludgeon Marilyn Sheppard to death. No weapon was found but Larry Houk, the mayor's sixteen-year-old son, did find a green cloth bag near the beach at the bottom of the hill. Inside the bag was Sheppard's bloodstained watch, which had stopped at 4:15, his college ring, and a key ring which had been ripped from his trousers.

To the Cleveland homicide detectives, the green bag bolstered their theory that Sheppard had staged a fake burglary and had hidden the bag of stolen items so that it easily might be found. Returning to the hospital, they subjected the young physician to a belligerent grilling. Sheppard acknowledged that the green bag was his but said he had no idea how it had gotten down to the beach below.

One of the Cleveland police detectives, Robert Schottke, delving for motive, asked Sheppard about a rumor that he had been having an affair with a former Bay View Hospital nurse who had since moved to California. Sheppard denied the charge, but in fact it was true. Schottke then accused Sheppard of killing his wife, to which Sam angrily replied, "Don't be ridiculous! . . . I loved my wife."

Questioned in depth about their relationship, Sam declared that Marilyn sometimes displayed "a little jealous streak," but that the couple did not have major problems. In fact, he said, reflecting the spirit of patriarchal authority in the fifties' household, their relationship was "ideal" in that Marilyn "respected my decisions on all matters."

Unconvinced, police ordered Sam monitored twenty-four hours a day and sealed off the home from the Sheppard family. He would be allowed to return to retrieve some clothing under police supervision, but otherwise Sheppard and his attorneys would be denied access to his home, now a crime scene.

Upon learning that the police had accused his son of murder, Sam's father summoned the family attorney, who soon recommended a criminal attorney, William J. Corrigan. This action gave rise to one of the enduring myths of the Sheppard case, that the family had hired an attorney well before anyone had suggested his responsibility for the murder.

On July 7 Sam attended Marilyn's funeral in a wheelchair. Around his neck was an orthopedic collar designed to relieve pressure to help heal his neck injury. To cynical newsmen and much of the public, the ever present collar would become a symbol of the lengths the Sheppard family would go to feign an injury in an effort to bolster a dubious tale of a mysterious intruder.

Although Gerber and the Cleveland police never shifted their gaze from Sam, an absence of evidence, including even the murder weapon, prevented them from making a quick arrest. By mid-July, however, the press and public opinion were becoming fed up with the lack of action on the Sheppard case.

As in any sensational case, the press would play a major role during the investigation and subsequent trial. In the Sheppard case, however, the role of the news media can scarcely be exaggerated. The newspapers and radio stations condemned Sam before he was even indicted. Before it was over, the Sheppard

In the days after the murder of his wife, Sam Sheppard (left) appeared in public wearing a neck brace as a result of the injuries he suffered in a struggle with the perpetrator of the crime. The police, coroner, and newsmen expressed skepticism about Sam's injuries, but they were well documented by attending physicians. Class also played a role in the Sheppard case, as much of the working and middle class public perceived the Sheppards as attempting to use their wealth and power to insulate Sam from the criminal justice system. Sam is pictured here with his equally nattily attired brother, Richard, and sister-in-law Dorothy Sheppard. Courtesy of Cleveland State University case would spur a landmark Supreme Court decision on conflict between a free press and a defendant's right to a fair trial.

Whereas Sam Sheppard remained silent on the advice of his attorneys, police suspicion of him quickly found its way into the newspapers. The city had three newspapers, including the especially hard-hitting Scripps-Howard paper, the *Cleveland Press,* the largest newspaper in Ohio with a circulation of 310,000. From the outset the *Press* published information that could only have been supplied by the police and which clearly had been intended to implicate Sheppard in his wife's murder. All other possible explanations of the crime, including Sheppard's consistent personal account, were virtually ignored.

An ongoing circulation war prompted competition among the newspapers, fueling sensational coverage of what was indeed, beyond question, a sensational murder case. Bold headlines referred simply to "Marilyn," like the glamorous movie star Monroe, and a salacious atmosphere prevailed in the large, yet provincial, Midwestern city.

Much of the public in Cleveland, a hard-working town of blue collar and middle management families, readily embraced the official view that Sam's wealthy family had been summoned to help him cover up the crime. While gender played a key role in the Lizzie Borden case, and ethnic prejudices in the Hauptmann case, class anxieties molded public opinion in the Sheppard case. Many believed that the Sheppards were brazenly thumbing their noses at the police. Sam "must be laughing secretly at the whole spectacle," the *Press* averred. An outraged public concluded that Sam Sheppard thought he could get away with murder simply because he was a rich and well-connected physician.

The *Press,* as its longtime editor Louis Seltzer later admitted, orchestrated a campaign to bring Sam Sheppard to "justice." On July 16 the *Press* condemned police and public officials for their "tragic mishandling of the Sheppard murder investigation." Rumors of Sheppard's alleged sexual liaisons with other women laced the published accounts, further inflaming public opinion.

The press reported, accurately, that Sheppard had declined requests that he take a lie detector test. The physician explained to police that he did not trust such a test, which, as he understood it, might not be reliable because of his "nearness to the tragedy." Sheppard's attorneys agreed that a lie detector test in the midst of the hostile public climate, and with their client still recuperating from injuries and trauma, would be unreliable and potentially misleading.

Moreover, Sheppard and his attorneys believed that officials convinced of his guilt would set up the test in such a way as to ensure his failure. Years later, Sam Sheppard would consent to a lie detector test.

Taking their cue from Gerber and the police, the *Press*, the *Cleveland News*, and the *Plain Dealer* joined with radio commentators to portray Sheppard as a womanizer who had a tempestuous relationship with his wife. The couple was said to have been on the brink of divorce. Rumor even had it that the child Marilyn carried was unwanted or fathered by someone else.

Although Sheppard had repeatedly told officials his version of events, media accounts charged that he had refused to discuss the murder with police, and that his powerful family continued to shield him from public accountability. Information that might have been favorable to Sam, or even the announcement that the Sheppard family was offering a reward for identification of Marilyn's killer, was invariably buried in a small story on the inside pages.

On July 20 the *Press* stepped up its campaign against Sheppard with the flagrant front-page banner headline: "**GETTING AWAY WITH MURDER**." The article insisted that the Sheppard family, with its influential friends in high places, had benefited from "extra-privileged courtesies that should never be extended by authorities investigating a murder." Only slightly more sedate, the *Plain Dealer* averred on July 22 that as a result of the "social prominence of the Sheppard family" Sam had been treated with "kid gloves."

The *Plain Dealer* even featured an editorial cartoon, with Sam's head placed on an animal's body. Around the cartoon figure's neck was a prominent collar, an obvious reference to Sam's oft photographed orthopedic neck brace. The cartoon depicted Sam as muzzled, unwilling to talk about the case, when in reality he had spent more than fifty hours responding to police questions as well as six hours responding to Gerber's questions in a public inquest at a high school.

Coroner Gerber conducted the public inquest, held on July 22, in such a way as not only to ensure a guilty verdict but to subject Sam and his family to the utmost humiliation. When Sam arrived voluntarily with his brother Steve, the two were ostentatiously patted down for weapons by a police officer at the door. A boisterous, virtual lynch mob atmosphere pervaded the high school gymnasium. A crowd of more than 500 persons gathered for the spectacle.

Once inside, Gerber displayed the sweeping powers granted to the coroner in Cuyahoga County. In a tradition dating to English common law, the coroner retained the type of broad authority over the investigation that had been dramatically reduced in most American communities by the introduction of the position of medical examiner. Yet in Cuyahoga County, for half a century, Gerber rejected such reforms and retained total control of the investigation. As coroner, he could rule not merely on the cause of death but, incredibly, possessed the power to identify the murderer in public as well.

During six hours of brutal questioning by Gerber, under the glare of television klieg lights, Sam Sheppard calmly reiterated his recollection of the events in his home on the night of the murder. However, he continued to lie about his affair with the former Bay View Hospital nurse, whose name was Susan Hayes. At that moment, however, authorities in Los Angeles were questioning Miss Hayes and acquaintances who had seen her and Sam together on various occasions.

During the proceedings Gerber was not obligated to follow any legal guidelines concerning the admissibility of rumor, gossip, innuendo, or hearsay evidence. Nor did he allow Sheppard's attorney, William Corrigan, to cross-examine witnesses. When Corrigan vehemently protested, Gerber ordered police forcibly to remove him from the gymnasium. The crowd erupted in delirious cheers as police literally dragged the distinguished, white-haired sixty-seven-year-old Cleveland attorney out of the gymnasium. After the inquest, the public descended upon Gerber with handshakes, kisses, and pats on the back for a job well done.

The public inquest was a performance worthy of Senator Joe McCarthy, whose reckless charges of communist subversion had destroyed the lives of hundreds of innocent people in the early 1950s. The anticommunist hysteria of the era was not just the product of one man. The federal government—and especially J. Edgar Hoover's FBI—led the campaign of hearings, prosecutions, and loyalty reviews designed to drive leftists from government, schools, private industry, and all walks of life. The federal government itself orchestrated repression and denial of civil liberties to thousands of Americans, the overwhelming majority of whom were not and never had been spies or criminals. Far from a justifiable response to threats to national security, the anticommunist hysteria of the postwar period represents the most sustained era of political repression in American history.

The witch-hunt atmosphere thus pervaded American culture at the time of the Sheppard case and clearly manifested itself in the investigation and trial of the Cleveland physician. Gerber, the police, and press—like Senator McCarthy and his subordinates on the national stage—willfully distorted the facts of the case and eroded Dr. Sheppard's right to due process under the law. With McCarthy, J. Edgar Hoover, and thousands of others emphasizing the existence of a vast communist conspiracy within the national fabric, Clevelanders were willing to believe that an evil force, Sam Sheppard, could live within an otherwise all-American family on the North Shore.

Historians have described the 1950s as an era of conformity in which the public bowed to authority and displayed little tolerance for diversity. Americans lived in similar styles of homes (described by one songwriter, Malvina Reynolds, as "little boxes . . . all the same") in suburbs that were laid out in similar patterns. They watched the same television programs, worshipped the same God, embraced the ethos of the Cold War, and condemned sexual immorality, including adultery, of which Sam Sheppard was guilty.

In this climate Gerber's "findings" after the public inquest were a foregone conclusion. First, the coroner determined that Marilyn Sheppard died from the blows to her forehead, a skull fracture, cuts and gashes on the top and back of her head, multiple bruises, and hemorrhaging. Marilyn had suffered thirty-five wounds, including fifteen blows to the head, a broken nose, and cuts on her hands, arms, and fingers.

As to the killer, Gerber concluded that the evidence of a burglary had been staged and that the possibility of a third party perpetrating the crime was "not probable or possible." The coroner's verdict declared bluntly that the "injuries that caused this death were inflicted by her husband Dr. Samuel H. Sheppard and that death in this case was homicidal in nature."

Without having been indicted or tried, and without a full investigation, Sam Sheppard stood condemned. Gerber, the Cleveland newspapers, and radio and television commentators had assumed the roles of judge and jury, making a mockery of the fundamental principle in American criminal law of innocent until proven guilty in a court of law. The real judge and jury in the 1954 Sheppard case, derived from the same prejudiced community, would simply follow the newspapers, the police, and the coroner in lockstep.

On July 26 Cleveland police reported that Susan Hayes had signed a state-

ment admitting to having had sexual relations with Sam Sheppard. This revelation sharply increased the prospect that Sam would be convicted of murder,
even though all that had been demonstrated was that he had committed adultery.

The next day the headline atop eight columns of the front page of the *Cleveland Press* read: "**WHY ISN'T SAM SHEPPARD IN JAIL**?"

At 10 P.M. on July 30, 1954, police placed Sam under arrest on the charge of
murdering his wife. A crowd had converged on Sam's father's home, trampling
the lawn, venturing onto the porch, and peering into the windows. When the
police arrived and took Sam away in handcuffs, the crowd cheered. People
chanted, "Murderer! murderer!" as flashbulbs popped in Sam's face.

A confluence of tragic events and cultural perceptions had landed Sam
Sheppard in jail on a charge of murder. Class prejudices against the wealthy
physician and his extended family had convinced many in Cleveland and
northeast Ohio that Sheppard was a guilty man using his influence in an
attempt to get away with murder. In these years before the Vietnam War and
Watergate eroded public trust, most Americans trusted the judgment of
authorities and elected officials. The police, the coroner, and prosecutors, and
perhaps above all the newspapers seemed so sure that Sam had committed the
crime. There seemed little reason to question their judgment. After all, his wife
had died in the home, with Sheppard there at the time, and it was now known
that Sam engaged in extramarital affairs.

As he languished in jail in 1954, Sam Sheppard, like Bruno Hauptmann
twenty years before him, could not benefit from the civil rights accorded to the
accused under the American criminal justice system as a result of the reform
decisions of the Warren Court in the 1960s. High court decisions in *Gideon*
(1963), *Escobedo* (1965), and *Miranda* (1966) guaranteed accused criminals the
right to an attorney, the right to remain silent, and the right to receive a warning from police that anything they did say could be used against them in court.
Hence Sam was charged, jailed, and denied the presence of his attorney for an
entire weekend following his arrest. Police subjected Sheppard to hour after
hour of the third degree. The police, Sheppard recalled, employed every tactic
short of physical abuse in an attempt to compel him to confess.

On August 16, Corrigan posted bail to free Sheppard from jail, but the young
surgeon knew he would not be out for long. The next day the grand jury

returned an indictment of first-degree murder. Sheppard was led back into the Cuyahoga County Jail in shackles. Ten years of debilitating incarceration had begun.

Common Pleas Judge Edward Blythin, chief jurist in the criminal division, assigned the case to himself. The silver-haired former mayor of Cleveland was softspoken, still betraying a hint of accent of his native Wales, but no one doubted that he was in charge. On September 20 Blythin denied Sheppard's request for bail and scheduled the trial to begin on October 18.

As a politician in the midst of a reelection campaign for another six-year term as judge, Blythin was hardly oblivious to the sensational publicity that the Sheppard trial offered. In an unprecedented move, the judge catered to the press frenzy by allowing two tables to be built inside the rail of the courtroom for television and newspaper reporters. He authorized installation of a new microphone and sound system to ensure clarity for the audiences that would fill the courtroom. Blythin formally banned photographs in the courtroom, but it was a ban that he often declined to enforce. Outside the courtroom, Blythin himself posed for television and newspaper cameramen.

The national media descended on Cleveland for a murder trial that, like the O. J. Simpson case forty years later, would feature wealth, sex, and bloody murder of a spouse (or former spouse, in Simpson's case). The major newspapers and magazines sent reporters to cover what *Time* called "the biggest murder story in the U.S. press since the trial of Bruno Hauptmann in 1935."

As the trial opened on schedule, three assistant prosecutors led by John J. Mahon—who was also a candidate for election to a judgeship that fall—conducted the state's case. Attorney William Corrigan moved for a postponement of the trial as well as a change of venue, citing massive and prejudicial pretrial publicity. Blythin rejected postponement and ruled that he would hold the venue request in abeyance while determining whether an unbiased jury could be selected.

During voir dire proceedings, several potential jurors were dismissed when they admitted to having been influenced by the massive pretrial publicity. But it would not have been possible to dismiss all of the jurors who had followed the case in the newspapers. Blythin drew praise from the press, which continued with daily banner headlines on the Sheppard case, when he determined that five jurors could be empaneled even though they admitted they had read a great

deal about the case in the local newspapers, all of which had long since condemned Sam as a murderer.

Jury selection, lasting almost two weeks, was tense and arduous. On the day
the trial opened Corrigan lashed out at prosecution efforts to make Sam's extramarital affairs "the main question in this case." Corrigan and his associate, Fred
W. Garmone, bitterly opposed the prosecution's tactic. Corrigan argued that
only those jurors who would acknowledge that extramarital sex would be irrelevant to their judgment in the murder case should be empaneled.

Mahon refused to back away from the decision to exploit Sam's marital
infidelity to its fullest. Blythin backed him up and refused to rule out jurors
who indicated the issue might affect their judgment. "I am ashamed of you,
judge," Corrigan barked at Blythin during a clash over the issue. "You are not
being fair."

Blythin rejected Corrigan's protests. Neither was there any chance, after
devoting nearly two full weeks to jury selection, that the judge would grant
Corrigan's demand for a change of venue. To no one's surprise, the judge
declared after a jury had been chosen that he was "thoroughly satisfied that we
have here a fair and impartial group of people."

With opening arguments at last set to begin, an anonymous caller revealed
that one of the twelve jurors had been convicted in 1943 of a sex crime involving
an underage boy. After several days of humiliating publicity, the juror, who by
then had married and become a father, was replaced by an alternate.

As to the public identification of the felonious juror, that was by no means
an exception, but rather the rule in the Sheppard trial. Astonishingly, the Cleveland newspapers published the names of the original pool of seventy-five
prospective jurors. When the seven men and five women were ultimately selected, their names, addresses, and photographs appeared in the daily press. The
jurors, who were not sequestered during the trial, thus received anonymous
phone calls as well as comments and a regular stream of advice from their
friends, family, acquaintances, and strangers. Opinion polls published in the
local press on the eve of the trial, and available to the jury, revealed an overwhelming public conviction that Sam Sheppard was guilty.

Only one of the twelve jurors had a college education, which did not bode
well for Sheppard, who not only had a medical degree but had been wealthy and
pampered throughout his life. The jury, well representing working-class and

middle-class Cleveland, would show little sympathy for Sam, who was widely perceived as rich, spoiled, and behaving as if he were above the law.

With the jury empaneled, court adjourned on Election Day, Tuesday, November 2, as both Blythin and prosecutor Mahon won their campaigns for the judgeships. Flush with his electoral triumph, Mahon opened the state's case the following morning by arguing that Sam Sheppard, engaged in an affair with another woman and on the brink of divorce, killed his wife in a fit of rage and attempted to cover up the crime by staging evidence of a burglary that in reality never occurred.

It was clear that the prosecution would focus on adultery in what was supposed to be a trial for murder. As the *Cleveland Press* averred in its coverage, "the state's case rests heavily on the theory that constant quarrels between Marilyn Sheppard and her husband over his amatory excursions provided the motive for her murder."

In his opening statement Corrigan focused on the rush to judgment against Sam by the police and the newspapers. Referring to the extramarital affair, Corrigan acknowledged that Sam was guilty of "human derelictions." He insisted, however, that the defendant and his wife were happy and looking forward to having the child that Marilyn carried at the time of her death.

In the afternoon, the jury left to tour the murder scene with a phalanx of reporters in tow and a press helicopter circling above. After Blythin ruled that only a single pool reporter could accompany the jury inside the Sheppard home, the reporter for the *Cleveland Press*, which had led the public campaign against Sam, won the distinction of being chosen. Sam went along, handcuffed at the wrist to a deputy, and broke into tears at the sight of a large teddy bear belonging to Chip in the family room of his home.

On November 4, Sam once again fought back tears as the prosecution began to introduce evidence from the autopsy. Allowed to turn his back to the screen onto which the autopsy photographs were projected, Sam, dressed conservatively in a dark suit, cried softly. The jurors, meanwhile, winced at the grisly color slides of Marilyn's head, marred by a series of brutal gashes.

Corrigan subjected Deputy Coroner Lester Abelson, who had performed the autopsy, to a long and aggressive cross-examination. The defense elicited that there had been no examination of a possible sexual assault, no analysis of the blood on the victim's face, and no explanation, in the absence of mouth wounds, of what caused two of Marilyn's teeth to be forced out of her mouth.

Gerber and the police had ignored these avenues of inquiry precisely because they raised doubts about the case against Sheppard. However, Corrigan's plodding style consumed nearly two full days on these issues, a tedious approach which tended to obscure rather than to highlight the points he was trying to make. The defense attorney continued to clash with Judge Blythin.

On November 8, prosecution witnesses Don and Nancy Ahern testified that they had enjoyed a pleasant July 3 evening at the Sheppards', who had seemed to get along quite well together. Nancy Ahern hurt the defense case, however, with her testimony that she believed that Marilyn had been more in love with Sam than vice versa. Over Corrigan's vehement protests, Blythin allowed blatant hearsay evidence from Nancy that Marilyn had expressed fears that Sam was contemplating divorce.

Esther Houk offered damaging testimony against Sheppard, including her recollection of a discussion months earlier in regard to an automobile accident claim. At the time, Sam had casually observed that it was a simple matter to fake head injuries. Here the prosecution sought to imply that Dr. Sheppard had faked his own head and neck injuries in an effort to lend credibility to his cover story.

Esther Houk also testified that she saw the Sheppards' dog, Koko, at the house on the morning of the murder. The prosecution argued that an intruder would have aroused the dog into a fit of barking, whereas actions by Sam, the dog's master, would not have done so. Neighbors had heard no barking during the night. Sam declared that he did not remember seeing the dog, which spent time both indoors and outdoors, on the night of the murder. Koko, or "Koke", as she was known, was a mild-mannered female. The Sheppards' neighbors had explained to police that Koke was "a poor watch dog and easily cowed." Another reported that Koko "welcomed strangers, and seldom barked at them."

Bay Village police officials testified that they had observed Sam's corduroy jacket lying folded on the living room couch where he had fallen asleep on the night of the murder. This was significant since the Aherns had testified that Sam had fallen asleep with the jacket on. Had he awakened to Marilyn's screams in the night, the prosecution suggested, he would hardly have stopped to carefully fold his jacket and lay it across the couch. Sam later explained that he might have removed the jacket sometime during the night. His brother Stephen declared that he had seen the jacket lying on the living room floor that morning and that someone had picked it up and placed it across the couch.

On November 16, after a brief appearance by Larry Houk, who described finding the green bag, the prosecution's lead witness, Sam Gerber, took the stand. In the course of three days of devastating testimony, Gerber—outspoken, resonating authority, and equipped with pieces of evidence, some of which he pulled from his pockets—carried out his mission to see that Sam Sheppard was put behind bars.

As the prosecution produced a pillowcase stained with blood, Gerber declared authoritatively that the imprint on it had been made by a "surgical instrument." Incredibly, although no such instrument had been found, nor could one even be identified, Gerber linked the crime to *Doctor* Sam Sheppard with this crucial testimony. Gerber dramatized this "evidence" through the provocative assertion that the imprint of the alleged surgical instrument was the killer's "blood signature." This testimony seems to have surprised even Judge Blythin, who questioned Gerber about the possibility that a weapon other than a surgical instrument could have created the wounds on Marilyn Sheppard.

Gerber's identification of the murder weapon as a surgical instrument was not merely baseless, but prejudicial. In an earlier public statement Gerber had allowed "we don't know" what kind of weapon had been used to kill Marilyn. "It was some kind of blunt object. It could be a piece of wood, a medical or surgical instrument, any one of a hundred things around the house." Such uncertainty had now been replaced with the authoritative assertion that a surgical instrument had recorded Sam Sheppard's "blood signature."

Gerber went on to testify that Sam's family had shielded him from questioning on the morning of the murder and thereafter, even though Sam in fact had calmly told his story both to the coroner and to the police. Invoking the public inquest, Gerber called attention to Sam's lie about the affair with Susan Hayes.

Corrigan, who had been forcibly removed from the inquest on Gerber's order, could barely contain his venom against the coroner, allowing his emotions to get the better of him during the two-day cross-examination. At one point the two antagonists grappled over who would hold a piece of evidence and, at another, doubled their fists amid angry shouts before Blythin restored order.

Schottke, the Cleveland policeman who accused Sheppard of killing his wife on the very day of the murder, testified that Sam had refused a lie detector test. The growing litany of errors in the Sheppard trial thus included prejudicial use of unauthorized lie detector evidence. Such evidence is not admissible in a criminal trial.

Lester Hoversten, a former medical school classmate of Sam's, who had actually been staying in the Sheppard home the week of the murder, testified next. Hoversten, who had traveled thirty-five miles to Kent, Ohio, for a golf outing and overnight stay on the night of the murder, testified that Sam had once spoken to him of considering a divorce. He added, however, that Sam and Marilyn had seemed relatively happy and that he "noticed nothing unusual or out of the ordinary" before the crime.

Of all the evidence in the Sheppard case, none was more crucial, nor handled more incompetently, than the blood evidence. On November 24, a police scientist described a blood trail from the upstairs landing to the basement. Next, Mary Cowan, the chief medical technologist in the coroner's office, testified that she had identified through testing seven spots on the blood trail as being human blood.

The prosecution argued that the blood had dripped from the "surgical instrument" as Sam carried it downstairs after the murder, yet, incredibly, no tests were made of the blood to determine whether it had been Sam's, Marilyn's, or that of a third party. Typing of the blood for a possible match with the victim, the defendant, or an unknown person should have been performed by the Cuyahoga County Coroner's office, but Gerber never bothered to order such tests.

In sharp contrast to O. J. Simpson's attorneys forty years later, Corrigan failed to make the most out of the state's negligence in handling the blood evidence. Instead of emphasizing Gerber's unfairness and incompetence, Corrigan entered into tedious arguments over the admissibility of blood evidence, with much of the discussion centering on arcane terminology over the chemicals used to identify blood. The net result appeared to be to confuse the jury and reinforce the impression that the defense had something to hide.

The case had gone smoothly for the prosecution even before it presented its most sensational witness, Susan Hayes. Twenty-four years old and attractive, Miss Hayes had been the focus of prurient press attention since the revelation of her affair with Dr. Sheppard. Testifying in a voice that was barely audible, never making eye contact with Sam, the former lab technician acknowledged a six-month affair after the two had become acquainted at Bay View Hospital. They had sex in a variety of places, she admitted, including automobiles and her parents' home. After she took a job in Los Angeles, Sheppard had visited and they spent seven days together. She had accompanied Sam as he had traded in his car for a Lincoln. He bought her a watch when she lost hers, an incident that Marilyn had learned about and with which she had confronted Sam. Susan Hayes testified that although Sam declared that he loved his wife, he had said he loved her, too, and he had considered a divorce.

The newspapers had a field day with Susan Hayes's testimony. Corrigan had continued his objections aimed at excluding evidence of extramarital affairs as "prejudicial" and "immaterial," but Blythin continued to overrule the defense objections. Since Sheppard was indeed guilty of adultery, the defense offered no challenge to Hayes's testimony. Mahon solicited additional evidence of Sheppard's efforts to arrange dates with other women, one of whom he had been seen kissing in public. Fittingly, the prosecution murder case rested on what it considered a high note: Sam Sheppard's sexual promiscuity.

After Blythin refused a pro forma defense motion for a directed verdict of acquittal, Corrigan began to present Sheppard's case. The first witness, brother Stephen Sheppard, testified as to the ransacked appearance of the home, including the overturned doctor's bag, which the police had not bothered to fingerprint. In fact, the police claimed to have found only one print in the house—of Sam's, on Marilyn's bed. Where were the prints of the four adults and three children who had spent the entire evening in the home on July 3? Obviously the police made little effort to seek out fingerprints that might point to an unknown person in the home.

Sam Sheppard began to cry aloud, his shoulders heaving, as Stephen Sheppard recalled a dinner on July 2 when Sam and Marilyn had told him and his wife of their plans to name their baby, if a boy, after Stephen, whose wife, Betty, had recently lost a child to miscarriage.

Sam's family was naturally expected to support him; hence Stephen Sheppard's testimony achieved little. Indeed, the Sheppard family, impeccably dressed in the latest fashions and sometimes openly contemptuous of the proceedings, probably had a negative effect on the middle-class and working-class people who predominated in the courtroom and on the jury.

As Stephen Sheppard stepped down, Corrigan knew he would have to do more if he were to succeed in freeing his client. Accordingly, Corrigan turned his focus to the injuries Sam suffered on the night of the murder. Corrigan set out to decimate the prosecution's contention that Sheppard's injuries were either faked or self-inflicted. He presented compelling medical evidence that the severity and extent of the injuries suggested that Sam, too, had been the victim of an intruder's violence.

The state's single witness on this issue, other than Gerber, had been Dr. Richard Hexter of Bay Village, whom Gerber had summoned to examine Sam Sheppard on July 4. On November 29 Hexter had testified that Sheppard had a black eye and minor cuts on his mouth, evidenced some neck soreness, and showed an absence of certain reflexes. He insisted that the patient "was definitely not in shock." Under cross-examination, Hexter, a general practitioner, had admitted, however, that he had little actual experience with patients in shock.

The defense now produced four physicians who testified that Sheppard's injuries had been far more serious than the prosecution suggested and could not have been self-inflicted. Sam's brother, Dr. Richard Sheppard, testified that in his opinion Sam had indeed been in shock when he examined him early that morning in the Sheppard home. Dr. Elkins, the neurologist who examined Sheppard at the hospital, testified that a small particle of bone had been separated in Sam's neck and that he had sustained a spinal cord contusion as well as a cerebral concussion. The type of injuries Sheppard received, Dr. Elkins testified, could not have been self-inflicted. Elkins determined that surgery was not necessary and that Sheppard's injury would heal if his neck remained immobilized in the orthopedic brace.

A radiologist and an eye, ear, nose, and throat specialist, plus a dentist, two nurses, and an X-ray technician also testified as to Sheppard's injuries, including a swollen eye and teeth loosened from a blow to the mouth. One of the nurses recalled that Dr. Sheppard was dazed and that his feet appeared badly shriveled, bolstering his story of awakening with his legs lying in the cold water of Lake Erie. Dr. Sheppard's body temperature had dropped and he had been on the verge of hypothermia.

The injury evidence might have begun to shift the trial in Dr. Sheppard's favor had the young physician proven to be a more effective witness in his own behalf. Just as Gerber had anchored the prosecution's case, Sheppard himself was the key witness for the defense. As the tall, balding osteopath took the stand, the jury fixed their eyes on the man about whom they had heard so much. Was he not only a philanderer, but a murderer to boot, or had the young surgeon who had seemed to have it all been tragically and unjustly accused?

For almost three full days beginning on December 9, Sam Sheppard had his opportunity to make an impression and win over the jury. Though his testimony was clear, articulate, and consistent with what he had said all along—with the exception of now admitting to his affair with Susan Hayes—Sam left the stand having failed to win sympathy from the jury.

Partly this was due to Sheppard's seemingly detached, unemotional language delivered in a high-pitched voice. As a witness and as a professional, Sheppard was undoubtedly trying to be precise. But his style did not appeal to the jury and probably reinforced their impression of him as a member of an arrogant and wealthy elite class. Although he had been overcome by tears earlier in the trial, during his testimony Sheppard did little to form an emotional bond with the jurors, who in the end simply did not particularly like him. They therefore made no special effort to save him.

Examples of stilted language included Sheppard's statement that he "visualized" a "form" when he went into the bedroom. Returning to consciousness after being knocked out, Sheppard said he was "stimulated" to go downstairs after the invader. During the struggle he experienced a "choking sensation."

These words gave the testimony more the character of a dry after-the-fact report rather than a horrifying actual experience. The hushed courtroom audience did listen with rapt attention, however, as Sheppard recalled his experience that morning as "like a nightmare or . . . a very horrible dream. . . . I was shaken beyond explanation."

Having lost the battle to exclude evidence of extramarital relations, Corrigan knew that he could not simply ignore the issue. At his attorneys' suggestion, Sheppard had long since passed some of his time in jail drafting an "autobiography" of his life, including the dalliances with Susan Hayes and Marilyn's attitudes about his affairs.

In the unpublicized document, Sheppard wrote that Marilyn had become less interested in sex after the birth of their son. She learned about his extramarital liaisons but "did not get extremely upset. . . . She didn't like my attentions to other girls at any time but she recognized my need for sex she had not recaptured since" Chip had been born.

Sam Sheppard now admitted on the stand what the jury already knew, that he had conducted an extramarital affair with Susan Hayes and lied about it to the police. He insisted, however, that he had denied the affair only because he had wanted to protect the reputation of Miss Hayes, not himself.

"**SAM ADMITS SUSAN DETAILS, ADMITS MARILYN UNHAPPY**" blared headlines in the *Cleveland Press*. The tabloid style, using only the first names in the manner of a soap opera or gossip column, had become the newspaper's standard fare. Sam denied that he had considered a divorce from Marilyn, insisting that both Hoversten and Hayes, and not he, had brought up the question of divorce. He was happy with his wife and son and the affair with Susan Hayes was behind them. Under cross-examination, however, he admitted that eyewitness accounts of him kissing yet another woman in a car about a year before were accurate, although he claimed not to have had sex with her.

Sheppard may have elicited some sympathy from the jury when he bitterly recounted the police third degree to which he had been subjected after his arrest. Working around the clock and in pairs, the police had thrust pictures of his battered wife in his face, used intense profanity, threatened to charge his family as accomplices, and lied about the evidence they possessed.

The day after Sheppard's testimony on the police third degree, the chief of the Cleveland police force publicly dismissed the charges as lies—a rebuttal accessible to the nonsequestered jurors. The prosecution did not, however, attempt to enter an official rebuttal into the court record, as it might have been expected to do had the charges been false.

The third degree treatment that Sheppard received, though not as violent as that accorded Bruno Richard Hauptmann, reminds us of the abject vulnerability of criminal defendants in the era before the Warren Court reforms of the 1960s. Before those decisions ensured rights such as to remain silent or consult an attorney, police routinely abused tens of thousands of accused persons across the country.

The widespread public perception of Sam Sheppard's guilt, together with the police chief's denial, defused whatever sympathy Sam's account of police mistreatment might have aroused.

At the end of the state's cross-examination of Sheppard, prosecutor Mahon went for the obligatory kill:

"Isn't it a fact that you beat your wife to death?"

"No, sir," the defendant replied.

"And after you killed her, didn't you run out of the house toward the beach and injure yourself by falling down the beach steps or jumping off the platform of the beach house?"

"That's absolutely untrue, sir, and I think it's very unfair."

Following Sheppard's testimony, the defense presented two witnesses who claimed to have seen a suspicious man near the Sheppard house on the night of the murder. One, a steelworker, described the man as "tall, with bushy hair." The prosecution disputed the veracity of the witnesses, noting that they came forth only after a $10,000 reward for Marilyn's killer had been offered, but the steelworker responded evenly that he was not motivated by reward money.

Another defense witness testified that Sheppard was a notoriously deep sleeper who might well have slumbered during the initial break-in and attack by an intruder. A friend of Marilyn's described her as "radiantly happy" about her pregnancy and future life with Sam. Marilyn's aunt, more like a surrogate mother since Marilyn's own mother was dead, offered similar testimony in Sam's defense.

On December 15, with the defense having rested, closing arguments began. Sam Sheppard's "brazen and open" affair with Susan Hayes remained the centerpiece of the prosecution murder case despite an absence of any evidence that Sam and Marilyn had fought bitterly over his affairs or that he had ever physically intimidated or struck his wife throughout their years together.

Confronting the adultery issue head-on in his close, Corrigan declared that "the fact that Sam Sheppard strayed is no proof that he did not love his wife, his child and his home." Sam had been able to have sexual relations with Susan Hayes for the asking. In other words, he had not needed to kill for her. He simply had no motive to murder his wife in such a brutal manner in his own bedroom.

Sam Sheppard had never in his life revealed even the slightest propensity for violence. As Sam had told the police three days after the murders, "I couldn't kill a squirrel or a rabbit much less someone I loved."

In addition to the absence of motive, Corrigan emphasized that no murder weapon had been found and no rational explanation provided for Sam's serious, documented injuries. These were the plain facts of the case, obscured amid the swirl of "lurid, misleading headlines," gossip, and innuendo linking adultery and murder. Corrigan begged the jury not to be swayed by the "trial by newspaper." The trial had gone on only because of the prejudicial publicity and the refusal of the police and Gerber "to admit their mistake."

On Friday, December 17, Judge Blythin clearly sided with the prosecution in the course of delivering his charge to the jury. It was a fitting end to what appellate justices later described as Blythin's incompetent handling of the trial. After explaining to the jury their options—first-or second-degree murder, manslaughter, or not guilty—Blythin attempted to demonstrate the difference between direct and circumstantial evidence. He did so by drawing upon a well-known American legend in such a way as to prejudice the case against Sheppard. Blythin explained that if the jurors had seen George Washington chopping down a cherry tree, that would be direct evidence, whereas if they merely saw a felled tree, and George Washington walking nearby with an axe, that would be circumstantial evidence. The message from the supposedly impartial jurist was clear: Sam Sheppard had been the only one in the house. Blythin was reassuring the jury that they might reasonably conclude that he had killed his wife despite the absence of any direct evidence that he did so.

Sequestered at last, as required under Ohio law during deliberations, the jury took three full days to decide the case. Near the end of the jurors' deliberations, Blythin declared publicly that they had taken long enough. On December 21, with everyone anxious to join Christmas holiday festivities, the jury returned to the courtroom with a verdict in hand.

True to the old saw, none of the jurors made eye contract with Sam as they filed back into the courtroom, prompting Corrigan to whisper to his client to prepare himself for the worst. Sheppard slumped in his chair when the jury rendered its verdict of guilty of murder in the second degree.

Brought before the judge and confronted with the verdict, Sam was given an opportunity to speak. "I would like to say, sir, I am not guilty. I feel there has been evidence presented before this court that definitely proves I could not have performed this crime."

With that, Sam was led away in handcuffs.

Many of the jurors later publicly acknowledged that they had embraced the prosecution argument that Sheppard had murdered his wife in a fit of rage. They did not find the young surgeon's account credible and were suspicious of his inability to recall details of the clash with the bushy-haired intruder.

Jurors later revealed to reporters that they scarcely considered the prosecution's call for conviction of first-degree murder, but that those who were reluctant to convict Sam at all were pulled on board by the initial majority that advocated conviction. Jurors said they were comforted by the state's and court's reassurances that the prosecution did not have to show a conclusive motive. Interviews revealed that neither Sam nor his brothers had left a favorable impression on the jurors.

Lasting more than two months, from October 18 to December 21, and with twenty-eight days of testimony, the Sheppard trial was twice as long as its most sensational predecessor, the Hauptmann trial. The Sheppard trial featured eighty-seven witnesses and some 300 exhibits. Media exposure, maximized by the extra space made for the press in the courtroom and the advent of television, had been unprecedented in American history.

Corrigan's defense had failed to impress the jury with the essential weakness of the state's case, especially the absence of the murder weapon and contradictory and missing blood evidence. Corrigan, whose legal career focused predominantly on labor issues, perhaps had done the best he could in the prejudicial climate that prevailed in Cleveland.

In Corrigan's defense, he could only react to the evidence presented by the prosecution and did not enjoy the right—not established as legal precedent until the 1963 Supreme Court decision in Brady v. Maryland—to gain access to the state's evidence. In fact, the state had literally taken possession of the Sheppard home, barring Sam, his family, and members of his legal team from examining the premises. Only after the trial was over, and Sheppard imprisoned, did the police return the house keys to the family.

Corrigan had faced a daunting task with the entire community prejudiced against Sam and primed for a conviction. The Sheppard trial did not occur in a cultural vacuum but instead reflected American society in the 1950s. Sam Sheppard's fast cars and "brazen" sexual promiscuity stood out in a decade that emphasized consensus, conformity, the sanctity of the nuclear family, and the rooting out of subversives within the community.

Although bitterly disappointed by the jury's decision, Corrigan and the

Sheppards knew Sam had been convicted in a virtual lynch mob atmosphere. They remained confident that he eventually would be cleared. Sam's parents, with their youngest son in jail for murder and their lives shattered, could not endure the crisis, however.

Less than a month after the end of the trial, Sam's mother shot herself to death. Dr. Richard A. Sheppard, the family patriarch, succumbed two weeks later from a bleeding ulcer and stomach cancer. While neither had been entirely healthy, clearly the ordeal of the murder and their son's trial had killed them.

While Corrigan requested a new trial and began preparations for the appeals process, by far the best decision he ever made in Sam Sheppard's defense was to retain the services of Dr. Paul Leland Kirk. A pioneer in a relatively new discipline then known as "criminalistics," Kirk was an eminent research scientist at the University of California at Berkeley. He defined criminalistics as the application of basic science, mainly physics and chemistry, to evidence at the scene of a crime.

Kirk's scientific analysis of the Sheppard murder would—after a legal struggle lasting more than a decade—finally turn the case around. By the mid-fifties, Kirk had established his reputation one of the nation's foremost experts on physical evidence at the crime scene. The recipient of a doctorate in biochemistry, Kirk was a veteran of the wartime Manhattan Project, which produced the atomic bomb. Since then he had published scores of articles, as well as four books, one of which was a celebrated text.

Kirk's pioneering work in criminalistics emphasized re-creation of the crime scenario, analysis of microscopic fibers and bits of evidence, and psychological profiling of the perpetrator—all of which were innovations in the fifties but have since become standard procedure in criminal investigations.

Kirk, who had no previous connection with the case, agreed to analyze the Sheppard murder scene on the understanding that he would not tailor his findings to satisfy the needs of Sam's defense. Privately, Kirk later admitted, he had assumed from his cursory initial knowledge of the case that Sheppard was probably guilty.

After assessing the evidence, Kirk changed his mind. Indeed, his investigation led inescapably to the conclusion that Sam Sheppard could not have been his wife's killer.

It quickly became clear to Kirk that the investigation by the police and the coroner's office had been abysmal, if not criminally negligent. Authorities failed to take control of the crime scene by sealing it off from all but a handful of official personnel in the crucial first forty-eight hours. Instead, scores of police, neighbors, newsmen, and photographers had tromped through the house and trod over footprints in the yard and on the beach.

Official handling of fingerprint and blood evidence had been botched. The house had been full of unidentifiable fingerprints but the official investigation produced one print, Sam's, on Marilyn's bed. There was no way to know how much evidence—footprints, fingerprints, hair, fibers, and more—had been irrevocably lost. Yet plenty remained, particularly in the bloodstained Sheppard bedroom. In a stunning indictment of the Cleveland authorities, Kirk found that they "did little or nothing toward analysis of blood in that room."

The blood evidence, virtually ignored by the Cleveland authorities, was the crucial evidence in the Sheppard case. Some of the blood that remained on the bed, the walls, and furnishings had flown from Marilyn Sheppard's head from the impact of the blows. But other blood spatter had come from weapon "throw off"—as the killer rained the thirty-five blows onto Marilyn, he flung her blood over the room and onto the walls in an identifiable arc. It was by this means, through analysis of the crime scene, that Kirk determined almost precisely where the killer had stood and with which hand—the left—he had struck.

It was clear from the blood spatter evidence that the killer himself would have been covered with the blood of his victim. Police reports noted that there was no sign of blood on Sam Sheppard the morning of the murder nor was he bleeding himself. Analysis of clothing turned over to Gerber revealed one spot of blood on Sheppard's pants. Sheppard's T-shirt had been missing, prompting the prosecution to argue that he had destroyed it, whereas the defense suggested it had been torn off in the struggle with the killer at the beach.

In any case, Kirk concluded from his reconstruction of the crime scene that Sheppard's pants and belt would have received blood spatters had he been the killer and that the blood could not have been washed out completely.

Even more decisive was evidence of a blood trail in the Sheppard home. Kirk found that the prosecution's theory with respect to the blood trail from upstairs to the basement had no credibility. Without even bothering to type the blood, the prosecution argued that blood all the way down to the basement stairs was

Marilyn's and that the blood had dripped from the murder weapon as Sam had carried it downstairs from the murder room.

Kirk knew that there could not have been enough blood on a weapon to drip continuously from the murder room to the basement. Only blood dripping from a wound could have left such a trail. And Kirk also concluded that Marilyn Sheppard had inflicted a wound on her attacker before she lost consciousness.

Kirk believed that two fragments of Marilyn's teeth, which had been found next to her body on the bed, had been broken off when the killer had covered Marilyn's mouth to stifle her screams. Kirk theorized that she had sunk her teeth into her assailant's fingers and held her grip until he forcibly wrested his fingers from the mouth. This aspect of Kirk's reconstruction was apparently wrong. In 1999, a forensic dental consultant concluded from an examination of Marilyn Sheppard's disinterred corpse that her teeth had not been pulled out but rather broken off from a blow to the mouth.

Kirk's reconstruction of the crime indicated that as Marilyn Sheppard tried to fight off her attacker the killer began pummeling her with the butt of a weapon in his left hand. The blows were rapid and vicious, but not as powerful as they would have been had the killer used his right hand. Although none of the blows was of sufficient strength to shatter the dura of the skull, Marilyn's jaw had been broken and her face battered.

Analyzing the gashes on Marilyn Sheppard's face and head, Kirk found no substantiation for Gerber's malicious argument that the killer had inflicted the wounds with a "surgical instrument." Kirk theorized that the killer may have used a flashlight to bash his victim's skull, but the end of a screwdriver would have fit the crime as well. Most telling of all, Kirk identified the blood of a second individual, besides Marilyn, in the Sheppard bedroom. Not only did that blood not match Sam's type A but, moreover, Sam had not been bleeding. Kirk identified a large, one-inch blood spot on the door of the wardrobe next to Marilyn's bed which the killer had brushed with his hand. Other, smaller blood spots contained spatter from the killer's hand as he continued to attack his victim.

Laboratory tests on blood samples taken from the trail leading downstairs from the bedroom ruled out the possibility that the blood on the trail had belonged to Marilyn Sheppard. This evidence disproved the prosecution's theory that the blood trail had been caused by Marilyn's blood dripping off a weapon as the killer walked downstairs. Neither could the blood on the trail have belonged to Sam Sheppard, as police, and even Gerber, who examined Sam personally on July 4, acknowledged that the physician had no cuts or wounds that could possibly have been the source of dripping blood. Tests also identified the blood of a third party on the wardrobe door.

In the final analysis, neither Sam nor Marilyn could have made the blood trail or left the other blood spots identified by Kirk in the bedroom—only the real killer could have done so. This crucial evidence in the Sheppard murder case had been completely misinterpreted by the Cleveland authorities.

Still more crime scene evidence bolstered Kirk's unambiguous conclusion that Sam Sheppard had not been his wife's attacker and killer. With all the lurid focus on Susan Hayes and adultery, the police and the press virtually ignored the real "sex angle" in the Sheppard case: Marilyn had been raped.

To Kirk it was obvious that the "motive of the crime was sexual." Her pajama bottoms had been pulled below her waist, one leg completely off, and the top had been pushed above her breasts. "Leaving the victim in the near nude condition," observed Kirk, was "highly characteristic of the sex crime." This type of crime is "completely out of character for a husband bent on murdering his wife."

Despite the obvious sexual nature of the attack, neither Gerber nor the police followed up with an examination for sexual assault. They made no analysis for evidence of semen. The refusal of the Cleveland authorities to analyze the sexual aspect of the assault offers another example of how crucial police and investigatory blunders can undermine the quest for justice.

The sexual assault, as well as other crime scene evidence, led Kirk to speculate that the killer had known the Sheppards and that Marilyn may have been the source of his erotic fantasies. A pioneer in the use of profiling techniques, Kirk concluded that the killer, likely of a lower class standing than the Sheppards, resented their wealth, prominence, and perceived arrogance. Evidence for this interpretation included the athletic trophies—Sam's 1941 high school cross country award and a bowling trophy of Marilyn's—which had been removed from their niches and smashed into pieces on the living-room floor. Officials lamely explained that Sam and Marilyn must have broken the trophies themselves in a fight that began downstairs and escalated to the bedroom.

A person who knew the Sheppards—and their house—fit the profile. The killer had seemed to know his way around. Since he was a thief as well, the killer loaded some possessions in the green sack, rifled Sam's physician's bag, pulled out drawers, and, perhaps in a psychotic or drunken rage, had smashed the Sheppards' athletic trophies. When Sheppard staggered down the steps after him again, the killer ran and ditched the green bag before turning on, wrestling with, and once again subduing the badly injured Sheppard, leaving him lying shirtless with his feet in the cold surf of Lake Erie.

While Sheppard had suffered no bleeding wounds, it was obvious to an unbiased, scientific investigator such as Kirk that the injuries Sam did suffer were real and not self-inflicted. It was fanciful to suppose that a physician would have subjected himself to a potentially paralytic or fatal neck injury, as the prosecution suggested, by hurling himself head first off a beach wall. Furthermore, Kirk noted, Sheppard's keys and chain had been forcibly ripped from his pants in a downward pulling motion that would have been difficult if not impossible for the man wearing the pants to have done. Sheppard's watchband had also been broken in a manner suggesting a struggle. Evidence of wet sand in the bedroom bolstered Sam's story that he returned to check on Marilyn once again after his struggle on the beach with the real killer.

While the profile of Marilyn Sheppard's murderer remained speculative, it was clear to Dr. Kirk that Sam Sheppard could not have killed his wife. The final report of the Berkeley criminalist was damning and unambiguous. "Analysis of the technical evidence offered by the prosecution shows it to be superficial, incomplete, and erroneous in interpretation." While some inference was unavoidable, Kirk averred, "in the main, the facts are clear and the conclusions inescapable." In conclusion, Kirk wrote simply that "the only explanation that is consistent with the facts is the one given by Dr. Sam."

While the defense immediately employed Kirk's bombshell report in an effort to gain a new trial for Sheppard, Cleveland officials scurried to downplay the findings of the eminent criminalist. The police and Gerber had leaped to the conclusion that Sheppard was guilty the day of the crime and they were not about to admit that they had been the architects of a great injustice. The Cleveland newspapers remained hostile to Sheppard.

Judge Blythin remained a willing accomplice as well, denying the defense motion for a new trial on May 9, 1955. His explanation represented a classic catch-22, well before author Joseph Heller had entered the term into the lexicon. Blythin ruled that Kirk's evidence should have been submitted for consideration in the 1954 trial, an argument that defied logic since the state had seized control of the crime scene, denying the defense the access it required in order for Kirk to have reached his conclusions.

Meanwhile, of course, Dr. Sam Sheppard was a condemned murderer and prisoner of the State of Ohio. Hoping that he would promptly receive a new trial, Sam chose to remain in the Cuyahoga County Jail until after Blythin's ruling. In June 1955, however, authorities relocated Sheppard to the state penitentiary in Columbus where he could take a prison job and assume an exercise regimen.

Prisoner number 98860 received visits from his brothers but preferred to correspond with his young son rather than expose him to the depressing reality of prison life. The two exchanged letters regularly as Sam Reese Sheppard, who lived with Steve and Betty Sheppard, grew from a small boy to a teenager. Father and son always concluded their correspondence with the Latin vincit qui patitur, "he who endures conquers." Sam would later entitle his ghostwritten autobiography *Endure and Conquer.*

Sheppard adapted to prison life as best he could. He won over most of his fellow inmates, whom he tended to view with sympathy rather than snobbery. Still a good athlete, Sam participated in prison team sports. No friend of the system, for understandable reasons, Sheppard refused to snitch on other inmates for rules violations, enhancing his popularity inside the walls. Inmates accorded him the honor of emcee at the annual prison pageant.

After first teaching auto mechanics, Sheppard accepted an offer to work in the prison hospital. He soon moved into the hospital dormitory, serving first as a nurse and then as a physician's assistant. Before long he was assisting in surgery and helping to save lives. Desiring to be useful, Sam went into solitary confinement for a NASA experiment and consented to have cancer cells implanted in his arm as part of a research study by Sloan Kettering. Other inmates followed his example.

Meanwhile, the Ohio criminal justice system remained hostile. Corrigan focused his appeal on the argument that prejudicial publicity drove Sheppard's arrest and conviction. "Day after day," the attorney explained, "newspapers were filled with accusations against him. His arrest was urged. One paper advocated the use of the third degree. Lurid headlines. Every fact of his private life

exposed. Every item that could be gathered that would make him appear unfavorably to the public repeated over and over again."

Oblivious to the argument, a three-judge panel of the Eighth District Court of Appeals ruled unanimously in 1955 that Sheppard had received a fair trial. The jurists paid scant attention to Dr. Kirk's affidavit or to the pervasive negative publicity.

In 1956, the Ohio Supreme Court affirmed the Court of Appeals verdict, but this time two dissenters emerged among the seven-member panel. The most vigorous, Kingsley Taft, a former U.S. senator, condemned Blythin's cherry tree analogy as wholly inappropriate by inviting the jurors to infer Sheppard's guilt, since all Americans learn as children that George Washington did in fact cut down the cherry tree. Taft also criticized the court for allowing into evidence Nancy Ahern's double hearsay evidence that Marilyn had supposedly heard that Sam was contemplating divorce.

Pursuing the case doggedly, Corrigan prepared a brief to appeal to the United States Supreme Court, which agreed to hear cases only if it deems that federal or constitutional law questions will be addressed. Corrigan appealed to the high court on grounds that pervasive and hostile press coverage had prevented Sheppard from receiving a fair trial. In a famous phrase, Corrigan wrote that a "Roman holiday" atmosphere had pervaded the judicial proceedings in Cleveland. "We believe that this case brings squarely before the court the widely debated question of fair trial and free press," he added.

In October 1956 the United States Supreme Court declined to grant a writ of certiorari under which it would review the case. Speaking for the Court, Justice Felix Frankfurter noted, however, that the decision "in no wise implies that this court approves the decision of the Supreme Court of Ohio."

His appeals seemingly exhausted, Sam and his family scraped for any alternative to waiting until 1964, when he would become eligible for parole. Although Sheppard had declined a lie detector test amid the turmoil of the initial investigation, Corrigan now arranged for one to be orchestrated by Erle Stanley Gardner, the *Perry Mason* series author and attorney who established his own Court of Last Resort for those who might be wrongfully accused. However, under pressure from Cleveland authorities the governor of Ohio canceled arrangements for the test to be administered to Sam in prison.

William Corrigan died on July 30, 1961, all of his appeals exhausted and having failed to free his celebrated client from wrongful incarceration. That same year, however, a key break came with the publication of *The Sheppard Murder Case* by Paul Holmes, a journalist and attorney who had covered the 1954 trial for the *Chicago Tribune*. With Erle Stanley Gardner writing the introduction, the book aroused national attention favorable to Sam's cause.

Holmes had little doubt as to Sam's innocence and, as an outsider, had been appalled by the pervasive hostility displayed toward Sheppard by the Cleveland media during the trial. The book recounted the lynch mob atmosphere in Cleveland, weaknesses of the state's investigation, the actual severity of Sam's injuries, Dr. Kirk's devastating revelations, and Blythin's errors.

One of the most interested readers was a recent graduate of Boston University Law School and an aspiring criminal attorney by the name of F. Lee Bailey. Introduced to the Sheppard family by Holmes, Bailey offered a youthful and aggressive approach to the Sheppard case. Bailey was willing to wait to collect fees, if any materialized.

Bailey's strategy was to jump-start the appeals process by filing a writ of habeas corpus, an ancient legal remedy dating to British common law for defendants who had been incarcerated without due process of law. The argument essentially held that since Sheppard's trial had been so blatantly unfair, his continued confinement in the penitentiary was also.

In 1963 Bailey, wanting no part of the Cleveland-area justice system, filed the writ in Ohio's southern federal district, where it would be considered by U.S. District Judge Carl Weinman of Dayton. Bailey's brief explained the weaknesses of the state's case; the "Roman holiday" atmosphere in and around the courtroom; publication of the jurors' names and photographs; Kirk's evidence; denial of defense access to the murder house; and the susceptibility of the judge and prosecutor to an inflamed public opinion in the midst of their electoral campaigns for judgeships.

Bailey also cited the memoirs published in 1956 by Louis B. Selzer, former editor of the *Cleveland Press*, who admitted to mobilizing "all our editorial artillery" to pressure authorities to call an inquest and charge Sheppard with murder. Bailey's central argument was that the hostile and pervasive publicity should have compelled Blythin to grant a continuance and a change of venue in order to ensure that Sam Sheppard received a fair trial.

In agreeing to hear the case, Judge Weinman emphasized that he would rule solely on the issue of whether Sheppard had received a fair trial, not on his guilt or innocence. With public opinion at last mobilizing behind Sam on the basis of Holmes's book and an adept publicity campaign orchestrated by Bailey, the perpetrators of the original injustice in Cleveland grew nervous. In an abrupt about-face, Gerber publicly recommended that Sheppard receive early parole. Still moving in lockstep with the establishment, the *Cleveland Press* offered editorial support for early parole. The state parole commission, however, turned down Sam's request, ruling that he would have to continue to serve the minimum sentence until he became eligible in 1964.

Thus the path was cleared for Judge Weinman's stunning decision on July 16, 1964. Weinman ruled that Sam, having been denied a fair trial ten years before, should be immediately released from prison on $10,000 bond. The decision, Sheppard's first victory in judicial proceedings, was a national cause célèbre.

Weinman ruled unequivocally, citing abundant evidence, that Sam had been denied a fair trial. The judge found it especially "startling" that jurors' names and photographs had been published in the midst of a celebrated murder trial. He echoed the defense charge that a "Roman holiday" atmosphere had prevailed as a result of the pervasive publicity. He declared flatly that the *Cleveland Press*, with its banner headlines suggesting Sam's guilt, had assumed "the role of accuser, judge, and jury. . . . If ever there was a trial by newspaper," Weinman concluded, "this is a perfect example."

Weinman also condemned the handling of the case by Judge Blythin, who had since died. Holmes and Bailey had publicized Blythin's comment, made in his chambers at the outset of the trial to New York columnist Dorothy Kilgallen, that Sam was "guilty as hell" and that the case was "open and shut." Weinman cited not only Blythin's bias, but his admission of hearsay and lie detector evidence as major errors.

Any one of the major errors, Weinman ruled, was sufficient to conclude that Sheppard had been denied a fair trial under the due process clause of the Fourteenth Amendment of the U.S. Constitution. "When these errors are cumulated," the judge declared in a sharply worded opinion, "the trial can only be viewed as a mockery of justice."

With the release of the eighty-six-page ruling, Sheppard gained immediate release from prison by posting the $10,000 bond. With his son away at boarding school, the person Sam most wanted to see was yet another remarkable figure in the Sheppard case, a German woman named Ariane Tebbenjohanns, with whom he had been corresponding for three years. Ariane, from Düsseldorf, Federal Republic of Germany, was a stunning platinum blond who had become convinced of Sam's innocence after reading about the case in Germany. The wealthy divorcée not only wrote letters but moved to the United States and began visiting Sam in prison.

At that point, the American press naturally went into a frenzy over the alleged wife killer's beautiful new love interest, especially when an enterprising reporter uncovered that Ariane's half sister had been the wife of the notorious Nazi propaganda minister Joseph Goebbels. Speaking openly with the press on that issue, Ariane handled herself well in insisting she had always detested the Nazis and Goebbels himself, who she claimed had once threatened to put her in a concentration camp after an argument.

Although Ariane herself was free of Nazi taint, Ohio prison officials had arbitrarily responded to the revelation of her family connection to Goebbels by summarily removing her from Sam's approved correspondence list and denying all future requests to visit Sam at the minimum security institution at Marion, to which he had moved in 1961.

Following his release from prison on July 16, 1964, Sam and Ariane, with the assistance of Paul Holmes, evaded the press and drove to Chicago, where they were married in a private ceremony. The couple then flew to New York for a brief honeymoon before Sam once again assumed the burden of fighting for his freedom.

On May 5, 1965, a federal court of appeals overturned Weinman's decision by a vote of two to one. Sheppard, living in a netherworld between freedom and captivity, kept a bag packed in readiness for his return to prison, although this time he remained free on bail. After failing on yet another plea to the same court, Bailey filed a petition with the U.S. Supreme Court.

At this time, the Supreme Court led by Earl Warren had begun to hand down several key decisions granting criminal defendants stronger legal standing, including the right to consult an attorney and to be duly informed of certain rights under the law at the time of arrest. Before it was done, the Warren Court would issue a series of decisions to limit the type of abuses to which both Sam Sheppard and Bruno Hauptmann had been subjected. Given this trend, perhaps it is no surprise that the court granted certiorari on November 15, 1965, thereby agreeing to hear an appeal of the habeas corpus Sheppard case.

On February 28, 1966, with Sam and Ariane sitting quietly in the gallery, Bailey outperformed Ohio Attorney General William Saxbe as each side presented its case for a half hour to the high court. Just over three months later, the Court ruled that Sam Sheppard "did not receive a fair trial." The vote was eight to one with Justice Hugo Black, offering no written explanation, the lone dissenter. The landmark decision, cited thousands of times since, granted new protection to defendants in highly celebrated public cases under the glare of the media spotlight. The high court found that because "inherently prejudicial publicity . . . saturated the courtroom, we must reverse the denial of the habeus corpus petition."

The court condemned Blythin's handling of the Sheppard case, declaring that the substantial and prejudicial pretrial publicity should have prompted the judge to grant a continuance and give strong consideration to the defense request for a change of venue. Citing the "carnival atmosphere" in the courtroom, Justice Thomas C. Clark, writing for the majority, criticized the "unprecedented" access accorded to reporters by the trial judge. Clark also cited public identification of the jurors, the election campaign of the judge and prosecutor, and the denial of counsel to Sam at the six-hour-long televised inquest as infringements on his rights of due process.

As a result of the 1966 Sheppard decision, the Supreme Court, while not challenging the freedom of the press directly, laid down guidelines for trial court judges to follow in an effort to insulate jurors from undue publicity.

While gratified at helping to establish an important national legal precedent to protect the rights of the accused, Sheppard realized that the Supreme Court decision did not make him a free man. In fact, the high court's action simply remanded the case back to district court—in Cleveland—where authorities wasted little time in deciding to subject Sheppard to a second murder trial.

Prosecutor John T. Corrigan—no relation to Sam's former defense attorney—could charge Sheppard only with second-degree murder, as under the double jeopardy prohibition in the U.S. Constitution a defendant cannot be tried twice for the same crime, in this case murder in the first degree. Publicly, Sam claimed to be eager for a retrial to exonerate himself once and for all. Privately, he remained terrified at the prospect of entrusting his life to another Cuyahoga County jury.

This time, however, the atmosphere would be different. Common Pleas Judge Francis J. Talty rejected Bailey's request for a change of venue, but he did order the jury sequestered throughout the trial and their phone calls to family members monitored. Just as important, Sheppard now entered the court a free man, rather than handcuffed and under armed guard.

The atmosphere in the country had changed as well. The McCarthy era hysteria had receded into history and the fifties emphasis on conformity had given way to the sixties—a decade of challenging convention and far less constrained public attitudes about human sexuality.

Sam Sheppard's second trial would be shorter, less emotional, and more businesslike. Cleveland press coverage remained hostile to Sam, but more subdued than during the first trial.

A week of jury selection once again produced seven men and five women, but this panel was younger than the original Sheppard jury, one of Bailey's goals, as its members had few memories of the pervasive prejudicial publicity of the first trial. Delivering his opening statement on November 1, 1966, Bailey promised an aggressive defense that would show that someone other than Sam Sheppard had been in the house to commit the murder in the early morning of July 4, 1954.

The prosecution put forth a familiar case, but with two important changes from the previous trial. Finally acknowledging the overwhelming medical evidence, the prosecutor jettisoned the argument that Sheppard's injuries had been faked or self-inflicted. His new argument was equally dubious, however: that the bone separation in Sheppard's neck, spinal cord contusion, chipped teeth, and cerebral concussion had been caused by Marilyn's resistance.

Another major difference between the two Sheppard trials was the absence of Susan Hayes from the list of prosecution witnesses. While Sam's affair with the former lab technician did enter into the record, she was not called to testify and the murder trial no longer centered on adultery.

Yet much remained the same. Cleveland detective Robert Schottke again testified for the prosecution, but Bailey took him apart on the stand. The aggressive young Boston attorney established that the police had failed to search for fingerprints, inquire as to the extent of Sam's injuries, or make practically any effort at all to consider alternative suspects.

Coroner Sam Gerber, looking older but still determined to pin the murder on Sam, was again the state's key witness. This time, however, Bailey cornered Gerber on his baseless identification of the alleged murder weapon. Decrying Gerber's "phantom impression [of] a surgical instrument," Bailey prompted the coroner to aver that a mere "object," rather than a "surgical instrument," had made the bloody imprint on the pillow. Gone was the inflammatory reference to the physician's "blood signature."

Bailey forced Gerber to acknowledge that he had never been able to define or identify such an object, although the lake had been dragged and he had spent a decade searching "all over the United States" for a medical implement that might match the imprint on the pillow. Bailey forced Gerber to acknowledge that he had not examined the blood spatter evidence in the murder room. Bailey's relentless cross-examination, conducted for six hours, highlighted Gerber's slipshod investigation as well as his animus against Sam Sheppard.

Although Gerber had been the key witness in the first trial, that distinction now belonged to the defense and to Dr. Paul Leland Kirk. After establishing Kirk's impressive credentials as a scholar and forensic scientist—including the presentation of evidence for both the prosecution and the defense in some 2,000 legal cases—Bailey drew from the witness his powerful blood evidence of Sam's innocence and the presence of a third person in the Sheppard home.

Kirk testified that blood from the murder room came from two different individuals (Marilyn and the killer), neither of whom could have been Dr. Sheppard, whose type A blood group was not represented in the murder room. Kirk demonstrated how the killer swung with his left hand. Kirk also discounted the potentially damning prosecution testimony of coroner's assistant Mary Cowan, who had asserted that a stain on Sam's watch was from blood spatter. Kirk, who had re-created blood spatter in his laboratory countless times, declared that a smudge rather than spatter had left the blood on Sam's watch.

As jurors later acknowledged, Kirk's testimony was impressive. Masking his strategy, Bailey hinted throughout the trial that he would put Sam on the stand, but actually he had no intention of doing so. He believed the jury would see that the prosecution had failed to prove its case, but Bailey also knew that Sam

Sheppard had been an ineffective witness in the first trial. His performance might have been even worse in the second trial, as Sam had begun to drink heavily and was popping a variety of pills to calm his nerves.

In his one-hour summation, Bailey emphasized Gerber's phantom identification of the murder weapon and "the story of the murder room." The Boston attorney declared that Sam would have been cleared in his first trial had the murder room evidence been presented.

On November 16, 1966, after eighteen days of testimony and fewer than half the witnesses of the first trial, Judge Talty instructed the jurors. Their options were to convict Sam of second-degree murder, manslaughter, or to find him not guilty.

With the jury excused at 10:45 A.M., Sam began perhaps the longest day of his life. Ariane and Bailey tried their best to soothe his jittery nerves. Just when it appeared the jury would be out for the evening, the bell rang announcing they would return with a verdict. A 9:20 P.M. the decision came and was read into the record by Judge Talty—not guilty. At last, after serving 3,575 days of wrongful incarceration, Sam Sheppard was a free man. "It's about time!" Sam exclaimed, slapping his hand on the table in front of him and drawing a sharp glare from the judge.

Most representatives of the Cleveland criminal justice establishment and press continued to believe Sam Sheppard was guilty. Some of them would continue to argue the case for the original guilty verdict for the rest of their lives. The initial prejudicial publicity and witch-hunt atmosphere left a profound and lasting impression. It would become increasingly clear that certain segments of public opinion in northeast Ohio were so wedded to conviction of Sheppard's guilt that no amount of evidence to the contrary would sway them.

Sam Sheppard was relieved, of course, but his acquittal in his only fair trial did not resolve the question that he and his followers had long been pondering: just who *had* killed Marilyn?

During the course of the trial, part of Bailey's strategy had been to establish in the jurors' minds potential alternative suspects in the Sheppard murder. Following up on suspicions first discussed by Sam and William Corrigan, Bailey believed that the murder might have been committed by Esther Houk and that her husband, also present at the scene, had clubbed Sam over the head when he came into the bedroom.

Sam Sheppard celebrates his 1967 acquittal upon retrial with attorney F. Lee Bailey (left) and his second wife, the former Ariane Tebbenjohanns of the Federal Republic of Germany, who had fallen in love with Sam during his imprisonment. Sheppard won his freedom in the second trial but, as Bailey later recounted, the family tragedy and a decade spent in the penitentiary had taken their toll on Sam, who already had begun to drink heavily and pop a variety of pills. Sheppard died just three years later, at age 46, of alcohol-related liver disease. Courtesy Associated Press Wide World Photos

It was well known that Spen Houk had a crush on Marilyn and had stopped over at the Sheppard home to have coffee with her on numerous occasions. In fact, according to Sam Sheppard, Houk had told Marilyn Sheppard that he had fallen in love with her during a trip the two couples had taken together to Canada. Marilyn had gently rebuffed the older man, who had conducted himself as "a gentleman" ever after.

According to Bailey's theory, Esther Houk, jealous over her husband's affections, had killed Marilyn, thus explaining why the blows had failed to crush the victim's skull—because they had been delivered by a woman. Spen Houk then helped his wife pin the crime on Sam. The theory of the Houks as culprits would help explain their damaging testimony in Sam's first trial. The truth was, however, that Sam and Esther Houk had never much liked one another. In his jailhouse "autobiography," Sam described Esther as "a complaining, rather ugly, argumentative female."

Although Bailey planted suspicions in the jurors' minds during his questioning of the Houks, the theory had no validity. In addition to the dubious motive—Spen Houk had indeed found Marilyn attractive but they had not been lovers—there was no physical evidence to implicate the Houks. Neither showed signs of cuts, bruises, or blood, nor did either have any personal history of criminality or violence.

After the trial Bailey shared his theory with Cleveland officials. In 1966 a Cuyahoga County grand jury did consider the evidence against the Houks, who had divorced in 1962, before concluding there was "no basis" for bringing charges against them. "We find the charges made by Mr. Bailey to be wholly unsubstantiated and without merit," the grand jury reported.

While still compelled to live with the haunting mystery of who had invaded his home and brutally murdered his wife, Sam Sheppard was at least a free man. He was still young, at age forty-three, but he felt the depressing sense of loss of the prime years of life. His son and namesake, raised by his brother, was in effect another man's child.

Sheppard tried to settle in with Ariane in the Cleveland suburb of Rocky River. The couple enjoyed only a "bitter happiness," Ariane recalled, as Sam continued to suffer from substance abuse as he "lived in the shadow of going back to prison. He never felt acquitted in everybody's eyes as long as the real killer was free." Seeking solace in a return to his medical books, Sheppard won renewal of his license to practice medicine. Life continued to prove burdensome, however, to the former Bay Village osteopath.

In addition to the considerable psychological scars of ten years' incarceration and the repeated judicial struggles, Sheppard found himself deeply in debt. He rushed out the ghostwritten *Endure and Conquer* in an effort to begin to pay Bailey's $150,000 legal bill, which no one considered unreasonable given the aggressive young attorney's effectiveness. In 1967 Bailey filed in Sam Sheppard's name a multi-million dollar action against Scripps-Howard, parent of the *Cleveland Press*, and editor Louis Seltzer, but a judge dismissed the suits in Cleveland District Court the following year.

Still considered a pariah by many in the community, Sheppard frequently heard the taunt, "Wife murderer!" when he went out in public. At one point, Sam announced after a European vacation that he and Ariane had decided to live abroad, but soon reversed himself. He then joined a hospital in Youngstown, Ohio, but soon resigned when he and the hospital were twice slapped with malpractice suits totaling more than $1 million. A target because of his notoriety, Sheppard learned that his medical insurance would be canceled.

Any and all activities in which Sam Sheppard engaged himself remained the subject of banner headlines in the Cleveland newspapers. That was true most especially when Ariane filed for divorce on December 3, 1968, declaring that Sam had threatened her with violence and that he habitually carried a pistol or a knife. Ariane acknowledged that her husband had never struck her, but she charged that he was "irrational" and a "maniac." She obtained a restraining order against him.

In a 1989 interview Ariane explained that "He threatened me but it was not him talking. It was the drugs, the uppers and downers and the alcohol he was on." Ariane added that "there was never a time when I believed he killed Marilyn."

Sheppard did not contest the divorce, but it drove him deeper into drink, drugs, despair, and indebtedness, as he was forced to pay Ariane $300 a month in alimony. A second marriage ending in tragedy only added to the psychological baggage with which Sam was compelled to live.

Moving to Columbus, Ohio, in the center of the state, Sam opened a small medical practice, but his heart was not in it. Newspaper headlines soon blared his decision to go on a national tour as an exhibition wrestler. Sam had loved wrestling in high school, and grappling with another man on the mat was the one activity he found truly liberating. One wonders, however, if Sam's desire to win wrestling matches did not reflect a deep-seated guilt, however irrational, over failing to subdue his wife's killer in the bedroom or on the beach outside their Bay Village home in the summer of 1954.

He called himself "Killer Sheppard." Toward the end of his life Sam Sheppard had become, as his son, Sam Reese Sheppard, later put it, "a satirical character of himself." During a trip to Mexico, Sam apparently married the nineteen-year-old daughter of his manager, a girl named Colleen Strickland. By this time he was estranged from his brothers and his son, who attended school overseas.

His substance abuse problems were out of control. "His spirit was finally broken," Sam Reese Sheppard explained.

On April 6, 1970, Sam Sheppard, aged forty-six, died of what the autopsy described as "liver failure." A buildup of fatty tissue, a prelude to cirrhosis of the liver, stemmed from alcoholism. He had refused medical treatment.

Neither his brother Stephen, nor his son, who was still overseas, attended the small ceremony in Columbus, although Richard Sheppard and his family joined Ariane and Colleen at the graveside. F. Lee Bailey attended as well. Sam's and Marilyn's former pastor at the Methodist church in Bay Village presided and chased away the ever present photographers and camera crews.

At the time of his death, the Internal Revenue Service had been pursuing Sheppard for payment of back taxes. The value of his estate was less than $5,000. As Bailey observed, Sheppard had "won back his freedom, and he won exoneration. But he couldn't win back his life." His life overwhelmed by an almost incomprehensible tragedy, Sam Sheppard in reality had proven unable to "endure and conquer."

To those familiar with the case, Sheppard's death was hardly the last chapter. The haunting question that he had taken to his grave—who killed Marilyn?—remained to be answered. While Bailey and others had once suspected the Houks, no evidence materialized to bolster the unlikely scenario of the Bay Village couple sauntering over to the Sheppards to batter Marilyn to death in the middle of the night. Another potential suspect was Dr. Lester T. Hoversten, Sam's friend and the Sheppard houseguest who had been away at Kent, Ohio, for the July 4 weekend in 1954. Marilyn did not like Hoversten and told Sam as much on several occasions.

Hoversten recently had been fired by a hospital and was struggling with depression at the time. Divorced but sexually active, Hoversten had made suggestive comments to Marilyn. Yet Hoversten had spent the weekend as a house guest and it is unlikely that he could or would have crept from the home where he stayed, driven more than seventy miles round-trip to murder Marilyn, arriving back unnoticed by his hosts in Kent. Hoversten also lacked motive, a history of violent behavior, or evidence of a bleeding wound after the crime.

In the early stages of the investigation, the Bay Village police compiled a list of potential suspects, but after Gerber and the Cleveland police decided on the first day that Sheppard was the killer, a follow-up investigation never transpired.

Number twenty-four on the Bay Village police roster of potential suspects was one Richard G. Eberling, proprietor of Dick's Cleaning Service, a window-washing business that served wealthy West Side customers, including the Sheppards.

An Elyria, Ohio, journalist first made the connection between Eberling and Marilyn's death after learning of an extraordinary admission by Eberling in the wake of an arrest for theft in 1959. Without being asked, Eberling told police that his blood was in the Sheppard house. Eberling explained that he had cut himself on a window lock while working there a few days before the murder.

With Sam convicted and ensconced in the penitentiary, Cuyahoga County authorities failed to follow up with an investigation into Eberling's connection with the Sheppards. As a result, Sheppard would continue to suffer unjustly— and still others would die.

The extraordinary story of Richard Eberling has been painstakingly pieced together over several years as a result of Sam Reese Sheppard's unceasing efforts to prove his father's innocence, a campaign aided by his attorney, Terry Gilbert, private investigators, and Cynthia Cooper, a writer and attorney and coauthor with Sam Reese Sheppard of *Mockery of Justice.*

What Cooper and others have unearthed in Richard Eberling is the story of an emotionally troubled, violently psychotic individual. During a series of interviews with Cooper at the Lebanon (Ohio) State Prison, where he was serving a life term for the murder of another woman, Eberling spoke freely but often cryptically about the Sheppard case. Between the truth, the lies, and the evidence, Eberling emerged as the compelling suspect in the murder of Marilyn Sheppard.

The overarching reality of Richard Eberling's youth was his illegitimacy. First known as Richard Lenardic, the boy never knew his father or his mother, a nineteen-year-old girl out of Cleveland's "Little Croatia" who gave him up for adoption after his birth in 1929. In and out of foster homes and rejected several times by potential adoptive parents, Richard suffered from severe emotional disturbances for which he was hospitalized repeatedly at a young age.

At school, Richard proved to be quite intelligent, but also a substantial disci-

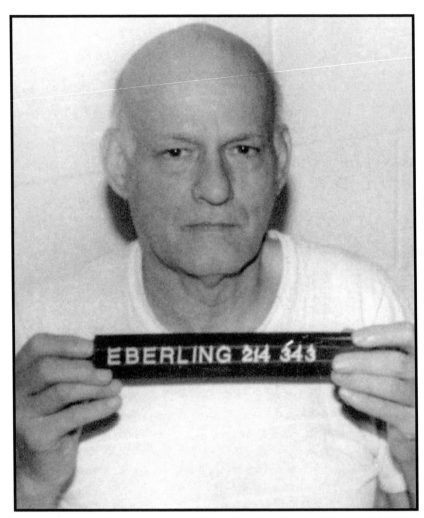

The Cleveland police mug shot of Richard G. Eberling. Busted as a petty thief and con man, Eberling was also a killer. Convicted of murdering one woman, Eberling was also suspected in the deaths of three others as well as Marilyn Sheppard. A former window cleaner at the Sheppard home, Eberling told police without prompting in 1959 that he had cut his finger and bled in the home just days before Marilyn Sheppard's murder. Although Eberling denied killing Marilyn Sheppard, he confessed or hinted at his own guilt in the murder privately on several occasions. Courtesy Associated Press Wide World Photos pline problem. He lied, cheated, stole, and constantly acted out in a quest for attention. After being placed with the Children's Aid Society in 1938, officials gave Richard a growth hormone because he appeared to behave in a manner that was insufficiently masculine for a boy. Reportedly, he had been found wearing girls' clothing. Conflicted over his sexuality throughout his life, Richard continued as a boy to betray signs of severe psychological and social disorder, including a diagnosis by at least one physician of schizophrenia. A child psychologist described Eberling as "active and nervous" as well as manipulative and deceitful. "He is very untruthful and will never admit he is wrong." In 1939 a Children's Aid Society report concluded: "We may see this child develop a definite psychotic state" which would compel him to be "institutionalized for the rest of his life."

Despite Richard's deeply troubled youth, sixty-nine-year-old George Eberling of Westlake, on Cleveland's West Side, adopted Richard, who had begun to emerge as a big, strapping teenager. He was just the sort of raw youth George Eberling sought to help him accomplish the hard work on the forty-acre Eberling farm. Richard, who would grow to be six-foot-one and 180–190 pounds, worked hard on the farm, but struggled through school and never dated, played sports, or participated in high school social events.

In 1948, during his last year of high school, Richard legally changed his name to Eberling. After his adoptive father's death, Eberling began to display his considerable talents as a manipulator, thief, and con artist. Virtually unnoticed, he outmaneuvered his adoptive relatives and, piece by piece through legal claims, gained complete control of the forty-acre farm.

By 1954, the year that Eberling began to work for the Sheppards, Richard had built Dick's Cleaning Service, the window-washing business he had started as a high school senior, into a going concern. Eberling targeted wealthy West Side customers, including Dorothy Sheppard, the wife of Sam's brother Richard, who then recommended Eberling to Marilyn. The wives of both Dr. Sheppards routinely handled all matters of household maintenance.

Speaking with author Cynthia Cooper and others from prison years later, Eberling recalled being attracted to Marilyn, who wore shorts and "California-type" fashions. "I was an orphan," Eberling recalled; "she was a golden girl." On one occasion, Eberling later confided in a fellow prison inmate, he had seen

Marilyn in the home wearing only her panties and had become sexually aroused.

To Eberling, the Sheppards, with their good looks, beautiful lakefront home, sports cars, and healthy young son, were the embodiment of the contented home life that he had been denied as a child. Years later, Eberling told Sam Reese Sheppard of having cookies and milk with him and his mother and walking down to the beach, Marilyn telling him that he could come swim at any time.

But there was another side to Eberling's feelings: anger, hostility, and class resentment. He had little contact with Sam Sheppard but from what he saw found him "arrogant" and "condescending." Dr. Sam, Eberling told Cynthia Cooper, "thought he was a gift to mankind." Marilyn, too, was "class-conscious" and typical of the people of Bay Village who "looked down on the people of Westlake," such as Eberling himself.

Through his work as a window washer Eberling gained intimate knowledge of the Sheppard home, located less than five miles from his own domicile. Decades later he offered a drawing of the layout of the home striking in its architectural accuracy. He got familiar with Koko, the family pet, which, as he recalled to Cynthia Cooper, was "the friendliest dog." In performing his work around the Sheppard house Eberling routinely used the entrance to the basement, where he would wash windows and carry them back and forth.

Richard Eberling possessed the intimate knowledge of the Sheppard home that enabled him to enter probably through an open basement door, creep up the steps to the landing, and then continue up to the bedroom. The angry, disturbed, and perhaps drunk intruder then carried out his sexual fantasies on Marilyn while paying back Sam, through the rape of his wife, for his upper-class snobbery. How perfect would their world be then?

"Why do women fight back when they are raped?" Eberling abruptly asked author Cynthia Cooper, investigating on behalf of Sam Reese Sheppard, during one of their many prison interviews. On another occasion Eberling described Marilyn as being stunned by a blow and then beaten to death. There was "blood all over." Troubled by the reminder that Marilyn had been four months pregnant, Eberling merely mused that "she didn't show."

That Eberling was a thief and a murderer of women is now a matter of public record. He would go on from the Sheppard murder to establish a clear pattern of theft, insurance fraud, relentless con artistry, and serial murder.

In 1955, with Sam in jail and Eberling going about his business unchallenged by police, fire destroyed a barn on the Eberling farm. Richard reportedly had removed valuable items from the barn—filing a claim on them afterward nonetheless—and had collected a sizable sum in the insurance settlement (setting fires has been identified by FBI profilers as among the characteristics of serial killers).

The next year a young woman whom Eberling was dating died in an automobile "accident" in eastern Michigan. With Eberling at the wheel, the right side of the car slammed into the left side of a truck parked on the side of the road. The truck driver insisted that he had pulled the vehicle six feet off the road.

The woman, Barbara Ann Kinzel, twenty-three, dark haired and pretty, like Marilyn, had been one of the nurses who had treated Sam Sheppard for his injuries the day after the murders. Although Kinzel's death was ruled an accident, an Ohio convict who became friends with Eberling in prison told Sam Reese Sheppard's attorneys that Eberling told him that he had gotten drunk with Barbara Kinzel and admitted that he and not Sam had killed Marilyn Sheppard. Eberling murdered Kinzel in the car crash the next day.

By that time, as Eberling later admitted to police, he had begun stealing cash, jewelry, sterling, and decorative items from the homes serviced by his cleaning business. He pilfered tens of thousands of dollars worth of items, including possessions of Marilyn Sheppard's, before finally being apprehended.

It was in the midst of confessing to these crimes, after his arrest in 1959, that Eberling offered the startling information that he was "positive" that he had cut his hand and "at various times dripped blood in various parts of the house" while working at the Sheppards' just before the murder in 1954. Eberling's unelicited statement that evidence of his blood might have been in the Sheppard home appears to have been a reckless effort on his part to provide a preemptive explanation for any effort to link him with the murder.

Additional evidence of Eberling's involvement with Marilyn Sheppard surfaced in the wake of his arrest. According to police reports in mid-November 1959, Eberling admitted that while cleaning the home of Richard Sheppard in 1958 he "ran across" several boxes of Marilyn Reese Sheppard's personal belongings. From one of the boxes he stole two diamond rings that he recognized as having belonged to Marilyn.

Eberling then offered up for the startled police investigators that "he cut his finger about four days prior to the murder and had dripped blood all over the downstairs of the Sheppard home." Eberling then "changed his statement, that he was all over the house with his finger dripping blood." Eberling claimed that during the initial investigation he had told two police detectives his whereabouts the night of the murder—at home alone in bed—but police could find no record of his ever having been questioned.

As a result of Eberling's striking and contradictory statements, Gerber himself questioned the confessed thief about the Sheppard murder for three hours. The coroner, who retained tight authority over the case, concluded that he "believed Eberling and didn't think he was involved in the murder." Gerber thus dismissed Eberling's clumsy efforts to fashion a false alibi in order to explain evidence—his own blood at the crime scene!—that he feared might have been uncovered in the Sheppard home. He need not have feared. Cleveland officials preferred that Sam Sheppard remain in jail rather than open an investigation into the patently suspicious statements of a known criminal.

Gerber at first opposed the suggestion of a lie detector test of Eberling, but apparently relented, as police did conduct the test in 1959. The analysis of the results concluded, "We do not find evidence of deception on his [Eberling's] graphs in answer to relevant questions" concerning the murder of Marilyn Sheppard. However, in 1989, after uncovering evidence of another murder committed by Eberling, Cleveland police sought second opinions of Eberling's 1959 lie detector test. A professional firm in Chicago concluded that Eberling "either murdered Marilyn Sheppard or had knowledge of who did." A Department of Defense analysis of the lie detector test results found the data insufficient to make a conclusive judgment.

In addition to the lie detector test, Eberling was evaluated by a psychiatrist in the wake of his 1959 arrest for theft. The diagnosis was "immature personality and obsessive-compulsive neurosis which is manifested by kleptomaniac tendencies." The psychiatrist recommended prolonged care, but Eberling received a ninety-day suspended sentence after pleading down to petty larceny. Gerber and Cuyahoga County authorities dropped the investigation of the Sheppard murder, leaving Sam languishing in jail and Eberling free to steal—and kill—again.

Eberling began to target vulnerable older women, especially a wealthy widow, Ethel May Durkin, with whom he had become close friends following her husband's death. Eberling attended to the wealthy old woman, whom he referred to as "Twinkletoes." Mrs. Durkin's sister, Myrtle Fray, saw through Eberling's mask. She objected to his presence in her sister's home, calling him a "creep" and denouncing him to his face. "He's an ex-con. He's taking you," Myrtle told her sister.

In May 1962 police found Myrtle Fray beaten to death. Eberling observed in a prison conversation with author Cynthia Cooper that Myrtle Fray had died the same way Marilyn had—"her face was beaten in" in the early hours of the morning. She had also been strangled and suffocated. A killer was never identified. Eberling described to Cooper how the killer burst through the night chain on the door and escaped after committing the murder by donning some of the dead woman's clothes and walking out unobserved. Ethel May Durkin's other sister also died suspiciously in 1970, falling down a set of stairs.

Eberling by this time had developed a homosexual relationship with a man named Obie Henderson, who had been named to serve as executor to Mrs. Durkin's estate in her will. On January 3, 1984, Ethel May Durkin died from injuries sustained in her home. Eberling was there. He had called 911 to report that Ethel May had fallen after drinking a cocktail he had prepared for her. The coroner—Sam Gerber—ruled it was an accident. He did not bother with an autopsy.

Mrs. Durkin's will left 70 percent of her estate to her "good friend and adviser" Richard Eberling. Soon thereafter, Eberling reported a break-in at Mrs. Durkin's empty home. Obie Henderson received a $17,000 insurance check. Altogether, Eberling may have received as much as $1 million.

By this time Eberling and Henderson were among the elite of Cleveland society, collecting art, hosting fund-raisers for the Cleveland ballet, and operating a successful decorating business. They once generated headlines by donating a $50,000 Arabian horse to a television fundraiser. After Ethel Durkin's death Eberling and Henderson moved to a twenty-seven-room mansion in Tennessee. However, Richard, suffering from alcoholism as well as emotional disabilities, was in and out of hospitals.

Former accomplices of Eberling soon informed police that Mrs. Durkin's will was a fraud and suggested that Eberling might have killed her. With Gerber having retired at last, the new Cuyahoga County coroner, Elizabeth Balraj, ordered Mrs. Durkin's body disinterred. An autopsy revealed that contusions and trauma on both the front and back of her head indicated homicide rather than an accidental fall. After their arrest in Tennessee, a grand jury indicted Eberling and Henderson on counts of fraud, forgery, theft, and murder. On July 7, 1989, a jury found Eberling guilty of fraud and homicide. He was sentenced to life in prison and ordered to pay a massive restitution.

In the 1990s, the ongoing investigation by Sam Reese Sheppard, Cynthia Cooper, and AMSEC International, a private investigative agency based in Virginia, uncovered still more damning evidence against Eberling. Vern Lund, a window washer who had worked for Eberling, told investigators that it was he, and not Eberling, who had cleaned the Sheppard windows on July 2, 1954.

Eberling, therefore, could not have cut his hand and dripped blood in the Sheppard house before the July 3 murder—he had not even been there in the days before the murder. The story, still uninvestigated by the police, had been ludicrous anyway—as if Marilyn Sheppard or the family maid would have allowed a blood trail to remain in the house as they prepared to entertain guests over the July 4 weekend.

Lund explained that he had kept quiet for years, not wishing to become involved, partly because he felt particularly vulnerable since he had engaged in homosexual activity. Lund insisted, however, that he could not be mistaken about having worked at the Sheppard house two days before her murder. Lund died on August 8, 1991. Eberling displayed agitation and refused to discuss Lund when Cynthia Cooper attempted to question him.

Another former worker with Dick's Cleaning Service surfaced to add another possible motive for the murder. Ed Wilbert, who worked periodically for Eberling for seven years, told investigators that Marilyn had caught Eberling stealing and threatened to turn him in. "Marilyn was going to blast him and told him so," Wilbert recalled. "She didn't like him."

Eberling had received a check from Marilyn dated June 24, 1954. He cashed it on the day of her funeral.

In the continuing absence of any public effort to investigate the Sheppard murder, the private investigation continued, now aided by new technology. Since the mid-1980s, DNA (deoxyribonucleic acid) tests of cells, which are unique to each individual, have been employed as a highly effective technique of criminal investigation. In only its first decade of existence DNA testing has already helped secure thousands of convictions of guilty defendants as well as exoneration of innocent ones—some of whom have been wrongfully imprisoned.

Sam Reese Sheppard and his investigative team successfully employed DNA in the investigation of Marilyn Sheppard's murder. Laboratory tests of DNA, conducted by Dr. Mohammad Tahir of Indianapolis in 1997, revealed that blood found on the Sheppard porch matched Richard Eberling's DNA. The quality of the dated sample was relatively poor, perhaps insufficient to convict Eberling in a murder trial, yet suggestive nonetheless.

Tahir also conducted tests on blood removed from the basement steps, sampled from a chip which had been kept over the years. The DNA test revealed that the blood could not have belonged to either Marilyn or Sam Sheppard. The same was true of the blood on Sheppard's pants.

The findings, released on May 4, 1997, showed that Richard Eberling's blood group had not been ruled out from the same tests. The type of test performed could not pinpoint that the blood was Eberling's, only that his blood matched the same broad typing found on the pants and the step, whereas Sam's and Marilyn's did not.

Stunningly, and for the first time, Dr. Tahir's DNA tests showed evidence of sperm from a vaginal smear taken from Mrs. Sheppard's body after the murder but ignored in the original investigation. In fact, tests revealed evidence of sperm from two donors within the last three days of Marilyn's life, presumably her husband and the rapist. The evidence that Marilyn had been raped, ignored during the original investigation—was now confirmed. Tests revealed that Richard Eberling could not be excluded as a possible match for the sperm sample.

In the final analysis, the tests showed that a third person had bled in the Sheppard home and that that person could have been Richard Eberling. On his left wrist, Eberling carried a scar consistent with a flap of skin being torn free by a fingernail. The ring finger and nail on Marilyn Sheppard's left hand bore signs of trauma consistent with such a struggle. It would thus appear that the blood that dripped through the Sheppard house stemmed from an injury inflicted to Eberling's wrist during Marilyn Sheppard's desperate efforts to deflect the killer's death blows.

Eberling denied any involvement in Marilyn Sheppard's death. He insisted that he had been home in bed on the night of July 3 and the notion that he had any involvement was "baloney." Eberling died on July 26, 1998. An autopsy the next day listed the cause of death as a heart attack.

Having amassed a substantial case against Eberling, Sam Reese Sheppard and his supporters worked tirelessly to clear his father's name. Despite massive evidence of injustice in the Sheppard case, Cuyahoga County officials remained obdurate. For years they fought efforts by Sam R. Sheppard to gain access to records that were supposed to be open under state law.

Finally, in 1994 a new prosecutor reopened the Sheppard case. At last, Cuyahoga County authorities acknowledged that the evidence showed that Eberling may have been the killer, but they declined to bring homicide charges against a man, already in prison for life, more than four decades after the crime. Meanwhile, Sam Reese Sheppard's attorney, Terry Gilbert, pursued a lawsuit under Ohio's Wrongful Imprisonment Law for restitution for damages incurred by Dr. Sheppard during his incarceration.

As the evidence mounted against Eberling, Cuyahoga County authorities now faced the prospect of a potentially damaging lawsuit. They allegedly responded by encouraging a prison informant to entice Eberling to declare that he had killed Marilyn—but that Sam Sheppard had paid him to do so. Such a solution would accommodate the evidence against Eberling while still not exonerating Sam Sheppard and thereby exposing the State of Ohio to a liability judgement.

The prison informant, Robert Lee Parks of Cleveland, who was serving a ten- to twenty-five-year sentence for aggravated robbery, sought to be removed from Orient Correctional Institute near Columbus, Ohio, where he believed his life was in danger because on several occasions he had implicated criminals through his work as a police informer— or "snitch", in prison lexicon. According to Parks, the prison warden informed him that he would be transferred only if he could entice Eberling to state that Sam Sheppard had paid him to kill his wife. Parks claimed that the warden, Alan J. Lazaroff, explained that the state of Ohio faced a potential $2 million judgment against it if Sam's son were to win his case for wrongful imprisonment. Lazaroff has denied Parks' account.

Parks befriended Eberling after they met in the prison hospital. Eberling, bald and sporting a long gray beard, was suffering from a variety of ailments that would soon kill him. As they became friends, Parks urged Eberling to implicate Sam in the murder of his wife as a means of getting the press and authorities to leave him alone and to stop trying to implicate Eberling himself in the murder. "Fuck it, man, why don't you just say Sam had something to do with it," Parks urged Eberling. Responding to written questions from Parks, Eberling scrawled down that he had killed Marilyn in return for a promise of $1,500, which Sam never paid.

Cuyahoga County authorities later acknowledged that in March 1998 they arranged for Parks to act as an informant, but denied Parks' allegation that he was given the specific mission of encouraging Eberling to implicate Sam. Parks insisted that warden Lazaroff "wanted information that Sam Sheppard was involved in that crime." Parks pleaded with authorities to let him wear a hidden microphone, but they refused, later stating that they had not wanted to risk Parks' life by wiring him.

Following Eberling's death in July of 1998, Parks received his transfer out of Orient, but he remained angry at authorities for having allowed him to remain in danger for so long a time. The convict also declared that he wanted to reveal the truth about the case in order to clear his conscience. Parks contacted Terry Gilbert, Sam Reese Sheppard's attorney, and in a videotaped interview from Southeastern Correctional Institute in Lancaster, Ohio, revealed that Eberling confessed his guilt, and his alone, in not only the murder of Marilyn Sheppard, but of the three Durkin sisters and Barbara Ann Kinzel as well.

Parks not only befriended Eberling, but smoked marijuana with him in prison and, after "he told me he was gay," allowed Eberling to perform oral sex on him. Eberling confessed to the murders in detail. "He told me everything about him killing Marilyn. . . . He told me everything Sam told the police was correct."

According to Parks, Eberling had seen Marilyn in her panties one day while washing windows at the home and had in mind ever after to rape her. On the early morning of July 4, Eberling, wearing overalls, makeup, and a wig, went to the home with the intention of raping Marilyn and stealing her jewelry. He used a Phillips-head screwdriver to break in through the basement door and came upstairs believing Sam was at the hospital for the evening because he saw a light left on upstairs. Eberling apparently knew that it was the Sheppards' habit to leave the upstairs light on for Sam when he worked late at the hospital.

"He covered her mouth, he was raping her," Parks recounted, when she "bit the shit out of him." Eberling told Parks he had not planned to kill Marilyn, but "lost control" when she bit him and "went berserk on her face" with the butt-end of the screwdriver. Eberling then explained that he "beat Sam's ass" in the bedroom and on the beach, wrapped the screwdriver in Sam's tee-shirt, which he had torn off in the struggle, and buried the weapon on a Lake Erie hillside.

Contrary to the Parks account, a 1999 forensic dental consultant concluded from an examination of Marilyn Sheppard's disinterred corpse that she had not bitten her assailant. As already noted, the wound on Marilyn Sheppard's attacker instead might have been caused by a scratch from a fingernail.

Although Cuyahoga County authorities have dismissed Parks as an unreliable convict, prosecutors from across the state had used such phrases as "very cooperative and truthful" to describe his activities as a prison informant. In fact, Parks' account of the murder fits many of the facts of the case. The inmate, who gained his release from prison in 1999, had no apparent reason to fabricate an account implicating Eberling.

It is possible that Parks' account is the closest we will ever get to the truth of the Sheppard case. Had Ohio authorities consented to a wire of Parks, or proceeded on an objective course of seeking out the truth, Eberling might have been induced to confess. "These serial killers are tormented by the inability to get it out," Terry Gilbert averred. "And I think he was on the verge of saying what happened and we just never got a chance to do it right." Sam Reese Sheppard condemned the actions of the Ohio authorities as "a disgrace—a political disgrace. We could have had the answers from this guy (Eberling)."

Sam Reese Sheppard and his attorneys believed that sufficient evidence had been uncovered to implicate Eberling and vindicate Sam Sheppard once and for all. "The system should have some accountability when people's lives are destroyed by wrongful convictions," Gilbert declared on the eve of the proceedings. "My dad was vilified to death by this state," Sam Reese Sheppard added.

Like the first two Sheppard trials, the civil suit promised to be a sensational media event. Sam Reese Sheppard, determined to redeem his father's reputation with a finding against the state, and Terry Gilbert both worked tirelessly to promote local and national media attention. "The media basically destroyed Dr. Sheppard," Gilbert explained, "so here we were . . . putting the media to positive use in a case that had been so infected by it. I didn't think there was anything wrong with that."

Sam Reese Sheppard and Gilbert cooperated with the public television pro-gram "Nova," which recreated the crime scene and analyzed the scientific evi-dence in an episode that aired in 1999. Consultants in the "Nova" program included Barry Scheck, the DNA expert who made a national reputation in the Simpson case. Gilbert and Sheppard served as consultants in a 1999 made-for-TV movie, a predictably melodramatic production that bore little resemblance to the realities of the case.

An aggressive new Cuyahoga County prosecutor William Mason fought back with press conferences of his own proclaiming that the evidence still strongly pointed to Sam Sheppard's guilt in the July 1954 murder. He sent a prosecutor and a video cameraman on the trail of Sam Reese Sheppard, record-ing his public statements with a view to challenging them in court. He ordered the disinterment and new tests of Marilyn Sheppard's corpse. The prosecutor had hoped to find that another man had been the father of the fetus she carried, but tests showed that the baby had been Sam and Marilyn's. Those who clung to the theory of Sheppard's guilt now had to argue that the seemingly mild-man-nered physician had brutally murdered his wife while destroying the life of his unborn child at the same time.

When discussions aimed at reaching an out-of-court settlement went nowhere, both sides prepared for what would be in effect the third trial of Dr. Samuel H. Sheppard. Sam Reese Sheppard and Gilbert had hoped, in essence, to put Eberling on trial, but as events would play out the question of Sam Shep-pard's guilt or innocence would be the one that riveted public attention.

A judgement for the plaintiffs in the wrongful imprisonment suit conceiv-ably could have cost the State of Ohio millions of dollars. Cuyahoga County authorities thus fought the Sheppard lawsuit with a vengeance. Prosecutor William Mason vowed that the state's defense against the plaintiff's lawsuit would center on demonstrating that Dr. Samuel H. Sheppard had in fact killed his wife.

Arguments in the wrongful imprisonment civil suit opened in Cuyahoga Common Pleas Court on January 31, 2000. Key decisions undermined the plaintiff's case from the outset. Sam Reese Sheppard declined to request a change of venue, as he sought to vindicate his father in the community in which Dr. Sheppard originally had been victimized. Yet the community remained poisoned against Sam Sheppard, as police, prosecutors, and many others insisted that the 1954 trial rather than the 1967 retrial had rendered the proper verdict in the case.

Scores of Cleveland police officers and reporters, those who have been utterly convinced of Sam Sheppard's guilt since 1954, remained very much alive and contemptuous of efforts over the years to establish the physician's innocence in the slaying of his wife. Despite the passage of almost fifty years the Sheppard case remained a neuralgic cultural issue in northeast Ohio.

Recognizing that they still enjoyed significant community support, the prosecution requested a trial by jury. No one could recall a single Ohio wrongful imprisonment suit being decided by a jury, rather than a judge, at this stage of the civil proceedings. Rejecting the plaintiff's protests, Cuyahoga County Common Pleas Judge Ronald Suster leaped at the chance to avoid the onus of decision-making in the third Sheppard trial. An eight-person jury from Cuyahoga County was duly assembled.

The plaintiff lost another key battle when Suster ruled that transcripts from the previous trials would be admitted into evidence. The judge hence forwarded for the civil jury the record of the 1954 proceedings, which higher courts had thrown out as a "trial by newspaper" and a mockery of justice."

Despite these setbacks Gilbert presented a strong case. Dr. Mohammad Tahir presented the compelling DNA evidence of the blood of a third person in the murder room as well as evidence that Marilyn Sheppard had been raped. Tahir testified that Eberling could not be ruled as the source of the blood but that Sam Sheppard could be eliminated. The Indianapolis scientist added that tests showed that the spot of blood on Sam's trousers had been neither his nor Marilyn's, but that it could have been Eberling's.

Nationally recognized experts on criminal investigation testified as to the botched handling of the crime scene and the flaws in Gerber's analysis. A forensic psychologist testified that the violent sexual nature of the Sheppard murder fit the pattern of a "sadistic intruder' rather than the victim's husband. Another expert testified that the scar on Eberling's wrist matched up perfectly with Marilyn Sheppard's damaged fingernails.

Gilbert declined to call Parks to the stand, realizing that the credibility of a convicted felon would be relentlessly attacked by the prosecution. However, a new witness surfaced to confirm much of Park's account. Cathie Collins Dial testified that in 1983, while in the employ of Richard Eberling, he confessed to her that he and not Sam Sheppard had killed Marilyn. Dial explained that she, only twenty years old at the time, had never heard of the Sheppard case, but that Eberling had explained it to her, including his motive. Marilyn and Sam "felt they were better than other people," Eberling had told her. Dial added more detail to the crime, noting that Eberling had explained that he had knocked out Sam Sheppard by striking him in the head with a pail. Dial said the conversation changed her relationship with Eberling and soon left his employ. When she heard years later that the Sheppard case was being investigated anew, Dial testified that she contacted Cuyahoga County authorities with her story, but they declined to follow up.

In presenting its own case, the prosecution employed the same tactics that had proven successful in the initial trial in 1954. Mason argued that Sam Sheppard had killed Marilyn in a fight that broke out over his extramarital affairs.

Susan Hayes—now a seventy-year-old grandmother of four—had to relive her affair with Sam, but this time on videotape rather than in person on Cleveland. Asked by the plaintiffs if she believed Sam had wanted to marry her or had loved her more than Marilyn, she responded with a definitive "No."

Mason and his associates called in their own experts to reject the plaintiff's scientific testimony. It was difficult for them to impugn Dr. Tahir's credentials, however, insofar as Cuyahoga County had been on record bringing him in to set up the county's own DNA laboratory. Mason told the jury to reject the blood evidence as too old and contaminated to be reliable.

The DNA contamination argument resonated with Americans as a result of the highly publicized trial of O. J. Simpson in the mid-1990s (see next chapter). The charge, bogus in both cases, was nevertheless successfully impressed upon juries in both the Simpson criminal case and the Sheppard civil trial. The blood evidence in the Sheppard case was indeed old, and susceptible to some legitimate questions about its handling, yet objective experts such as Tahir found it compelling.

The bottom line, Mason repeatedly hammered to the eight jurors, was that the wealthy and adulterous Dr. Sheppard had murdered his own wife and tried to get away with it. The scientific evidence was so much "mumbo jumbo" and the evidence of the so-called experts need not be considered at all.

The lawyers presented closing arguments in the second week of April 2000. Recounting the painstaking efforts over nearly half a century to clear Dr. Sam Sheppard's name, Gilbert pleaded with the jury, "Give us justice, please." The prosecution insisted that the jury was "being asked to reward the killer's son for the killer bludgeoning his wife."

The third Sheppard trial came to an end on April 12, 2000. After three-and-a-half hours of deliberation, the jury ruled unanimously in favor of the state, rejecting the plaintiff's claim of unlawful imprisonment. It was not only the verdict but the rapidity with which the jury returned it that stunned courtroom observers, especially Gilbert, who slumped to the table, his head in his hands. Sam Reese Sheppard, no stranger to family defeats in Cuyahoga County courtrooms, consoled his attorney with pats on the back.

"Everything just didn't add up to enough," explained one juror, one of the few to comment after the trial. It was more likely, however, that the jury—much like the panel in the O. J. Simpson criminal trial—had its mind made up and declined to conduct a systematic review of the evidence. "It was like a joke," the bewildered Gilbert recounted. "It was like invalidating what so many people had worked for and believed in."

"I'm shocked with the jury, quite frankly," echoed Sam Reese Sheppard. "To shrug it [the evidence] off—which seems to be what they did—it just seems curious." Judge Suster acknowledged that the jury had not taken the time to consider the evidence. "I don't think they could have gone through it all in three-and-a-half hours," the judge commented.

In the final analysis, it had proven more difficult than the plaintiff imagined to prove the negative—that Sam Sheppard had not committed the murder. The decision of the jury in the civil proceeding did not obviate the fact that Sam Sheppard had been acquitted in his last criminal trial, but it did reveal that Sheppard's son and attorney had come up short in their effort to convict, in effect, a dead man, Eberling, of the crime.

The prosecution went much further in its own triumphant summation of the meaning of the case. Mason declared that the jury's verdict in the civil case had proved nothing less than that Sam Sheppard had murdered his wife early in the morning of July 4, 1954.

Cuyahoga County authorities thus claimed victory, culminating a nearly

Sam Reese Sheppard (left) and his distraught attorney, Terry Gilbert, backed by supporters, meet with the press following their defeat in a civil trial in Cleveland in April, 2000. The son of Dr. Sam Sheppard had sought to win a judgment for wrongful incarceration of his father from the State of Ohio. Cuyahoga County authorities insisted to the end that Sam Sheppard had been guilty of murdering his wife despite the 1967 acquittal and the evidence which had accumulated implicating Richard Eberling. Courtesy Associated Press Wide World Photos

half century-long vendetta against Dr. Samuel Holmes Sheppard. The authorities remained determined to deny that an injustice had occurred in the Sheppard murder case, and to spend well more than one-hundred thousand dollars to do it. In reality, however, the evidence strongly suggests that a man's life and family had been destroyed by murder, official incompetence, malicious press coverage, class tensions, community prejudices, and vengeful prosecutors.

While Sam Reese Sheppard contemplated an appeal of the verdict in the civil trial, the Sheppard case appeared destined to remain a tragedy of Shakespearean proportions.

Nothing can change the fact that Dr. Sam Sheppard died without knowing who had killed his wife and ruined his own life in the process. And yet, he may have had an inkling. Not long before his own death, a broken man at age 46, Sheppard encountered Richard Eberling outside an ice cream parlor on Cleveland's West Side. Eberling pulled over in his car and took Sam aside for a few words. No one knows what was said, but something prompted Sam to look over at his son and observe: "This guy could have done it."

IV   A HOUSE DIVIDED: RACE AND THE
O. J. SIMPSON CASE

Orenthal James Simpson, flanked by defense attorneys F. Lee Bailey and Johnnie Cochran (right) exults in triumph as the jury announces the verdict of "not guilty" at the conclusion of his trial for double homicide on October 3, 1995. The Simpson jury, sequestered for almost a full year during the nationally televised trial, spent less than two hours discussing the mountain of evidence assembled in the case. The jury in the subsequent, and much shorter, civil trial deliberated for 13 hours before issuing three judgments against Simpson totalling $33.5 million. Courtesy Associated Press Wide World Photos

IV A HOUSE DIVIDED: RACE AND THE O. J. SIMPSON CASE

A cool night breeze filtered through the suburban streets of Los Angeles, but the killer's rage was white-hot.

When she opened the door he grabbed her and pulled her out onto the cobblestone walkway. He battered her forehead with his fist and then plunged the single-edged knife into her neck. The blond woman screamed, as nothing so terrified her as the specter, now a deadly reality, of a killer wielding a stainless steel knife.

Suddenly another man walked into the scene, blurting "Hey! Hey . . . Hey!!" Before the onlooker could react, the large man, in a homicidal rage, was upon him. He drove the younger man into an iron fence, cornering him, and delivered a series of deadly knife thrusts to his thigh, torso, and neck. Muscular and fit, the young man fought briefly, twisting his body, deflecting what blows he could with his bare hands, slapping out at his assailant, but in reality it was over before he could even comprehend the astonishing fact of his own murder. The killer severed the younger man's jugular vein, lifted him by his shirt, and plunged a final thrust deep into his body.

The killer turned back to the blond woman, now lying facedown at the foot of the stairs. Her blood was already cascading down the cobblestone walk.

He grabbed her by the hair, lifted her up toward his waist, his boot on the small of her back, and pulled the knife across her throat. In this final act of rage, he cut deep, to the vertebra, ensuring that she would never cause him pain or humiliation again.

He jogged back to his car, oblivious to his finger dripping blood from a gouge he received in the brief struggle with the younger man. The killer jumped into his vehicle and sped away from the scene of one of the most sensational murders in American history.

About 10:15 P.M. on Sunday, June 12, 1994, the continual barking of a dog disturbed Pablo Fenjves, a writer who lived behind Nicole Brown Simpson's house at 875 South Bundy Drive in L. A.'s elite Brentwood section. The dog, Fenjves later testified, gave a long "plaintive wail" and sounded like "a very unhappy animal."

About an hour and a half later, a Turkish immigrant named Sukru Boztepe and his wife, Bettina Rasmussen, took a stray Akita into their apartment before deciding to take the agitated dog out again in search of its home. Out on Bundy, a busy north-south artery in the heart of suburban Brentwood, the dog pulled harder as they neared the address marked 875. The big dog tugged them around the corner by a black iron gate.

Looking into the small yard, the horrified couple saw Nicole Brown Simpson's corpse lying in an immense pool of blood. They ran next door to bang on the door of the neighboring home, whose occupant promptly dialed 911.

Shortly after midnight, Officer Robert Riske of the Los Angeles Police Department (LAPD) arrived at the scene and found not only the dead woman, but the young man with his head virtually covered by his shirt. He was also clearly dead, up against a tree by the fence separating the Bundy residence from the condominium next door. He had lost a shoe in the struggle. His eyes were open.

On the ground at the crime scene Riske observed a black hat, a brown leather glove, and a white bloodstained envelope.

Opening the door to Nicole's house, his gun drawn, Riske went in and found candles still burning, upstairs and down. A bath, by now as cold as the bodies outside, had been drawn. In odd juxtaposition to the terrifying scene below, two children, a boy and a girl, slept peacefully in separate bedrooms inside. Riske noted bloody footprints down a pathway and out to the back alley.

The LAPD soon descended on the scene of what promised to be a sensational murder in the heart of a posh L. A. suburb. When they learned the identity of the female victim, the former wife of the famous actor and football star, Orenthal James ("O. J.") Simpson, everyone knew it would be a cause célèbre of epic proportions. The nineties was a decade that reveled in glitz, sleaze, and tabloid journalism, all of which the Simpson case would feature in abundance.

By the time Detective Mark Fuhrman, on call that night at the West L. A. detective-homicide unit, pulled up at 875 South Bundy, he was at least the

fifteenth cop to arrive at the scene. The case, however, would be handled by **199**
detectives Philip Vannatter, a grizzled twenty-six-year LAPD veteran, and his
partner, a younger, balding man, Tom Lange, both of whom made their way to
the Bundy crime scene.

As the detectives discussed the situation, Vannatter and Lange decided that
the next step would be to go personally to inform O. J. Simpson of his ex-wife's
death. Fuhrman—whom neither Vannatter nor Lange had ever met before, the
LAPD being a huge force, more like an army—volunteered that he knew where
Simpson lived. Fuhrman explained that he had been there years before on a
domestic violence call, and that the house on Rockingham Drive was only a few
miles away.

With Fuhrman leading the way, the cops arrived at Simpson's estate at 360
North Rockingham, where they immediately noticed a single car, a white Ford
Bronco, parked somewhat askew, as if hurriedly, outside the gates. Inside the
compound, two other cars were parked in the driveway. The detectives rang the
bell outside the gate, but received no answer. Lights burned inside the home. A
telephone call got a response only from the answering machine.

The cops later testified that they did not at that time consider Simpson a suspect. These statements could not have been true, as it is a venerable axiom of
police work that when a woman dies the first suspect to be considered is her
husband or another significant man in her life. Studies have shown that as
many as a third of female homicide victims are killed by their husband or
boyfriend. Moreover, since Fuhrman knew about the history of domestic violence in the Simpson home, he would have been a fool not to consider Simpson
a suspect.

While the police undoubtedly speculated that Simpson might have murdered his ex-wife, they also considered the possibility that he or someone else
might have been a target for violence and could be lying dead or injured inside.
At this point Fuhrman, who relished nothing more than being at the forefront
of a big case, observed blood on the Bronco—a few spots just above and below
the driver's side door handle. After conferring, the detectives put in a call for an
LAPD criminalist and decided to enter the Simpson estate. That decision
became a critical element in the Simpson case. If the police considered Simpson
a suspect, they were required to obtain a search warrant before entering the
premises. The cops justified their decision to enter the grounds by insisting that

Simpson was not a suspect and that their primary concern was the possibility, given the crime scene they had witnessed, that there might be other victims inside the Rockingham gates.

Fuhrman, the youngest and, as a regular participant in pick-up basketball games, the most fit, offered to go over the six-foot-high brick wall. After doing so, he opened the gate for Lange, Vannatter, and Detective Ron Phillips. Looking into guest houses at the back of the estate, Phillips saw someone sleeping inside the first of three bungalows.

A groggy man with tousled long blond hair opened the door. The police entered the room and asked the man if he knew whether O. J. was at home. Kato Kaelin, soon to be labeled by one wag as "the world's most famous house guest," said he did not know. While looking at the soles of shoes in the closet for signs of blood, Fuhrman asked Kato if anything unusual had happened during the night. Kato said yes, that at about 10:45 P.M. he had heard a loud thump outside his room wall, on the other side of the window unit air conditioner. He remembered because he had experienced the natural Californian initial reaction to a shaking wall—fear of an earthquake.

While the other cops stayed with Kato, Fuhrman went out to the back to try to ascertain the location of the wall behind the air conditioner. He found a long dark path covered by leaves and went down it. After covering twenty feet or so, he saw a dark leather glove on the ground. Fuhrman later testified that it appeared sticky and "looked similar to the glove at the Bundy scene." He walked on, encountering cobwebs which he hadn't felt before, and decided to back his way out, still not touching the glove on the ground.

Meanwhile, at Kato's suggestion, the detectives had awakened O. J.'s daughter by his first marriage, Arnelle Simpson, who soon let them into the main house. Finding that Simpson was not home, the police next conferred by phone with the celebrity's personal secretary, who informed them that he had flown to Chicago that evening for a golf tournament sponsored by Hertz Rent-A-Car, which had long employed Simpson as the "superstar of rent-a-car" in a series of well-known television commercials.

Detective Phillips telephoned Simpson in his Chicago hotel room and informed him of his ex-wife's death. "Oh my God, Nicole is killed?" Simpson responded. Phillips assured Simpson that his two young children who had been sleeping upstairs at Bundy had been taken safely from the crime scene. They had seen none of the carnage and no one had yet explained to them why they had been removed from their home in the middle of the night. Simpson declared that he would catch the next available flight to L. A. As Phillips hung up, he realized that Simpson had not asked how or even when his wife had been killed.

As dawn came to Rockingham, Vannatter observed blood drops inside and on the exterior of the locked Bronco. The blood drops led to the iron gate, then to the front door, and inside to the foyer. As in the Sheppard case, the killer's blood trail would be critical to the murder investigation. In fact in the Simpson case there were two blood trails, at Rockingham and at Bundy, and the detectives immediately took note of their similarity.

LAPD criminalist Dennis Fung arrived at the scene at 7:10 A.M. and performed a preliminary test which strongly suggested that the spots the detectives had discovered on the outside of the Bronco were indeed blood. Vannatter now had sufficient cause to obtain a search warrant, but he thought to check first with an assistant prosecutor with whom he had recently worked on a case. Her name was Marcia Clark. Astonishingly, Clark, an avid reader of true crime cases, but who rarely watched television, and obviously was not a sports fan, told Vannatter she had "never heard of" O. J. Simpson.

By the time Simpson arrived back at his home, shortly after noon, he was clearly the number one suspect in the murder case. The police assumed that this was a fairly typical case in which a husband, or ex-husband, consumed with rage, had murdered his former spouse. Acting on Vannatter's orders, police handcuffed O. J. , but soon freed him after Simpson's attorney, Howard Weitzman, assured them that his client had no intention of fleeing and planned to cooperate in the investigation. By that time, however, photographers and cameramen had captured pictures of Simpson in handcuffs. The media frenzy had begun. Word quickly spread across the country that O. J. Simpson had been arrested as the suspect in the murder of his ex-wife.

Noting the bandage on Simpson's left hand, Vannatter asked O. J. if he would agree to come to the police station to make a statement. After conferring with Weitzman, who accompanied Simpson to LAPD headquarters, Simpson agreed to a tape-recorded interview with Lange and Vannatter.

In marked contrast with the third degree treatment of Lizzie Borden, Bruno Richard Hauptmann, and Sam Sheppard, the LAPD treated Simpson with deference befitting his status as a Hollywood celebrity. Nonetheless, the 32-minute police interview produced devastating evidence against Simpson. The former football star offered contradictory explanations as to the cut on his finger, at first stating that he cut it at home while rushing to get ready to fly to Chicago the evening before. Moments later Simpson said he suffered the cut in Chicago, on broken glass in his hotel room, when he received the news of Nicole's death.

Simpson had no alibi for his whereabouts from 9:35 to 10:55 P.M. when a limousine driver had picked him up for the trip to the airport. During the same time period when the murders had taken place, Simpson admitted to dripping blood around his home, driveway, and car and yet couldn't recall how he had cut himself.

Simpson's police interview, characterized by halting and contradictory statements, served to confirm police suspicions that he had killed his wife. Simpson denied doing so, or knowing anything about her death, yet he displayed no sign of outrage over being falsely accused, nor did he evidence a desire to get on with the business of finding the real murderer.

Despite the consensus that there was probable cause to arrest Simpson and charge him with murder, the LAPD and the L. A. District Attorney's office decided to wait a few days to marshal evidence, including the results of blood tests. On the advice of Robert Kardashian, an attorney but also one of O. J.'s closest friends, Simpson dropped Howard Weitzman in favor of another highly respected L. A. attorney, Robert Shapiro.

Shapiro negotiated with the DA's office to ensure that Simpson would be allowed to attend his ex-wife's funeral, which he did together with his children on June 16. At Shapiro's request, Simpson privately underwent a lie detector test, which he failed completely. A psychiatric evaluation revealed that Simpson might be approaching an emotional breaking point.

Shapiro repeatedly assured the DA's office that he would deliver Simpson to them the moment they chose to arrest his client and charge him with murder. Simpson, meanwhile, secretly holed up at Kardashian's home, where he could avoid the press while keeping company with a few close friends, including his girlfriend, model and aspiring actress Paula Barbieri.

At 8:30 A.M. on Friday, June 17, Lange called Shapiro and asked him to bring in Simpson on a warrant alleging double homicide with special circumstances, a charge which meant under California law that the death penalty had not been

ruled out and that there would be no bail for O. J. until his case had been concluded. Unlike Bruno Richard Hauptmann or Sam Sheppard, the celebrity
defendant would not be hauled into custody under the glare of the media spotlight—or so it appeared at the time—but rather would be allowed to come in
quietly under his own volition.

After being informed of his imminent arrest, however, Simpson weighed his
options, which apparently ranged from suicide to flight. O. J. decided to do
what he had done best in life: run. When the attorneys discovered that Simpson
had fled, and left what sounded like a suicide note, they called a press conference at which Kardashian read Simpson's letter to the astonished throng of
media.

In the note Simpson denied killing his ex-wife, lamely offering that just
being a suspect had destroyed his life. "I can't go on, no matter what the outcome people will look and point. I can't take that." Simpson insisted he had
been "totally loving and understanding" of Nicole and it was he who had
suffered in their relationship to the point that he "felt like a battered husband."
Simpson added that he was "sorry" for the family of Ronald Goldman, the
young man slain along with Nicole Brown Simpson. Simpson went on to thank
his closest friends. "Don't feel sorry for me," Simpson concluded. "I've had a
great life. . . . Please think of the real O. J. and not this lost person. . . . Peace +
Love O. J."

Soon after the press conference ended, just after 6 P.M., police spotted Simpson's 1993 Ford Bronco heading north on a Los Angeles freeway. One of the
most bizarre chase scenes ever—in a city that had practically invented the chase
scene—began to unfold. At the wheel, Simpson's close friend and former football teammate A. C. Cowlings turned on his emergency flashers. At one point,
when police drew their guns and began to approach the Bronco as it rested at a
traffic signal, Cowlings quickly called 911 to explain that O. J. was "still alive" but
"has a gun to his head." Cowlings succeeded in convincing the police to back
off.

As television helicopters got in on the act, all three national networks broke
into regular programming to cover the surreal scene. Crowds gathered at the
roadside and on bridges along the Bronco's route. Before it was over, more than
an hour later, the spectacle of the slow-moving white Bronco followed by a phalanx of LAPD black and whites would be the most watched television event of

the year. A crowd comprised mostly of sympathetic African Americans gathered at Simpson's driveway at Rockingham to shout "Free the Juice."

After Cowlings pulled into the Rockingham driveway just before 8 P.M., Simpson sat in the car for almost another hour before finally agreeing to get out and submit to arrest. Even after his flight from justice, the police allowed Simpson to visit the restroom, drink a glass of juice, and place a call to his mother before they took him in.

Cowlings, arrested along with Simpson, had in his possession almost $9,000, his passport, a loaded pistol (given to him by one of many friends on the LAPD), a fake mustache, and a goatee. These items suggested that rather than committing suicide Simpson had decided to become a fugitive.

After spending the weekend in jail, Simpson was arraigned on Monday, June 20. Appearing depressed, he muttered an unenthusiastic "not guilty" plea.

Despite Simpson's morose appearance, the L.A. District Attorney's office realized that the accused man remained a popular public figure. Sports fans knew him as the winner of the prestigious Heisman Trophy as a college running back at the University of Southern California. After starring in the 1969 Rose Bowl, Simpson was the number one pick by the Buffalo Bills in the National Football League draft. In 1973 he became the first running back ever to amass more than 2,000 yards rushing in a single season.

After a sterling career, Simpson employed his good looks, sculpted build, and an ever smiling public image to amass a fortune in endorsements, most notably in his commercials for Hertz. He had carried the Olympic torch in the 1984 Los Angeles summer games and established himself as a popular broadcaster of sporting events for two major networks. A brilliant businessman and self-promoter, Simpson was worth an estimated $11 million a year before the murders.

Simpson seemed to have put behind him a difficult childhood in which he had grown up in a rough neighborhood, the Potrero Hill section of San Francisco, where he had been a juvenile delinquent, engaging regularly in shoplifting, fights, and other criminal activity. Even then Simpson had risen to the top—as a gang leader. "I was Al Capone—I was the boss," he boasted years later.

Now known to the public simply as "O. J.," the use of initials conjuring up an image of affection, Simpson appeared regularly in movies, including the series of comedic Naked Gun spoofs. Simpson relished his role as a brain-dead police officer in the Naked Gun movies. In reality, he looked down on the police, whom he had manipulated many times in real life.

As they began to build their case, the L.A. prosecutors realized that Simpson was a celebrity whose popular public persona could be a serious obstacle in what promised to be a sensational murder case. In any celebrity case in modern jurisprudence, public perceptions would play fully as significant a role as the actual evidence in the case. To combat Simpson's appeal, Gil Garcetti, the elected district attorney of Los Angeles County, and prosecutor Marcia Clark began to offer statements and leak information to condition the public to see the other side of O. J. Simpson—a chronic wife beater who had finally resorted to murder. As in the case of Sam Sheppard, public officials depicted Simpson as a Jekyll and Hyde personality to explain to the public how an otherwise respected citizen could have been the perpetrator of a heinous crime.

The prosecution's actions marked the opening salvo in what would become an ongoing battle to "spin" public perceptions in the sensational mediated trial. One of the tactics employed by the DA's office was to release to the public a 1989 tape of a 911 call made by a terrified Nicole Brown Simpson during an incident of spousal abuse. The incident, occurring at 4 A.M. on New Year's Day, transpired at the Simpson home on North Rockingham. Simpson, who had divorced his first wife, Marguerite, with whom he had two children, Jason and Arnelle, had lived at the estate since 1977. That same year, he began dating Nicole, who was eighteen years old at the time. She moved into the Rockingham home in 1979. In 1985, with Nicole pregnant with Sydney, the first of the couple's two children, she and O. J. Simpson were married.

On the 911 tape, the sounds of screams and slaps could be heard. After arriving at the scene, police were being told by a housekeeper that there was no problem at the home, whereupon a blond woman wearing only a bra and sweatpants emerged from behind some bushes, screaming "He's going to kill me! He's going to kill me!"

Nicole flung open the gate and cowered into the arms of the police. Her face was cut and an eye had been blackened. She told the cops that O. J. had hit and slapped her and pulled her hair. Simpson then emerged in a bathrobe screaming that he no longer wanted Nicole in his bed. He denied beating her, stating that he merely had pushed her out of bed.

Simpson reacted with astonishment when the L.A. cops informed him that they would have to arrest him as a result of the incident of domestic violence. After all, he explained, they had been to the estate for the same reason many times before—including the call to which Mark Fuhrman had responded in 1985, an incident in which an enraged Simpson had smashed the windshield of his own Mercedes—and had never put him under arrest before.

"You've been out here eight times before and now you're going to arrest me for this?" the outraged Simpson declared. He insisted that he had done nothing wrong and that the incident was "a family matter." Not buying it, the cops asked Simpson to go back inside and change in preparation for a trip to the police station. Instead, Simpson hopped in his Bentley and fled the scene, successfully evading four police cars.

Nicole attempted to drop the matter the next day but, after looking into the history of abuse, prosecutors were determined to pursue the case. With attorney Weitzman acting in his defense, Simpson reluctantly pleaded no contest in return for a probated sentence and community service. Simpson then skirted the community service provision by arranging for a fund-raiser to be organized rather than actually doing anything himself. He also avoided counseling sessions that were typically required in spouse abuse cases.

As a result of his wealth and fame, Simpson had evaded punishment for his abusive behavior. Such incidents encouraged his contempt for the police and the criminal justice system. Ironically, in view of later charges of a police conspiracy against Simpson, the truth was that the LAPD and local prosecutors had treated the celebrity with kid gloves. Rather than rushing to judgment against Simpson, the police had allowed him to violate the law with impunity.

Simpson's and Nicole's relationship continued to sour before ending in divorce in October 1992. Under terms of the settlement, she received $10,000 a month in child support for Sydney and their younger child, Justin. Nicole purchased the condo on South Bundy, but continued to list Rockingham as her official address for tax purposes.

On the eve of the murder, the relationship deteriorated further over financial disputes and O. J.'s feeling that Nicole was trying to minimize his access to the children, although he enjoyed regular visitation. In the days before the murder, Simpson threatened Nicole, using the terms "bitch" and "cunt" repeatedly. He became even more enraged when she hung up on his telephone calls. On

June 7 Nicole informed a Santa Monica battered women's shelter that Simpson was stalking her.

As the prosecution began to present this evidence to a grand jury, Simpson's defense team objected. By this time Shapiro, who had never tried a murder case before, was soliciting the help of some of the top defense attorneys in the country. These included F. Lee Bailey, the hero of the second Sam Sheppard trial, and Alan Dershowitz, a Harvard law professor who was particularly well known for his defense of such wealthy celebrities as Klaus von Bulow and Mike Tyson. Gerald Uelman, dean of the College of Law at Santa Clara University, also joined the defense team.

These men understood that the outcome of a trial could often be determined by the legal maneuvering that occurred before the courtroom proceedings actually took place. They promptly seized the initiative, which they would not relinquish throughout the long ordeal of the Simpson criminal case. Documenting Garcetti's myriad press conferences and the prosecution's systematic leaks of the 1989 911 tape and other evidence, the defense argued that the grand jury proceeding had been prejudiced by the publicity and that a preliminary hearing should be held instead.

To their surprise, Superior Court Judge Cecil Mills agreed, issuing a decision on June 24 that the grand jury case be disbanded in favor of a preliminary hearing. The defense then pressed for a hearing to be scheduled as soon as possible in hopes that the prosecution would have to present a hastily prepared case to which they would then be committed in the subsequent criminal trial.

Having seen his publicity campaign backfire, Garcetti committed a far more fatal mistake in his choice of the courtroom venue for the trial. Although it is normal practice to file a case in the district where a crime occurs, the Simpson case would not be heard in Santa Monica Superior Court, the normal venue for a murder in Brentwood.

Garcetti mistakenly believed that once the prosecution had begun to present a case before the grand jury, which met in the downtown L.A. Criminal Court Building, the criminal case had to be continued downtown. This was not true. Certainly the facilities as a whole, though not the courtroom itself, were superior in the downtown facility than in Santa Monica, where an earthquake had done some damage to the court building. But under normal circumstances the trial would have been held in Santa Monica. The celebrity of the Simpson case was having a profound effect well before the trial had even begun.

Months later it would become obvious that the problem with conducting L.A. County Superior Court Case BA#097211, *The People v. Orenthal James Simpson*, in downtown Los Angeles was that a predominantly African American jury would prove so suspicious of the official version of events as to overlook the evidence against Simpson. Garcetti and Clark, convinced that the evidence against Simpson was overwhelming, were not worried at the time that the outcome of the case might hinge on perceptions of race. They did not yet know that the defense would build its case around that very issue. To the extent that he considered race, Garcetti, the son of Mexican immigrants, believed that strengthened "perceptions of justice" would flow from a downtown trial that would be sure to attract a substantial black jury pool.

Racial perceptions could hardly be ignored in any case involving an African-American defendant and the LAPD. Like most American cities, Los Angeles had long reflected racial tensions, especially in incidents involving police violence against African Americans. The 1965 Watts riot, in which thirty-four people were killed and rioters and police did $35 million in property damage, began with an altercation between police and a black motorist charged with drunk driving.

Strained relations endured between blacks and the LAPD, a gigantic and quasi-military force headed by a series of police chiefs who, if not outright racists, were at best insensitive to injustices against the African-American community. Race relations between the police force and African Americans hit an all-time low in the early eighties when, in an effort to combat a crime wave fueled by drug trafficking and gang warfare, the LAPD went on a collective rampage against the black community. The police victimized hundreds of innocent people through illegal raids, beatings, and frame-ups. Some of the cops carried out their mission in cruel and sadistic fashion, yet few were brought to justice for their crimes.

Excessive force by the police, notorious within the African-American community itself, usually escaped the attention of an oblivious, predominantly white public. On March 3, 1991, however, when a citizen with a video camera taped police administering a brutal beating to a black suspect, Rodney King, the issue of police brutality and racism became a prominent national story. On

April 30, 1992, violent riots once again erupted in Los Angeles when a predominantly white jury in Simi Valley, where the case had been tried, acquitted the white police officers of brutality charges in the King incident.

A distinguished commission, headed by Warren Christopher, who would become President Bill Clinton's first secretary of state, investigated in the wake of the widespread rioting in south L.A. The Christopher Commission called national attention to what all African Americans in Los Angeles already knew: that the LAPD frequently employed "excessive force" against blacks and that "racism and bias" were rife among its rank and file. The King incident, shocking in its brutality, was atypical only because it had been captured on videotape. Such incidents of white-on-black police brutality were routine in Los Angeles. The LAPD, virtually an army unto itself, had never previously been brought to account by the mayor, city hall, or public opinion.

The subsequent outcome of the Simpson case stemmed directly from the profound mistrust on the part of the black community of not only police but the entire criminal justice system in Los Angeles and in the United States itself. While the Simpson *crime* had no apparent connection with race, the Simpson *case* would be decided in a community and nation driven by racial tensions. Once again, cultural dynamics would overwhelm a celebrated criminal proceeding.

Many African Americans, in Los Angeles and nationwide, immediately rallied around Simpson, who was after all a black icon. The *Sentinel*, the African-American newspaper of L.A., decried the handcuffing of Simpson after his return from Chicago as an example of the LAPD's desire to seize upon a black suspect. The charge of a "rush to judgment" would become the theme of Simpson's criminal defense team.

The African-American community in L.A. knew that other black sports stars, including Hall of Fame baseball player Joe Morgan and Olympic track star Al Joyner, had been wrongfully detained by the LAPD in past incidents solely on the basis of their race. Across the country countless African Americans had been similarly victimized because racism among the ranks of predominantly white police forces was not just an issue in Los Angeles, but a pervasive national problem. Hundreds of thousands of black men across the country had been pulled over on roads and highways by police, not for DWI (driving while intoxicated) but DWB—driving while black.

While most whites remained indifferent to such discrimination, African Americans were being targeted for crimes and incarcerated at alarming rates. Particularly in the wake of efforts to crack down on drug offenders in the late eighties, the U.S. prison population soared from 900,000 in 1987 to 1.4 million inmates in 1994. Almost half of the prisoners were black men. African Americans routinely received harsher sentences than whites, with an especially noteworthy disparity between blacks convicted for possessing crack cocaine while white offenders received more moderate sentences from the predominantly white justice system for powdered cocaine offenses.

Nothing better symbolized white phobias of blacks as criminal predators than the infamous 1988 campaign commercial launched by Republican candidate George Bush against Massachusetts Democrat Michael Dukakis. The national television ad focused on the case of Willie Horton, a convicted black rapist who had been paroled during Dukakis's term as governor only to perpetrate violent crimes again. The political ad angered blacks and white liberals, but seared into the national consciousness the perception of blacks as violent offenders who should be caged.

Despite widespread condemnation of the Willie Horton incident, *Time* magazine proved equally insensitive in the wake of the Simpson murders when it placed a surreal darkened mug shot of O. J. on its June 18 cover. The darkened image invoked stereotypical nineteenth-century depictions of African Americans as violent and unpredictable, animalistic. The cover outraged African Americans, and millions of others, across the nation.

By the time the preliminary hearing began on June 30, the Simpson case had become inextricably linked with one of the most explosive issues in American history—race relations. The defense attorneys were not about to let pass the only opportunity they had to deflect attention away from the realities of the crime itself. The defense team determined to take an aggressive approach. It would concede nothing, fighting virtually every motion, no matter how routine. At worst this strategy would drag out the proceedings and deflect attention away from the core realities of the crime. Unable to refute the evidence against Simpson, the defense would try to show that the evidence was tainted or had been manufactured by a racist LAPD that sought to destroy O. J. Simpson, presumably because he was a wealthy black celebrity.

With the issues of sex, race, and murder at the forefront, unprecedented media attention enveloped the Simpson case. Like its predecessors, this latest trial of the century would be conducted in a carnival atmosphere.

By the 1990s tabloid journalism influenced print media and dominated television coverage. Crime had become a big story in local and national news. Local television stations across the country featured "action cam" reports from crime scenes on the nightly news. Broad public access to video cameras had given rise not only to incidents such as the Rodney King beating, but "reality TV" shows such as *COPS, America's Most Wanted,* and *Hard Copy.*

Already in the 1990s Americans had been mesmerized by a series of sensational celebrity crime cases, some which had been broadcast live on national television. These included the William Kennedy Smith rape case in Florida and the Menendez brothers murder trial of two teenagers accused of killing their parents in Los Angeles. Sensational criminal cases involving prominent blacks—heavyweight boxer Mike Tyson for rape and pop icon Michael Jackson on charges of child abuse—preceded the Simpson case.

Fueled by the national obsession with crime, celebrity, and race, the Simpson case would morph into a compelling daily national soap opera. Networks such as CNN and Court TV, boasting millions of subscribers, would provide blanket "gavel-to-gavel" coverage. The burgeoning Internet would proliferate with Simpson case chat lines and a variety of Web sites.

The Simpson case, in short, became a national obsession.

Crucial to the unprecedented public access to the Simpson trial was the presence of cameras in the courtroom. After the Warren Court had barred cameras from legal proceedings in the 1965 *Estes* decision, a new Supreme Court ruling in 1981 in effect reversed the decision by leaving the matter to the discretion of individual states. Under California law, cameras could be allowed into the courtroom, thus enabling blanket coverage of the Simpson case.

With cameras rolling as the preliminary hearing unfolded on June 30, Judge Kathleen Kennedy-Powell received a normally routine prosecution request that hair samples be taken from Simpson's head for matching with those found on the knit cap left at the crime scene as well as other evidence. The defense vigorously opposed the motion, giving new meaning to the cliché about splitting hairs. The focus of the long debate was just how many hairs would be taken from Simpson's head. The defense strategy of relentless challenge was under way.

Uelman began to argue the "rush to judgment" defense by charging that the police conduct revealed a presumption of Simpson's guilt. The defense attorney called into question the decision to go over the wall at Simpson's estate. Vannatter, Lange, and Fuhrman played into the strategy by denying that they considered Simpson a suspect. Vannatter went so far as to make the absurd comment to Shapiro that the cops had no more suspected O. J. of the murder than Shapiro himself! Had Simpson been considered a suspect, the police would have needed a search warrant to enter the premises. By stating that they had not considered Simpson as a suspect, the police were trying to ensure that the evidence they had uncovered could be entered into the record, but their actions instead had the effect of undermining the prosecution's case. Once again, as in the previous cases analyzed in this book, police errors played a key role in skewing the outcome of a prominent murder case.

By lying after having sworn to tell the truth, the police enhanced the case for the defense, which intended to make the credibility of the LAPD, rather than the murders themselves, the focus of the trial. It was the first, but far from last, example of the police and prosecution laying the groundwork for their own defeat.

The cops insisted that they had gone over the wall out of concern that Simpson himself, or someone else, might have been victimized inside. This consideration was indeed legitimate, given the carnage they had just witnessed at Bundy. Nevertheless, the defense had demonstrated to the attentive public—especially the African-American community, including the downtown L. A. jury pool—that the LAPD would brazenly lie about having considered Simpson a suspect. If the police would lie, it might be logical to assume that they might manufacture evidence as well.

Uelman attacked the police explanation that blood had been seen on the Bronco. He called attention to the very small amounts of blood outside the vehicle and demanded that the police explain why they had not considered that the blood may have been from a "hangnail" or even juice from a "dripping taco."

The defense sought to throw out the evidence obtained in the police search of Simpson's estate and automobile. Vannatter nearly gave them cause by stating in his affidavit to obtain a search warrant that Simpson had gone out of town "unexpectedly." Actually, the flight to Chicago for the Hertz promotion had been long planned. Vannatter's false statement was yet another example of a police error, or lie, that the defense would exploit in an effort to construct a plausible theory of a conspiracy to frame O. J. Simpson.

In the preliminary hearing, however, Judge Kennedy-Powell rejected the defense motion and allowed admission of the evidence obtained from Simpson's estate and from the Bronco. Despite losing on this point, the defense had tapped into public suspicion of LAPD motives, especially strongly felt by African Americans. Moreover, the aggressive defense at the preliminary hearing prompted Marcia Clark to call many of the prosecution's main witnesses— Vannatter, Lange, Fuhrman, and Kato Kaelin, among them. Hence the prosecution's case was "locked in" and the defense could know exactly how to begin the process of destroying it.

Although Kennedy-Powell ruled on July 8 that sufficient evidence existed for Simpson to stand trial for murder, the defense had already reversed the momentum of the case. As a longtime professional athlete, Simpson himself was no stranger to shifts in team momentum. His friends and attorneys convinced O. J. that all was not lost, that he actually might be able to win the case. Arraigned once again in superior court, Simpson this time appeared dapper and upbeat. The ebullient personality that had enabled him to achieve wealth and celebrity was back in force. Asked for his plea, the once morose defendant now declared that he was "absolutely, 100 percent not guilty." If the fan letters he received were an indication, tens of thousands of people believed him.

Although the defense had scored some victories in the preliminary hearing, much more work remained to be done if they actually hoped to win what the press promptly dubbed the "trial of the century." A coterie of Simpson's friends and advisers, while respecting what Robert Shapiro had done, still believed that what O. J. lacked was an experienced defense attorney who could sway a jury. Shapiro's reputation was that of a skillful plea-bargainer, but O. J. wanted no part of a deal. In football parlance, it was fourth and long but he intended to go for it. One possible candidate for star litigator, favored by Simpson himself, was Gerry Spence. The rawhide-wearing Westerner, successful in the defense of a white supremacist in Idaho, was hardly the right fit, however, in the defense of a black L.A. celebrity.

Ultimately the rather obvious choice was Johnnie L. Cochran Jr., the most prominent African-American defense attorney in Los Angeles. Cochran was not only a skilled defense attorney, but was well known to the potential jury pool of the downtown Los Angeles court. Cochran had the most visible African-American firm in L. A. and had provided opportunities to young black attorneys to work under him. Deeply respected in that community, Cochran had represented many African American clients, ranging from total unknowns to pop star Michael Jackson in the child molestation case.

Although Cochran did not invent the Simpson team's race-based defense, which had already begun to unfold under Shapiro, he alone could turn it into an art form. After a falling-out with Cochran, Shapiro himself later charged that not only would Cochran play the race card, but that he would do so "from the bottom of the deck." In fact Cochran had already spearheaded several successful defenses of African-American clients by seizing upon illegal activities and racism on the part of the LAPD. He knew precisely how to win such cases with predominantly black juries and had done so again and again, making millions of dollars in the process.

Johnnie Cochran, rather than the soon-to-be infamous Aris Isotoner glove, was the perfect fit in the Simpson case.

As true believers in the American adversarial justice system, neither Cochran—nor Dershowitz, Bailey, or Uelman—would be impeded by the guilt or innocence of their client. The American justice system operates on the premise that it is the obligation of the prosecution to demonstrate guilt and that the accused, no matter what crime he may have committed, deserves a vigorous defense. They would offer the most aggressive defense possible and make the state prove its case against Simpson.

On July 18, Simpson himself formally invited Cochran, a longtime acquaintance, to join the defense team. The two had much in common. Both were transplanted Bay area Californians who had risen from humble beginnings to use their considerable talents to achieve wealth and success amid the glitz of L.A. The two men liked and respected one another. Cochran's confidence furthered the process of bucking up O. J. for the long haul.

In addition to Cochran, two more high-profile attorneys completed the composition of the defense team. Barry Scheck and Peter Neufeld, experts on the use of DNA blood evidence, were hard at work in what would become a successful effort to convince the jury that the incriminating blood evidence against Simpson was somehow tainted.

Securing the services of the two New York attorneys was a brilliant stroke. Bright, aggressive, and morally flexible, Scheck and Neufeld had been the first attorneys to challenge the results of DNA evidence in a 1989 murder case by attacking the handling and testing of blood evidence in the laboratory. By the time of the Simpson trial, Scheck and Neufeld had built a national reputation in legal circles for their expertise on DNA evidence, which they had also used to free wrongly convicted defendants.

Defense attorneys never tire of arguing that the prosecution enjoys distinct advantages that accrue from having the power of the state, including the police, and its vast resources behind them. While this is true in most cases, it is not true in a high profile trial featuring a wealthy defendant. No rational observer can dispute that wealth plays a role—often a decisive role—in the administration of American justice. Wealthy clients can retain powerful legal talent and employ their own vast array of investigators and expert witnesses. The rich enjoy extraordinary opportunities to defend themselves which the middle class and certainly the poor do not. While possession of wealth can help to even the playing field for the accused, this is not always true, as demonstrated in the Sheppard case in which a uniquely hostile environment in Cleveland doomed even a well-heeled defendant.

The media dubbed Simpson's coterie of attorneys the "Dream Team," an appellation in which they delighted and which could only help the defense cause. Great teams—like the original Dream Team of NBA basketball players who won the Gold Medal at the 1988 Olympics—are expected to win. The same media representatives who had once peppered Gil Garcetti with hostile questions about the DA's initial kid-glove treatment of the celebrity suspect now depicted the defense attorneys in glowing terms. As in the three previous cases analyzed in this book, media coverage, which had now become more favorable to the defense, would play a critical role in the evolution of the murder trial.

The momentum in the Simpson case had turned sharply in favor of the defense before the trial even began. The prosecution found many of its initial advantages negated and compounded its plight with a series of questionable decisions. Early on Garcetti announced that the state would not pursue the death penalty against O. J. Simpson. This decision probably represented good public relations, but it hurt the prosecution in jury selection, to which matters now turned. Statistical studies have shown that jurors who do not oppose the death penalty are also those more likely to convict.

The lawyers for both sides knew that jury selection in a criminal trial is often more important than the evidence itself. After the preliminary hearing, both sides spent the balance of the summer consulting experts and testing focus groups and mock juries. Both the prosecution and the defense hired nationally known consultants on jury selection, which they knew could make or break their case. The highly sophisticated analysis of potential jurors produced essentially the same result in both camps. It was readily apparent that race would play a role in jurors' perceptions and that African Americans were inclined to be far more sympathetic than whites to Simpson. The most sympathetic group was African-American females.

The defense took this information and used the jury selection process to seek as many African American, and particularly African American female, jurors as possible. The prosecution, however, now dominated by Marcia Clark, chose to ignore the expert consultants' warning that African-American women would prove hostile to the prosecution. Moreover, Clark refused to credit the experts' conclusion, based on questionnaires and analysis of mock jurors, that black women did not like Marcia Clark herself.

Again and again the data showed that African-American women were turned off by Clark's assertive style and her aggressive, rapid-fire pattern of speech. However unfairly, many of them perceived that the thin, dark-haired attorney was embarked on a vendetta against a hero of the African-American community. Asked to select one word to describe Clark, several of the black women chose "bitch." These women, many of whom perceived themselves as occupying a traditional role as mother-protectors of African-American men, would be inclined to doubt the prosecution's case as a result of their dislike and distrust of the lead prosecutor herself.

To the extent (not very great) that Clark believed any of the consultants' evidence, she concluded that she would be able to overcome their suspicions. In her defense, Clark quite rightly understood that the physical evidence against Simpson was overwhelming and she believed that the truth inevitably would win out over the jurors' prejudices and sympathies. Clark naively believed also that she could appeal to black women jurors as a woman, calling attention to the victimization, through years of spousal abuse and ultimately murder, of a female victim. Here she ignored the consultant's evidence that most of the African-American women were not sharply prejudiced against Simpson as a result of the domestic violence evidence. Many adopted the attitude that such "trouble" in a marriage was not that unusual and did not necessarily lead to murder. When the time came to select the Simpson jury, Clark had rejected most of the consultant's recommendations in deference to her own instincts. As a result, the defense won a crucial victory in the jury selection.

On September 26, 1994, the first day of jury selection, Los Angeles Superior Court Judge Lance Ito, who had been assigned the case, told prospective jurors that the trial might last through February. In fact, because of a torturously slow pace sanctioned by Ito himself, it was to last an entire year.

Within three days, as both sides excused potential jurors from service, the original pool of more than 900 had been whittled down to 304. But the remainder of the jury selection process would take more than two months. Prospective jurors completed lengthy questionnaires and submitted to the lawyers' questioning.

During this process, scores of white males, whom the consultants' analyses showed were those most likely to convict, were summarily dismissed by the defense. While the defense blatantly screened out as many prospective white jurors as possible, Cochran showed himself to be a master spin doctor by charging publicly that it was the prosecution that was pursuing a racial agenda by screening out blacks. In reality, both sides were fully aware of the racial divide, but only the Dream Team placed race at the forefront of its courtroom strategy.

Finally, on December 8, a jury of twelve, with an additional twelve alternates, ten of whom would in fact serve, was selected. The jurors were far more African American and more female in composition than the jury pool as a whole. Of the twenty-four selected, fifteen were African American, including eight women. By comparison, Los Angeles County as a whole was eleven percent black.

Only two of the jurors were college graduates. Most relied on television, and often tabloid television, for their news and information rather than reading newspapers and news magazines. Some believed that use of force was acceptable within the family. Many had acknowledged negative perceptions of the LAPD and thought that O. J. Simpson was less likely to be guilty because he was a sports hero. No wonder Johnnie Cochran later wrote that the day of final jury selection marked one of his great triumphs in the case.

Although Marcia Clark had failed to recognize it at the time, she had already gone a long way toward losing the case. The actual Simpson jury would behave very much like the expert jury consultants who Gil Garcetti had hired—but whom Clark had chosen to disregard—had said that they would.

Another move backfired when the prosecution requested that the jurors be sequestered to avoid the saturation of media coverage. On January 11, 1995, Ito ordered the jury sequestered in L.A.'s Inter-Continental Hotel. The jurors were thus forced to live in a world apart from their communities and families, with the exception of weekly conjugal visits. For their service they would receive a pathetic five dollars a day. Sequestration was certainly logical in view of the heavy media coverage of the Simpson case. The problem, however, would arise with the inordinant length of the criminal trial. No one at the time appreciated just how interminable the Simpson trial would become and the dramatic impact the ordeal would have on the jurors.

Despite having lost the battle over jury selection, the prosecution entered the case with a high degree of confidence. They believed that the rock-hard evidence of Simpson's guilt ultimately had to prove decisive. The evidence, based largely on DNA tests, was alone enough to convict a defendant in a "normal" case. In fact, criminal defendants nationwide, when confronted with far less DNA evidence than arrayed against Simpson, routinely pleaded guilty and had their cases cleared from court dockets in a matter of minutes.

Since its spectacular introduction into forensic science in a 1987 murder case in England, DNA (deoxyribonucleic acid) had emerged as a powerful tool of criminal investigation. In the British case, DNA tests had exonerated a wrongfully accused man and provided the critical evidence that identified the real rapist and murderer of two young women. DNA testing was particularly effective in solving cases of rape and murder in which there were no witnesses, yet evidence remained in the form of blood or semen. When such evidence could be matched with an individual's unique genetic code, DNA had the potential to remove virtually all doubt from a criminal case.

In the Simpson case, the blood evidence at the Bundy crime scene, at O. J.'s Rockingham home, and in the Bronco, had left the defendant's genetic fingerprints all over the crime. Through testing the prosecution had secured a series of positive matches linking Simpson with the murder victims. The evidence demonstrated not merely that Simpson was guilty beyond a reasonable doubt—the American legal standard—but that in reality there was virtually no doubt at all.

DNA tests confirmed that the blood drops the killer had left while leaving the crime scene matched Simpson's type and excluded well more than 99 percent of the human race. For one drop in the Bundy driveway there was a one in 170 million chance that the blood belonged to someone other than Simpson. There was a one in fifty-seven billion chance that blood on the rear gate at Bundy belonged to someone other than Simpson. (More matches that are found within each sample of DNA multiply the probabilities.) DNA tests confirmed that the blood found inside and outside the Bronco matched Simpson's type and those of his victims. DNA tests confirmed that the glove found behind the cottage on Simpson's estate matched the mixture of the defendant's blood and that of his two victims. Socks found in Simpson's bedroom contained one spot that matched O. J.'s blood and another that matched Nicole's.

Understandably, the prosecution had to believe that this evidence alone proved Simpson's guilt beyond a shadow of doubt, much less a reasonable doubt. The defendant had motive: his rage against his ex-wife for whom he had bought everything, from a luxurious home and cars to enlarged breasts. In return, Simpson demanded absolute control of Nicole, including her submission to violent abuse. Her total rejection of her ex-husband in the days before the murder led to her murder. In addition to the motive and the conclusive physical evidence, Simpson also had opportunity: no one could account for his whereabouts at the time of the killings.

Perhaps the prosecution might not be faulted for believing that all it had to do was to present this overwhelming evidence to a jury—any jury—and it would have no choice but to convict.

The defense, of course, understood these realities all too well. Simply put, if the case went forward on its merits their client was a condemned man. The rather obvious strategy, then, was to do everything they could to take the case away from its merits and to provide an alternative issue—LAPD racism and planting of evidence—to seize center stage in the nationally televised courtroom drama.

The battle began after the completion of jury selection. Prior to the opening statements, however, the defense won an important victory when Judge Ito barred evidence of O. J.'s "confession" to former football great turned evangelist Rosy Grier. On November 13, 1994, as Grier visited Simpson in jail and urged him to confess his sins to God, Simpson blurted out, "I didn't mean to do it. I'm sorry!" A deputy heard the confession and was prepared to testify, but Ito ruled Simpson's statement to his spiritual adviser inadmissible.

The defense then turned to the heart of its case and won an even more important battle on the admissibility of evidence as to LAPD racism. As the defense's race-based strategy emerged, Clark summoned Christopher Darden, a close friend but, more importantly, an African American, to work with her on the case. The prosecution, while hardly a "dream team," now featured a tri-umvirate of Clark, veteran prosecutor William Hodgman, and the relatively inexperienced Darden. In an effort to trump the race card, Darden would serve to counterbalance Cochran's efforts to appeal to the predominantly black jury on the issue of race. Darden and Cochran clashed almost at once. Older and far more accomplished than Darden, Cochran ruthlessly depicted the young black prosecutor as little more than an Uncle Tom.

In arguments before Ito on January 13, the two black attorneys argued bitter-ly, with the jury dismissed, on the crucial issue as to whether race should be allowed to take center stage. At issue was the defense effort to ask LAPD detec-tive Mark Fuhrman whether he had ever used the term "nigger" to describe African Americans.

Darden argued that use of the word should be excluded because it would "inflame the passions of the jury." If Cochran were to be allowed "to play this race card," Darden contended, "the entire complexion of the case changes. It is a race case then. It is white versus black . . . us versus them, us versus the system."

The young prosecutor had clearly perceived the defense strategy, and its potential effectiveness, but Johnnie Cochran lashed back with venom. Simp-son's lead attorney charged that Darden's comments were offensive and that he wanted "to apologize to African Americans across this country" for Darden, whom he dismissed as an "apologist" for Fuhrman and the racist LAPD. Dard-en and the prosecution lost the battle when Ito ruled that Fuhrman could be asked whether he had used the word "nigger." Lacerated by Cochran's personal attack, Darden remained wounded, defensive, and often ineffective through the rest of the trial.

The clash over the word "nigger"—and Ito's dubious decision to allow it to be invoked—set the stage for race, rather than murder, to become the centerpiece of the Simpson murder trial. By the time the trial opened in L.A. Superior Court on January 2, the Dream Team's race-based defense was firmly in place.

The attorneys and the families—the Browns, the Goldmans, and the Simpsons—had to fight their way into the crammed courtroom through packs of reporters and cameramen. Representatives from CNN, Court TV, *Hard Copy, Current Affair, Larry King Live,* and *Geraldo* scrambled for seats in the courtroom. Trailers, network trucks, and scaffolding abounded outside the superior court building. As many as seven helicopters managed to avoid running into one another as they hovered in the skies above the mad scene outside the L.A. courthouse.

In a step that acknowledged the role that race had assumed in the case, the prosecution elected to have Darden speak first to the predominantly African-American jury. Establishing a rapport with the jurors, Darden referred to his own upbringing in the black community in Richmond, California, as he tried to convince the African-American majority that it would be their duty to convict brother Simpson.

Darden eloquently explained that there was another O. J. behind the smiling public persona, an angry man who had controlled, abused, and ultimately butchered his wife and an innocent man. "And the evidence will show," Darden concluded, "that the face you will see and the man that you will see will be the face of a batterer, a wife beater, an abuser, a controller . . . the face of Ron and Nicole's murderer."

After Darden sat down, Clark focused her opening argument on the hard evidence, explaining to the jury how the DNA results demonstrated Simpson's guilt. While the Brown and Goldman families wept, and Simpson averted his eyes and squirmed in his chair, Clark showed the jury the grisly crime scene photographs. The sheer quantity of blood and the horrible savagery, which had shocked even the hardened homicide veterans, had less effect on the jury than the prosecution had hoped. The jurors were "the most stone-faced group of people I have ever seen," Darden later observed.

The prosecution's opening, carefully planned and well delivered, failed to dampen the ebullience of Johnnie Cochran. Much to Robert Shapiro's chagrin, Cochran by now completely overshadowed him. Even Shapiro's old friend, F.

Lee Bailey, whom he had brought into the case, sided with Cochran during the often-bitter internecine conflicts of the Dream Team. Bailey understood that Cochran offered not only the best hope for Simpson, but for Bailey himself to get an opportunity to return to the limelight.

While Shapiro migrated to the far end of the defense table, Cochran opened the race-based defense. Bright, dapper, and radiating confidence, Cochran went well beyond the usual admonition to the jurors to presume the defendant's innocence. He implied that Nicole lived—and died—in a world of sexual promiscuity and drug abuse. In its "rush to judgment," the LAPD overlooked the likelihood of a drug-related murder to blame the crime on an innocent Simpson. "Injustice anywhere is a threat to justice everywhere," Cochran intoned, quoting the African-American national hero, civil rights leader Dr. Martin Luther King Jr.

Stepping beyond the bounds of legal propriety, Cochran claimed he would present a variety of witnesses to prove Simpson's innocence. Under rules of discovery, however, Cochran was obliged to provide the prosecution with a list of such witnesses, which he had not done. Judge Ito sanctioned Cochran for his unprofessional conduct, but he had succeeded in planting doubts in the jury's mind. Many of the witnesses he promised to call—including ones who were supposed to testify that the murders were a drug-related hit, or refute the charges of domestic violence—never took the stand.

While the defense used phantom witnesses to plant seeds of doubt, the prosecution had to contend with witness problems of its own. One was Faye Resnick, a close friend of Nicole Brown Simpson, who had already sold her sensational account, *Private Diary*, to publishers. Resnick, who understood the Simpson family situation well, could have been a valuable witness. Among other things, she would have testified that Simpson had openly threatened to kill Nicole and that Nicole had repeatedly predicted that he would in fact someday do so. But the defense would have undermined Resnick's credibility by charging that her testimony reflected a quest for publication profits rather than the pursuit of justice. Moreover, Resnick had admitted to using drugs. Even though Simpson used marijuana and other drugs, drug abuse and sexual promiscuity on the part of Nicole and her friends would have been ruthlessly exploited by the defense.

The defense capped its own publicity campaign with the release of Simpson's ghostwritten first-person account, *I Want to Tell You.* The book became a huge bestseller and moneymaker, especially—in what would come as no surprise to the expert jury consultants—among African-American women. Simpson's account declared that his beloved ex-wife had been murdered as a result of her unfortunate connection with Faye Resnick's drug world. Months later, Simpson would generate an additional $3 million in sales from a $30 video in which he proclaimed his innocence.

Another potentially useful prosecution witness lost to the publishing industry was Jill Shively, a woman who while driving her car in Brentwood on the night of the murders saw Simpson driving erratically and honking his horn at a motorist who impeded his path. But Shively had already sold her story to the television tabloid show *Hard Copy,* thus compromising her credibility as well. As Darden later explained, the prosecution had to compete with the press and publishers, who could offer prospective witnesses money, while the state could offer them only an opportunity to be "carved up by ruthless defense lawyers while Ito looked on."

The unfortunate reality of Ito "looking on," instead of taking charge of the high profile case, was apparent from the outset. Indeed, in the minds of many legal experts, Ito was arguably the single greatest impediment to justice in the Simpson case. Typically, the instincts of the defense proved superior in the selection of a presiding judge. Because Ito's wife, Margaret York, was a captain of the LAPD, Shapiro could have vetoed the decision to assign the case to Ito. But Shapiro, a close friend of Ito's, shrewdly calculated that Ito would overcompensate in order to demonstrate that he was not protecting the police.

The son of Japanese-American parents who had been forced into a Wyoming relocation camp during World War II, Ito had become thoroughly at home in L.A. One of the principal problems with the bearded, forty-four-year-old judge was his comfort before television cameras and among celebrities. Ito never seriously considered barring cameras from the courtroom, but even had he done so nothing could have prevented media coverage from saturating the case.

Gavel-to-gavel television coverage by the networks, CNN, and Court TV converted seemingly minor developments into supposedly major turning points. Scores of attorneys assumed roles as expert commentators, many of them casting the Dream Team in a glowing light. Attorneys such as Lesley Abramson, Greta Van Susteren, and Gerry Spence left the courtroom behind for new roles as celebrity commentators.

Judge Ito joined the attorneys in pandering to the television cameras. He granted press and television interviews and posed for pictures with souvenirs and stacks of fan mail he received. Ito entertained celebrities and talk show hosts in his chambers and offered courtroom passes to his favorite Hollywood stars. In the assessment of Marcia Clark, whose relationship with Ito deteriorated throughout the course of the trial, the judge was nothing less than "a total starfucker."

It was one thing to be starstruck, quite another to prove unable to conduct courtroom business in an efficient manner. By failing to move the case at an appropriate pace, Ito committed the jurist's gravest sin: he lost control of the courtroom. The defense took full advantage while the prosecution bore the brunt of the judge's ineptitude.

As the defense understood, the longer the case dragged on and the more side issues and irrelevant information that entered the record, the more obscure became the core reality of the case: the massive hard evidence against their client. It was Ito, through his rulings, who allowed the defense to challenge minor points and call into question normally routine procedures, sometimes for days on end. Perceiving that the evidence against Simpson was overwhelming, Ito undoubtedly decided to grant the defense as much leeway as possible in his rulings in order to avoid having his handling of the case called into question on appeal.

Much of the Simpson case involved the attorneys on both sides engaged in extended, and often bitter arguments. Sidebar conversations between the attorneys and the judge actually began to consume more time than the trial itself. Forced into sequestration, and spending more than half their service time outside the courtroom while the lawyers debated, the jury became increasingly frustrated. Many of the juror revolts and dismissals, which ultimately threatened to result in a mistrial, can be traced to the tortoiselike pace of the trial and the judge's refusal to rein in the attorneys.

While the jury languished in their hotel with nothing to do but watch movies, Ito allowed the attorneys to argue and trade recriminations over

Cochran's violation of the discovery rules during his opening statement. Ito had previously allowed debate to drag on interminably over the admissibility of evidence pertaining to Simpson's spousal abuse.

Once the case began, Ito dismissed the jury for an astonishing nine days and presided passively while the two sides contended bitterly over a defense effort to interrupt the prosecution's case to present testimony by Rosa Lopez, a maid who worked in the house next door to Simpson's and who at one point claimed to have seen O. J.'s Bronco in front of the Rockingham home at about the time the murders took place. Insisting that she was suffering as a result of media harassment, Ms. Lopez threatened to leave the country for her native El Salvador, hence the defense sought to get her on the stand even though it was not yet time for them to present their case.

While the jurors sat in their hotel, Ito let the debate drag on, finally ruling that Lopez's testimony could be videotaped and played later as part of the defense case. When the taped testimony was taken, Lopez proved to be unsure of the precise time she had seen the Bronco and in essence offered nothing of substance. The defense, which chose not to show Lopez's testimony to the jury, had succeeded in disrupting the prosecution's case for more than a week.

By early March the prosecution had managed to introduce damaging evidence of a history of Simpson's physical abuse of Nicole during their marriage. After the lengthy arguments, Ito had ruled that the prosecution could present evidence of abuse dating to 1977, including the 1989 New Year's Day beating for which O. J. had successfully eluded arrest.

The jury also heard a tape of Nicole's voice, choked with tears and terror, as Simpson menaced her on October 25, 1993. "He's O. J. Simpson," she told the 911 dispatcher. "I think you know his record. Could you just send somebody over here?" Ito, however, ruled inadmissible evidence that Nicole had reported to a battered women's shelter that Simpson was stalking her in the days before the murder.

While the prosecution exploited Simpson's history of domestic violence, it proved clumsy in handling the forensic evidence. Because the deputy medical examiner who had performed the autopsies on Ron Goldman and Nicole Brown Simpson had acknowledged making mistakes—none of which was crucial—Clark decided not to call him. Instead, the prosecution summoned the coroner and spent eight days eliciting fairly routine evidence from him. The prosecution thus needlessly dragged out its own case and, by not presenting the man who had performed the autopsy, played into the defense conspiracy theory. Why, the defense asked, was the state afraid to produce the official responsible for the autopsy? What were they hiding?

The prosecution was equally ineffectual, but not as long-winded, in its handling of Nicole's sister, Denise Brown. The emotional testimony of Simpson's threats and abuse failed to make the desired impact, in part because of Darden's poor handling of the witness and in part because the jury did not care for the L.A. party girl lifestyle that Denise, who had repeated convictions for driving under the influence of alcohol, and her deceased sister had lived. Denise cried genuine tears of grief and anger over her sister's murder, yet failed to move the seemingly implacable jurors.

The defense wisely offered only a cursory cross-examination of the victim's sister. The Dream Team also declined to attack other minor witnesses, such as the staff at Mezzaluna, the restaurant where Ron Goldman worked and where Nicole ate her last meal. The testimony of the dog walkers who discovered Nicole's body also received little play from the defense, although Simpson's attorneys would later launch an effort to challenge the prosecution's time line for the murders.

But much to Johnnie Cochran's delight, he found Ito willing to grant him almost complete latitude to ask questions and interject his own comments to depict the murders as a drug hit. Through the words he used in formulating his questions, Cochran also implied that Nicole had been sexually insatiable and habitually targeted black men as the object of her desires.

All of this, it would become evident, played well with the jury, which also proved susceptible to the theory of an LAPD conspiracy against Simpson. As became evident when Detective Tom Lange took the stand, the defense was conserving its energies for an all-out assault on the LAPD. The defense had been unhappy with the decision to admit the evidence gathered in the Rockingham search, even as Ito noted acidly that Vannatter's affidavit in obtaining a warrant had been written with "reckless disregard for the truth."

Cochran raised myriad issues with Lange about police handling of evidence, going out his way repeatedly as he framed questions to draw the jury's attention to the fact that Lange resided in Simi Valley. Simi Valley, as all the jurors knew, was a conservative and predominantly white community and home to hundreds of LAPD officers. Moreover, the officers who had administered the brutal beating to Rodney King were exonerated by an overwhelmingly white Simi Valley jury.

During his four-day cross-examination of Lange, Cochran took full advantage of the wide latitude granted by Ito. Angry and unnerved by Cochran's tactics, the prosecutors—and particularly Darden—lost their cool. During a sidebar with Ito, Darden responded sharply to a baiting comment by Cochran. Ito promptly sided with the defense attorney, even though Cochran had instigated the incident, and demanded an apology from Darden for interrupting him. Darden at first sullenly refused before he finally issued the apology.

The incident reflected the strained relationship between the judge and prosecution, which Ito often, and inexcusably, treated with contempt, sometimes in front of the jury. By contrast, the judge showed far more deference to the Dream Team.

Indeed, while the defense continued to gain momentum, the prosecution struggled to maintain its equilibrium. The prosecution compartmentalized its case by farming out various avenues of inquiry to individual attorneys. Marcia Clark failed to exercise overall authority for the case in its entirety. The individual prosecutors began to buckle under the strain. Suffering from stress, fatigue, and heart problems, William Hodgman could no longer participate directly, thus removing from the courtroom the most experienced attorney on that side of the aisle. Marcia Clark, a notorious chain-smoker who had suffered in the past from eating disorders, strained to balance the demands of the trial with her responsibilities as a mother in the midst of an impending divorce from an angry husband. Darden, in addition to being depicted as an enemy of his race by Cochran, and suffering the wrath of Ito, had to contend with his brother's deteriorating health en route to death from AIDS.

Just when it appeared that things could not get much worse, they did just that with the swearing in of Detective Mark Fuhrman. The forty-three-year-old officer, a marine combat veteran of Vietnam, was the answer to the defense prayers. He had long been targeted as the centerpiece of the race-based defense theory of an LAPD effort to frame Simpson for murder.

The Dream Team seized upon LAPD records of a psychological evaluation which bolstered the depiction of Fuhrman as, in Shapiro's words, a "bad cop" and a "racist cop." The assessment found that Fuhrman coveted the "big arrest" and that he seemed to enjoy opportunities to use violence against "low class" (and often black) people. The detective had waged a long legal struggle with the LAPD in the early eighties as he sought retirement and disability benefits based on the claim that he was suffering from stress.

After it became public knowledge that the defense was pursuing a race-based defense targeting Fuhrman, more evidence poured into the Dream Team files. Kathleen Bell, a former real estate agent, wrote Cochran that she had worked in an office next to a marine recruiting station where Fuhrman often visited friends and engaged in racist talk. According to Bell, Fuhrman expressed hatred for African Americans and crowed that he routinely used his police powers to harass black men when he saw them out with white women.

Although the prosecution had ample warning of the defense's planned assault on Fuhrman, Clark had not even bothered to conduct a routine mock cross-examination to prepare this key witness for the defense onslaught. Appearing for the prosecution, Fuhrman repeated the testimony given at the preliminary hearing, explaining how he had gone over the wall at Simpson's estate and found the bloody glove behind Kato Kaelin's cottage.

Cochran by this time had decided to reward F. Lee Bailey for his support by offering him the limelight in the cross-examination of Fuhrman. After pledging to reporters that he would take apart Fuhrman on the stand, Bailey made little headway in efforts to impeach Fuhrman's testimony or offer a plausible scenario of how he might have planted evidence against Simpson.

Failing at that, the defense sought to confront the predominantly African-American jury with evidence of Fuhrman's racism. Backed by Ito's prior ruling in the defense's favor, Bailey now asked Fuhrman if he had "addressed any black person as a nigger or spoken about black persons as niggers in the past ten years?"

Fuhrman denied having done so, another blatant lie, and one which would be disproven to the detriment of the prosecution. Together with other police lies—notably the absurd claim by Lange, Vannatter, and Fuhrman that they had not considered Simpson a suspect—as well as procedural errors, these missteps would give a jury sympathetic to Simpson the opportunity to set him free.

That, combined with an abundant supply of smoke and mirrors from the defense over the blood evidence, was the essence of the Simpson case.

The prosecution still had plenty of compelling evidence to present. Clark summoned her best witness, limousine driver Alan Parke, who had taken Simp-son to the airport on the night of the murders. Parke was clear and objective and, remarkably, had even spurned offers to sell his story to the tabloids. As he had done in the preliminary hearing, Parke testified that he arrived at Simp-son's estate at 10:25 P.M. on the night of the murders. He saw no white Bronco and no one answered the doorbell when he rang it. Parke then saw a well-built African-American man jog across the lawn and up to the front door. Moments later he rang again and Simpson answered, explaining over the intercom that he had overslept, was taking a shower, and would be down in a few minutes. When Simpson emerged, he insisted on handling a black duffel bag himself. Never seen again, the black duffel bag presumably contained the weapon and other incriminating evidence that Simpson disposed of later.

As they pulled out of Simpson's estate, Parke testified, he found his view obstructed by a vehicle that had not been there before: Simpson's white Ford Bronco. Cochran could do nothing to challenge the incriminating circumstan-tial evidence of Simpson's guilt offered by Parke.

With Parke's testimony having stabilized its case, the prosecution now pre-sented the decisive DNA evidence. The hard scientific evidence through DNA analysis could actually prove the guilt or innocence of a defendant. To attorneys of guilty defendants, DNA can be a frightening evidentiary tool making it vir-tually impossible to argue their clients' innocence. For this reason DNA had been challenged in court and in the press for years, yet the evidence is so pow-erful in its ability to deliver the truth that genetic fingerprinting is now a staple ingredient in criminal justice cases.

The Simpson attorneys understood, of course, that the DNA evidence—lots of it, in several locations—could be marshaled to demonstrate Simpson's guilt beyond a reasonable doubt. The only way to challenge such evidence was by mounting an all-out assault on the handlers of that evidence.

The architects and executioners of this portion of the defense case were Bar-ry Scheck and Peter Neufeld. The two DNA experts attacked on several fronts. Scheck, who took the lead role, had identified a series of procedural and han-dling errors which he exploited to argue that some of the DNA evidence against Simpson had been contaminated and was therefore invalid. The defense declined to challenge other DNA evidence linking Simpson's blood with the defendants, but charged that this blood had been planted by the LAPD.

The primary victim of Scheck's relentless attack was Dennis Fung, the thirty-four-year-old LAPD criminalist who had been responsible for collecting the crime scene evidence at Rockingham and Bundy on the morning after the murders. Hank Greenberg, part of the compartmentalized prosecution team, elicited the DNA evidence from Fung, but failed during his direct examination to anticipate the witness's vulnerabilities in order to preempt the impending defense attack.

Animated and confrontational, Scheck intimidated and destroyed Fung during nine interminable days on the witness stand. Scheck exploited procedural errors, misstatements, and shoddy record keeping in an effort—which proved successful with the jury—to discredit the decisive DNA evidence.

As Scheck exaggerated a series of procedural errors, converting them into a dark conspiracy, Fung appeared increasingly nervous, failed to defend himself well, and began losing sleep as his ordeal continued. Scheck's systematic destruction of Fung and the LAPD test laboratory was crucial to the Dream Team's ultimate success. No wonder O. J., in a blatant violation of courtroom decorum, reached out and shook the befuddled Fung's hand when he left the stand for the last time.

Indicative of what transpired was the issue of the blood found on the back gate at Bundy. DNA analysis established conclusively that the blood matched Simpson's type—and that of no one else on Earth—but Scheck suggested that the blood had been planted by police. Scheck showed a blown-up photograph, grainy and inconclusive, that purported to show there had been no blood on the gate the morning after the crime. In fact, myriad witnesses had seen the blood on the gate that morning. Scheck was on target, however, when he pointed out that Fung had erred in allowing the blood to remain on the gate for days before testing.

Similarly, Scheck argued that socks found in O. J.'s house, which contained deadly incriminating spots of both his and Nicole's blood, had been planted. Scheck showed the jury a photograph from Simpson's bedroom in which the socks were not seen, but this was merely because, as several persons had witnessed, the socks had already been removed in an evidence bag. Because the socks were black, and only a few drops got on them, the blood had not been immediately noticed. Still, by hammering away the defense had achieved its goal of raising doubts in the jurors' minds.

Given careful consideration—which the jury ultimately would decline to supply—the defense theory of planted evidence was absurd. It would have required a massive LAPD conspiracy to frame Simpson. Fung and his assistants would have had to conspire with Fuhrman, Lange, Vannatter, and other cops— many of whom did not even know one another—to plant evidence against a defendant who for all they knew at the time had an airtight alibi.

But Fung and his young assistant, Andrea Mazzola, who had worked only three crime scenes before, had made a number of errors. They should have changed their gloves more often in taking blood samples. Not all of the blood samples were taken as quickly as they should have been nor maintained under ideal temperatures and conditions. Fung had mistakenly reported that he collected certain evidence when in fact Mazzola had taken it—misstatements which Scheck ruthlessly exploited to undermine Fung's credibility. Although the DNA evidence had been tested in as many as three laboratories, all of the blood had been processed through the LAPD facility, which defense experts characterized as a shoddy operation.

The coup de grâce for Scheck was his artful presentation of a scenario in which he suggested that Vannatter had removed some of Simpson's blood from a sample and then planted it to incriminate Simpson. The basis for this claim was a report that eight cubic centimeters of blood had been drawn from O. J. for testing but only six-and-a-half cubic centimeters were accounted for in lab tests. The reality was that the amount drawn in such samples was not typically measured precisely. No evidence existed to suggest that any of the blood had been removed and planted. Vannatter, however, after receiving the vial of blood taken from Simpson at police headquarters, had kept it on his person to deliver personally to the criminalist instead of logging it in, as police procedure required. The jury would follow Scheck's lead in concluding that Vannatter, supposedly obsessed with destroying Simpson, might have seized this opportunity to plant evidence.

The defense bolstered its conspiracy theory through its own witness, Dr. Henry Lee, director of the Connecticut state forensic science laboratory. In a phrase that resonated with the jury, Scheck led Lee to declare there was "something wrong" with the blood evidence in the case because of contamination. The same witness, who unlike Fung was highly compensated for his expert testimony, declared that according to his analysis of the evidence the bloody footprints of a second person were present at the scene. During the prosecution cross-examination it became clear that Lee's footprints were those of a construction worker who had left them when the concrete had been poured at the Bundy residence!

Employing such tactics for days on end, Scheck emphasized the "something wrong" theme and the contamination of the blood samples. But as DNA expert, New York attorney Harlan Levy, has explained, "DNA is far more robust, and less subject to contamination, than the [Simpson] defense suggested."

In reality, no sample is pristine—all are "contaminated" to some extent—yet the essential result remains discernible. Indeed, the jury failed to understand, and the prosecution failed to explain to them, that contamination would have made a match *less likely*. That is, had the blood samples been contaminated, the contamination could have impeded a match but could not produce a false positive. Contamination would make it more difficult to determine whose blood was in the sample. Contamination could not make a sample of blood bear the DNA of O. J. Simpson. In reality, given the matches between Simpson's blood type and that found at Bundy, Rockingham, and in the Bronco, any contamination would actually mean that it was more rather than less likely that Simpson was guilty.

Given the complexity of DNA and the intricacies of laboratory testing and procedures, the jury and most of the national lay audience quickly became lost in confusion. The torturously slow and detailed prosecution presentation of the evidence proved more tedious than effective. The complexity of the issue, combined with Scheck's relentless assault and repeated charges of conspiracy and cover-up, raised enough questions with the receptive Simpson jury to call into question the credibility of the very evidence that in reality proved the defendant's guilt beyond doubt.

The prosecution tried but failed to overcome the doubts planted by Scheck. The amount of conclusive DNA evidence in the Simpson case was far more than normally available to prosecutors. In many instances, a single speck of blood has produced sufficient DNA evidence to condemn or exonerate defendants. In the 1993 World Trade Center bombing cases, authorities produced crucial evidence against one of the defendants through successful DNA tests from his saliva on the flap of an envelope he had mailed threatening additional destruction.

In the Simpson case, the amount of blood, found in several distinct places and belonging to the defendant and his victims, was overwhelming and incriminating. The jury, however, would choose to ignore it.

The pattern of overwhelming evidence of Simpson's guilt blowing up in the prosecution's face continued with the infamous Aris Isotoner leather glove, which Nicole had purchased for O. J. One glove had been left at Bundy; the other was found by Fuhrman behind Kato's cottage at Rockingham. The brown leather gloves were of such high quality that they were sold at only one chain of stores in the United States, Bloomingdale's. A credit card receipt showed that Nicole bought the gloves in New York around Christmas 1990.

Christopher Darden botched this compelling evidence by deciding on the spur of the moment, in direct contradiction of agreed-upon prosecution strategy, to have Simpson try on one of the gloves in court. O. J., a decent actor, strained and kept a straight face as he mumbled "too tight" loud enough for the jury, and millions of Americans watching on television, to hear.

"Expert" analysts, talking heads, and tabloid reporters converted this actually inconsequential bit of courtroom theater into a major disaster for the prosecution. Newspaper headlines blared a breakthrough in the Simpson defense case.

Darden had erred in the maneuver since the blood-soaked gloves had shrunk and Simpson attempted to pull them on over latex gloves which he wore to prevent contamination of the evidence. Furthermore, Darden failed to stand with Simpson and ensure that he actually tried to pull on the gloves, rather than sticking his thumb out to impede their path while acting as if he were straining to get them on.

While media coverage gave enormous publicity to the botched effort to have Simpson try on the gloves, it devoted far less attention to prosecution witness Richard Rubin, a real expert on the gloves, who calmly explained the impact of the shrinkage and of the layer of latex. "At one point in time," Rubin explained, "those gloves would be actually, I think, large on Mr. Simpson's hand." Indeed, when Darden brought out a new pair of the gloves, they fit nicely, but the damage had already been done.

The most famous line of Johnnie Cochran's summation now had been written: "If it does not fit, you must acquit."

The prosecution had still more compelling evidence to present but it was questionable at this point how much the jurors, already languishing in their prolonged confinement, were willing to hear. A shoe expert testified that the killer was over six feet tall and wore $160 Bruno Magli shoes, size twelve, the same size that the six-foot-three Simpson wore. Impressions from the shoes had been found at the scene and on the rug on the floor of the Bronco as well. Chillingly, a print from the same shoe had been identified on the back of Nicole's dress, where the killer's foot had been placed when he lifted her head to slit her throat.

Hair and fiber experts testified that hair in the blue knit cap found at the scene matched Simpson's, as did hair found on Ron Goldman and deposited by "direct contact." Experts testified that they found Nicole's hair on the bloody glove left at Rockingham. Fibers from Goldman's shirt were found on each of the gloves. Fibers matching those in Simpson's Bronco were found at the scene. Cumulatively, the evidence was devastating and would have required an implausible conspiracy among officials in order to manufacture it.

By midsummer, with Ito having allowed the case to drag on already half a year, the prosecution made the decision to wrap up the presentation of evidence against Simpson. The decision reflected the state's awareness that the jury was becoming fed up. The prosecution itself had wasted a great deal of time, particularly by dragging out routine evidence, and Ito had allowed superfluous issues and petty arguments to consume weeks of court time. Because the case had been so poorly handled, the state in effect had run out of time.

The decision meant that the prosecution rested without presenting any information about the infamous Bronco chase, seen by millions, and Simpson's suicide note. Why would O. J. write what his own attorney at the time described as a "suicide note" if he were not guilty? Why did Simpson take with him a passport and a fake goatee and mustache, changes of clothes, and $9,000 in cash if he had not been running from something?

Even more inexplicable was the decision not to introduce the thirty-two-minute statement Simpson gave to Lange and Vannatter the day he flew back from Chicago. Clark ignored this valuable evidence when she should have played for the jury the taped interview, in which Simpson soundly edgy, defensive, and contradictory.

Asked in the police interview how he had received the three bruises and seven cuts, including one deep gouge, that were visible on his left hand, Simpson could only mutter, "I don't know." He then explained that he had cut his hand on a glass in his hotel room in Chicago when he got the "news" of Nicole's death. In the same interview, however, he said he cut his hand at his house—though he didn't remember how—as he hurried to make his flight at the airport on the night of the murders.

Having decided not to introduce Simpson's own contradictory and self-incriminating behavior into evidence, Clark brought an end to the state's case. On July 5, 1995, after 92 days of testimony, 58 witnesses, 488 exhibits, and the expenditure of at least $6 million in public funds, Clark stood before Ito and declared: "The People rest."

Given the poor performance by the prosecution, the defense might have been wise to consider putting on only a modest case of its own. Instead, Cochran summoned a series of witnesses, many of whom backfired, but others who proved crucial in setting his guilty client free. The Dream Team began by summoning Simpson's sisters, his daughter Arnelle, and his mother, all of whom Cochran anticipated would appeal especially to the African-American women on the jury.

Subsequent witnesses, however, failed to bolster the defense effort to undermine the time line for the murders. One defense witness, Brentwood resident Robert Heidstra, who had heard loud voices about the time of the murders, blew up in Cochran's face. He testified that one of the voices he had heard coming from the area around Nicole's courtyard sounded white and another sounded like the voice of a black person. Cochran exploded in protest, insisting predictably that it was "racist" to allege that African Americans might have a distinctive speech pattern.

Another defense gambit backfired when Cochran tried to suggest that Simpson was so limited by his football injuries that he lacked the physical capability of killing Ron and Nicole. The prosecution gleefully took up this challenge, producing a copy of a workout video in which O. J., who was an avid golfer as well, appeared running in place, jumping, and pumping his arms. Eerily, Simpson joked on the tape about keeping adequate distance from a workout partner unless a man wanted to punch his wife and blame it on the exercise, "if you know what I mean."

Cochran's inexperience with murder cases was showing, hence the defense attorney returned to his most effective theme—race. Simpson's lead attorney now played his trump card by subpoenaing Laura Hart McKinny. A North Carolinian, McKinny, like thousands of others, had once lived in L.A. in pursuit of a career as a screenwriter. Working on a movie project in the mid-1980s, McKinny had made twelve hours of tapes with an L.A. policeman she had interviewed to gain insight into cop culture. The officer was Mark Fuhrman.

On the subpoenaed tapes, Fuhrman delighted in playing the role of a bigoted and even sadistic cop. He did it so well that it obviously reflected his own real personality to a considerable extent. The tapes, some of which were played in court with the jury excused, were incredibly crude and included Fuhrman's repeated use of the term "nigger."

Fuhrman also admitted to manufacturing and planting evidence against defendants he "knew" to be guilty. Ito also allowed public airing of a sickening excerpt in which Fuhrman described in detail systematic police abuse and torture of black L.A. gang members. In one segment, not played in court, Fuhrman had even maligned Judge Ito's wife, a police officer, in crude sexual tones, raising the issue of whether Ito could rule objectively on the admissibility of McKinny's evidence.

On August 29, Ito ruled that some of the taped excerpts could be introduced as a means of discrediting Fuhrman's denial earlier that he had used the word "nigger" in the past ten years. Once he had made the earlier decision to allow the defense to question Fuhrman about whether he had used the word, Ito's decision to admit McKinny's evidence could hardly be avoided.

Still, the decision allowed the case to focus once again on race rather than murder, and in effect put Fuhrman on trial rather than Simpson. Additional witnesses came forward to declare they had heard Fuhrman use the word "nigger." Not satisfied, Cochran expressed outrage that Ito had not allowed still more of the tapes into evidence. He complained bitterly to the press that "the cover-up continues" and called for the people of Los Angeles to remain calm, as if there was cause for another riot like the one that erupted after the verdict in the Rodney King case.

Despite Cochran's protests, the defense had won yet another round in the case. One of the prosecution's chief police witnesses had been revealed as a liar and a racist. The defense knew it was but a small step to convince the jury that with such characters prevalent in the LAPD, an otherwise implausible theory of planted evidence against Simpson might gain credibility and set their client free. The defense wisely closed its case on the high note of revelations of Mark Fuhrman's racist character.

Marcia Clark tried to pick up the pieces in the prosecution's presentation of evidence to rebut the defense case. The prosecution produced photographs of Simpson snapped over the years by amateur photographers. One proved conclusively that Simpson possessed and was wearing a pair of the rare Aris Lights style gloves on the sidelines at a 1990 football game.

The case may already have been lost by that time, however. At the same time, the defense continually impeded the flow of the prosecution rebuttal evidence with interruptions and objections without cause, actions that Ito failed to rein in.

An event in the last week of the trial epitomized the entire case and paved the way for Simpson's acquittal. The Dream Team gave no real consideration to allowing Simpson to take the stand, knowing at that point that opening their client to cross-examination was about the only way they could in fact lose the case. Cochran, however, sought and received Ito's assent to allow Simpson to speak briefly about waiving his constitutional right to testify. Knowing what was coming, Clark implored Ito to reject the request. "Please don't do this, Your Honor," she intoned. "I beg you."

But Ito continued to be the defense's best friend. On September 22, with the jury excused, the judge asked Simpson if he was indeed waiving his right to testify on his own defense. As Lizzie Borden had done a century before, Simpson seized the opportunity to declare that he declined to testify on his own behalf, but quickly added that "I did not, would not, and could not have committed this crime."

The denial captured national media attention and could not have escaped the attention of individual jurors through conjugal visits. Ito had to have known this would happen but inexplicably had given Simpson an opportunity to speak on his own behalf without being subject to questioning by the prosecution. By allowing the case to center around race rather than murder, and enabling Simpson to proclaim his innocence, Ito had gone a long way toward deciding the outcome himself.

On September 26, 1995, after a full year in court, Marcia Clark tried to salvage the prosecution case in her summation of the evidence against Simpson. It represented her last opportunity to change the momentum of the trial. Here was the chance for Clark—with patience, clarity, and conviction—to demonstrate the compelling evidence against Simpson and the dubious defense conspiracy theory. Instead, she often appeared disorganized, imprecise, and inarticulate, an inexcusable performance considering that the closing statement, for which she had had months to prepare, should have been the prosecution's finest hour.

Clark did take the jury back through what should have been the decisive evidence against Simpson. Simply put, the scientific evidence through DNA testing of blood matches, as well as of hair and fibers, placed Simpson, and him alone, at the crime scene. Moreover, the irrefutable evidence showed that Simpson had taken the victims' blood evidence with him on his clothing and in his car. Scheck's obfuscations notwithstanding, the sheer number of DNA matches between Simpson and his victims offered compelling evidence against the argument that it was all a result of laboratory error.

The closing argument was the time to highlight Simpson's guilty behavior after the fact, including the writing of the suicide note, had that evidence been introduced, as it should have been. Why, since the defense alleged Simpson was being framed, had he not once made that claim himself, in terms of indignant outrage that only the innocent can express? How could the LAPD and the criminalists be so incompetent, as Scheck had charged, and yet the architects of the intricate conspiracy that Cochran alluded to? And just where was that black duffel bag that neither Kato Kaelin nor Alan Parke had been allowed to touch?

The classic ingredients of murder were all there: motive, means, and opportunity. The evidence, albeit circumstantial, proved beyond a reasonable doubt that Simpson was a double murderer. Yet Clark failed to present a compelling closing argument to that effect.

Christopher Darden was more effective in his part of the closing argument, which he delivered in one of the evening sessions ordered by Ito in a hopelessly belated effort to speed up the proceedings. Darden offered a poignant reminder to the jury of the contents of Nicole's safe-deposit box, which had been drilled open by the prosecutors after her death. There, along with her will, she left notes of apology from Simpson for some of the beatings he had administered, as well as photographs of her face after enduring an attack by her husband in 1989. Darden explained convincingly that Nicole had left this evidence in safekeeping because she knew that one day Simpson might well murder her. "She knew in 1989," he explained. "She knew it. And she wants you to know it."

Darden's work was the most effective part of the prosecution summation, but the overall effort had been weak and left plenty of opportunity for Johnnie Cochran to maneuver. Unlike the prosecution, Cochran made the most of his opportunities.

The prosecution should have preempted Cochran's argument by pointing out—step-by-step, in clear, systematic, and simple terms—that the defense theory in the Simpson case was implausible. The same LAPD which had systematically overlooked Simpson's violent abuse of his wife—including Fuhrman, who had actually responded to one of Nicole's 911 calls—was supposed to have orchestrated a conspiracy against the man they had previously shielded from prosecution. Even had the LAPD wanted to conspire to incriminate, the facts of the case showed that it could not have been done.

Fuhrman, the focus of the conspiracy theory, was somehow supposed to have obtained one of Simpson's gloves, dipped it in the victims' blood, and transported it from the murder scene at Bundy to the cottage in back of Rockingham, where he then disingenuously claimed to have found it. Clark should have hammered home to the jury that Fuhrman was at least the fifteenth cop at the scene at Bundy and that none of the other officers had seen a second glove there—the one that Fuhrman supposedly removed and transported to Simpson's estate—before he arrived.

Had fourteen other cops seen two gloves and merely looked on gleefully as Fuhrman picked one of them up and put it in a baggy? Which one of the cops happened to have a size twelve shoe and, knowing it was Simpson's foot size, decided to walk it through the crime scene, stepping on Nicole's back, and dripping Simpson's blood, which they had somehow obtained? How did Fuhrman and his co-conspirators—some of whom, such as Lange and Vannatter, he had never even met—know Simpson did not have an alibi? For all they knew he could have been with scores of people at a party at the time of the murders. Did they set up an elaborate frame just hoping that Simpson happened to be home alone with no alibi? Was it plausible that twenty-six-year LAPD veteran Vannatter would remove two cubic centimeters of blood—with Dennis Fung and his aides as his willing accomplices—and paint it onto the gate at Rockingham out of a racist, previously undetected desire to destroy a wealthy and popular public figure?

In fact, under California law the perpetrators of such a conspiracy could have themselves faced the death penalty for planting evidence incriminating another person in a murder case. What was it about O. J. Simpson that cops who had previously shielded him would now go to such lengths to destroy him? Was there none among this vast conspiracy who might fear betrayal by one of their members, a betrayal that would send him to the gas chamber?

After dissecting the implausible defense theory in an organized, articulate, and compelling fashion, Clark would then have been in position to address the weaknesses in the prosecution case, none of which should have threatened the a verdict of guilty. The chief problem, of course, was Mark Fuhrman, who through Simpson's good fortune happened to have been summoned to the scene by his superior and also happened to have been the subject of audio tapes demonstrating that he personified the type of racism and police abuse for which the LAPD was infamous. The prosecution compounded its bad luck by bungling the Fuhrman issue. As one of their key witnesses, Fuhrman should have been prepared for Bailey's questions about use of the word "nigger." Once Ito had admitted the question itself into evidence, Fuhrman and the prosecution should have considered a response in which Fuhrman would admit that he had used the term "nigger" during the course of his work on the streets, but that he did not consider himself a racist. The McKinny tapes would never have been introduced to refute his ill-conceived lie that he had not used the term in the past ten years.

Moreover, in its own rebuttal, the prosecution could have bolstered its witness by pointing out that he had willingly taken on a black female partner and that they had respected one another; that he regularly played basketball with African-American friends; and that, as was true, he had energetically pursued evidence in a case which had resulted in freeing a wrongly accused African-American suspect. It would not have been desirable or necessary to invent information to attempt to glorify Fuhrman, or even to deny his racism, but the prosecution should have made some effort to call into question Johnnie Cochran's subsequent depiction of Fuhrman as Adolf Hitler reincarnate.

Instead, Clark played into Cochran's hands by herself denouncing Fuhrman as "the worst the LAPD has to offer" and in effect apologizing for having called him as a witness.

Instead, Clark played into Cochran's hands by herself denouncing Fuhrman as "the worst the LAPD has to offer" and in effect apologizing for having called him as a witness.

Generally speaking, when a prosecutor in a criminal trial ends up denouncing her own key witness in no uncertain terms, the cause is usually lost.

The prosecution should have devoted more energy to explaining to the jury that it was a giant step from acknowledging that racism existed within the LAPD to alleging a conspiracy to frame Simpson. Yes, Fuhrman and other cops harbored racist sentiments but the only LAPD conspiracy that existed pertaining to Simpson was the one which had resulted in his repeated ability to avoid being brought to justice for abusing his wife. *That* LAPD conspiracy was real and it was documented. The other was fiction.

Since race had been intruded so heavily into the case, the prosecution might have taken the opportunity, as former Charles Manson prosecutor Vincent Bugliosi has suggested, to point out that Simpson himself had long since virtually abandoned the black community. One of the reasons for O. J.'s mainstream popularity was his image as a "non-threatening" African American. Unlike other African-American athletes in the 1960s—men such as Muhammad Ali, Kareem Abdul-Jabbar, and another great NFL running back, Jim Brown—O. J. pointedly renounced taking positions on politics or race relations. No major African-American organization—for example the Urban League, NAACP, United Negro College Fund—could report receiving a major contribution from the wealthy actor and retired athlete. Simpson had little connection with the African-American community and himself once remarked: "I'm not black—I'm O. J."

Finally, Clark should have calmly explained to the jury that small irregularities, inconsistencies, and procedural errors—those that Cochran and Scheck tried to convert into a police conspiracy—always occur in criminal cases. No body of evidence is ever pristine or handled perfectly. The legal standard of reasonable doubt reflected awareness that inconsistencies and errors in gathering and processing evidence would occur in criminal cases. Although the LAPD and its forensic scientists made such errors, and even lied, the evidence in the case remained no less compelling.

The prosecution should then have concluded not by *asking* the jury to return a verdict of guilty, but by reminding them that it was their *sworn duty under the law* to do so. The prosecution's failure to marshal the evidence or charge the jury in a compelling fashion, especially in its summation, opened the door for Johnnie Cochran. In sharp contrast with the weary and disorganized prosecution effort, Cochran displayed style, flair, and confident aggression in his closing argument.

The fact that his argument had little connection with reality did not dissuade Cochran or the jury. As he had done throughout the case, Cochran proceeded as though the police and a racist justice system, rather than his own client, were on trial. Emphasizing the alleged LAPD "rush to judgment," Cochran argued that the racist cops had been out to frame an innocent man, a role model for African Americans.

Cochran in effect told the jurors they could ignore the evidence in the case since it had been gathered by the LAPD. Fuhrman and Vannatter were "twin demons of deception," Cochran declared, exhibiting a chart entitled "Vannatter's Big Lies." While Vannatter was merely a liar and conspirator, Fuhrman was nothing less than a "genocidal racist." Equating the police force with Hitler's Germany, Cochran declared that the jury had an opportunity to rein in the police.

The verdict they would render, Cochran emphasized, "goes far beyond the doors of this courtroom. . . . Stop this cover-up. If you don't stop it, then who? . . . You are empowered to say that we are not going to take it anymore. I'm sure you will do the right thing. . . . You police the police."

Here, Cochran came very close to encouraging what the prosecution later charged occurred in the case: jury nullification. Jury nullification occurs when a panel deliberately chooses to ignore the evidence in a case in order to render a verdict that satisfies their sentiments or emotions rather than the facts. Even as Cochran came close to encouraging nullification, the beaten prosecutors could not muster the energy even to object.

With his energy and aggression still fully mobilized, Barry Scheck complemented Cochran's close by hammering away once again at the supposedly tainted DNA evidence. The blood evidence, whether planted or contaminated, should be considered worthless. Everything that went through the LAPD laboratory was "garbage in, garbage out," Scheck asserted. "Something is terribly wrong with the evidence in this case," he emphasized, offering the jurors a veneer of justification they were looking for to post a verdict of not guilty.

Marcia Clark had one last opportunity to cut through the myriad distortions, inconsistencies, and illogic of the defense arguments but, tired and beaten, she again failed to rise to the occasion. The defense ensured that she never developed a flow in her rebuttal argument by interrupting her an astonishing seventy-one times. Such behavior was not only rude but virtually unprecedented. Ito sustained only two defense objections but, as usual, he failed to rein in the illustrious Dream Team.

The jury, understandably fed up with the yearlong case, took few notes throughout the closing arguments. The overwhelming majority had their minds made up when they finally retired on Friday, September 29. The fourteen remaining Simpson jurors, including at the end only two alternates out of the original twelve, were survivors who had weathered a long ordeal that they now intended to bring to a rapid conclusion.

Sequestered for almost a full year, they had lived apart from their communities and families, except for a once-a-week, five-hour conjugal visit with a spouse or significant other. They had lived without television—though they watched more movies than anyone could bear—and had their telephone calls supervised by sheriff's deputies. Some of the African Americans on the jury charged that the predominantly white deputies were racist and had treated them with disrespect.

They had seen eleven defense attorneys and nine prosecuting attorneys parade in and out of the court case. They had listened to an astonishing 16,000 objections, most of them frivolous, as Ito had allowed the proceedings to drag on interminably. They had seen Marcia Clark pushed to the breaking point, but had seen her disappear from court for almost three months only to return refreshed, whereas they had received no such break themselves. Incredibly, the judge at one point insisted on taking his own vacation in the midst of closing arguments, thus further delaying the trial, before at last being talked out of it.

The issue of race had been at the forefront of the jurors' minds from the outset. They knew that they were the survivors of a selection process in which both sides had empanelled and dismissed prospective jurors on the basis of race. During the long trial, as alternates replaced ten jurors for a variety of reasons, charges of racism surfaced repeatedly.

In April Cochran publicly denounced the proceedings when an African-American woman, Jeanette Harris, a strong proponent of Simpson's innocence, was dismissed for having lied about her personal experience with spousal abuse. Cochran charged that racial politics lay at the root of Harris's dismissal, a viewpoint that may well have gone back to the jury through conjugal visits and worked against the prosecution. Cochran could not hide his glee, however, when Ito dismissed a white juror on grounds of improper conduct.

In the end the defense, as usual, came out on top. The Simpson case began with eight black jurors and ended with nine, none of whom could be expected to ignore the pressure from the African-American community to free O. J. As Jeanette Harris had explained in a television interview following her dismissal, "An African American might say, 'I can't say he's guilty because I want to walk out of here.'" Just as Darden had predicted when he implored Ito not to admit testimony on Fuhrman's use of the word "nigger," the case for the African Americans on the jury inevitably boiled down to "Are you with the Man or with the Brothers?"

The stunning rapidity with which the jurors reached their verdict clearly revealed that their minds were made up and they had not deliberated at all. After electing a foreman, the jurors spent less than two hours discussing the evidence in the latest "crime of the century." They requested verdict forms and voted twelve to zero for acquittal before returning to their hotel for one last night of confinement while the attorneys whisked their way back to Los Angeles to receive the results the following morning.

Having learned the night before that the jury had reached a verdict, an unprecedented 150 million viewers worldwide—the most ever to watch a television event—tuned in the next morning. Shortly after 10 A.M. on Tuesday, October 3, 1995, the jury rendered its verdict of "not guilty" to a tense and jam-packed courtroom.

Simpson clenched his fist in victory while a smiling Johnnie Cochran gripped the powerful athlete's shoulder. While Simpson, his family, and his attorneys celebrated, the prosecution sat in stunned silence. Kim Goldman, the dark-haired sister of Ron Goldman who had sat through the entire trial, sobbed on her mustachioed father's shoulder as he shook his head in anger and disbelief.

Across the nation, Americans reacted with divergent emotional responses to the jury's verdict. African Americans celebrated the jury's decision while most whites expressed shock at Simpson's acquittal. Many wondered how the jury

Reactions to the verdict in the Simpson criminal case underscored the significance of race relations in the outcome of the trial. According to one poll, 85 percent of African Americans concurred with the verdict of the predominantly black jury compared with only 32 percent of whites. The man pictured here, Robert Graham, reflected the elation that typified the reaction of millions of African Americans to the acquittal of a popular black defendant. Courtesy Associated Press Wide World Photos could have overlooked the physical evidence against the defendant. As subsequent statements from the jurors themselves demonstrated, they had behaved just as the defense had encouraged them to do: they had dismissed the overwhelming DNA evidence against Simpson. "I didn't understand the DNA stuff at all," one of the jurors later explained in a devastating indictment of the prosecution's handling of the key evidence. "To me, it was just a waste of time." Barry Scheck's assault on the DNA evidence could not have been more successful.

On the first ballot, Anise Aschenbach, one of the two remaining whites on the jury, declared that she had been offended by Cochran's call to send a message to the police rather than deciding the case on its merits. A leader among the African American jurors shot back that the LAPD had been out to get Simpson from the start. The first ballot went ten to two in favor of acquittal.

Aschenbach and her cohort quickly gave in, in part because the prosecution case had been so poorly presented. Several jurors declared after the trial that had the prosecution case been more compelling, they would have convicted Simpson. A stronger prosecution case may not have produced a conviction, but should have at least won a hung jury and another trial, or possibly a plea bargain, for Simpson.

The African-American majority seized the opportunity that the prosecution and Ito, through his weak administration of the case, had given them to respond to the chants of "free O. J." As one of the black women muttered after the verdict, "We've got to protect our own." The African-American women had little sympathy for Nicole who, despite being savagely murdered, had been perceived as the type of predatory woman who "takes one of our men."

As they filed out of the courtroom, an African-American male juror flashed a black power salute to the defense table, a pointed indication that the case had been about racial solidarity against the white-dominated system.

No one, aside from Johnnie Cochran, understood the racial dynamics of the case better than Chris Darden, who later declared that from the outset of the proceedings he "could see in [the jurors'] eyes the need to settle some score." Well before the drug wars of the 1980s, which had underscored their reputation, the LAPD had been infamous for riding roughshod over civil rights in the African American community. The sickening Rodney King incident and the terrible riots that followed in the wake of the acquittal of the cops who perpetrated the beating marked the height of black-white polarization in Los Angeles.

The time had now come to lash back against the system, and the chief beneficiary of that backlash was Simpson. The irony was that a pampered and narcissistic celebrity—a man who had long since distanced himself from the black community—had become the focal point of an African-American struggle for equal protection under the law.

With the news that the jury had reached a verdict, the LAPD and federal authorities prepared to respond in the event of another wave of rioting in Los Angeles and other major cities in the event of a guilty verdict. Given the jubilant reaction on the part of the overwhelming majority of African Americans, it seems entirely possible that riots may well have erupted had Simpson been convicted.

The public reaction was the latest shocker in a case that had featured more than its share of twists, turns, and surprises. Across the country, the unrestrained jubilation of African Americans contrasted sharply with the anger expressed by most whites over the injustice of Simpson going free. According to one poll, 85 percent of blacks concurred with the verdict compared with 32 percent of whites. The reaction to the Simpson verdict revealed evidence, shocking to many whites, of the profound alienation of African Americans from the justice system.

In retrospect, the reaction of the African-American community, and the decision of the jury, are understandable. The justice system had been made to work for a black man in a celebrated case. African Americans knew all too well that police harassment, violence, and tampering with evidence against African-Americans were everyday occurrences in the United States.

Why were not those whites who protested the outcome of the Simpson case upset that African Americans suffered daily injustices under the law?

On the other hand, many of the African Americans who celebrated the Simpson verdict, including, incredibly enough, some members of the jury, ignored the realities of the case. The DNA fingerprinting offered evidence of Simpson's guilt that went well beyond the legal standard of reasonable doubt. The Simpson case might well be cited for the salutary effect of calling attention to racial inequality under the law, but Simpson himself was no hero to the black community.

Outraged by the verdict, the majority of white Americans paid little attention to the historic reality of a racist justice system. For example, it has long been demonstrated through statistical analysis that African-American offenders are far more likely to receive the death penalty than whites who commit comparable crimes. African Americans, hundreds of thousands of whom are of lower socioeconomic standing than most whites, lack the means to combat a system stacked against them. Harsher sentences and a greater propensity to deny parole to black prisoners have long been realities of the American system of injustice.

Police prejudice against minorities is another aspect of the racist justice system. The main reason for Simpson's acquittal was the total absence of LAPD credibility in the African-American community. The black jurors knew the cops were lying when they said Simpson was not a suspect when they went over the wall at Rockingham. It was also clear that Vannatter dissembled in obtaining the warrant for Simpson's arrest and committed procedural errors in his handling of the blood evidence.

The prosecution and the two judges—Kennedy-Powell and Ito—winked at the police lies, which have become accepted as routine. Across the nation, police and prosecutors see themselves fighting against a "liberal" system that they believe now favors criminals as a result of the Warren Court reforms, which had ensured the civil liberties of the accused. To combat this supposed liberal bias, cops routinely plant evidence and lie, especially in cases of search and seizure, to implicate alleged criminals. There is even a term for such police behavior— "testilying."

Juries have traditionally accepted the official version of events, thus helping to convict the overwhelming majority of defendants in criminal cases. In the Simpson case, however, the defendant's wealth, the racial composition of the jury, and the LAPD's absence of credibility in the black community produced an acquittal. Police lies and evidence of Fuhrman's blatant racism prompted the jury to give credence to implausible defense theories and to dismiss the overwhelming evidence of Simpson's guilt.

In light of the Simpson case, police and prosecutors across the country should understand that lies and illegal searches ultimately do not serve the interests of justice. If officials themselves flout the law, the public has no reason to support a corrupt system. And juries will be more likely to nullify the evidence and set guilty defendants free.

Finally, the Simpson case served to undermine further the standing of the legal profession in a nation already accustomed to telling jokes at the expense of attorneys. The prosecution, led by Marcia Clark, was little short of incompetent. Johnnie Cochran, by contrast, provided Simpson with a defense that was as shrewd as it was cynical. Cochran invoked the legacy of Martin Luther King Jr. and the cause of racial injustice in behalf of a man who had long since abandoned the black community for a life in the fast lane with his rich white friends. The other key defense attorney, Barry Scheck, performed a national disservice by calling into question the reliability of DNA evidence, which has the power to reveal guilt or innocence—as it did in the Simpson case.

Neither cynicism nor incompetence precluded most of the attorneys involved in the Simpson case from cashing in on million-dollar book deals and starting new careers as cable TV personalities. By contrast, the biggest losers were, of course, the families of the victims. O. J. and Nicole's two young children will be scarred for life. The Brown family lost a daughter, yet faced the repellent prospect of negotiating with the man who killed her to retain access to the children she bore. In December 1996 Simpson won custody of the children in a courtroom battle with the Browns. The Goldman family not only lost a son and a brother but witnessed, day after day in the courtroom, the perpetration of a grotesque injustice.

Although he won acquittal and obtained his freedom after spending sixteen months in jail, Simpson did not escape unscathed. Sued for monetary damages over the deaths of their children by the Brown and Goldman families, Simpson faced the seizure of his possessions and financial assets in damages turned over to the victims' families.

The plaintiffs enjoyed significant advantages in the civil proceedings. The jury's decision was to be based on "a preponderance of evidence," a lower standard than guilt "beyond a reasonable doubt" in the criminal proceeding. Unlike the criminal trial, the defendant could be forced to testify in the civil proceeding. This time Simpson would prove to be a disastrous witness for himself.

The votes of only nine of twelve jurors, rather than unanimity, were required for a judgment in favor of the plaintiffs. In addition, the only thing Judge Hiroshi Fujisaki had in common with Lance Ito was his Japanese-American ancestry. Stern and unsmiling, Fujisaki disdained the type of publicity that "Judge Ego" had reveled in. Before the trial began Fujisaki issued gag orders and banned TV coverage as well as still photographers from the courtroom.

New evidence surfaced in the civil trial. Unlike Ito, Fujisaki allowed Nicole's diary and her phone call to the battered women's shelter reporting that Simpson was stalking her to be admitted into evidence. Authentic photographs surfaced of Simpson wearing the size twelve Bruno Maglis he had once described as "ugly-ass shoes" that he would never have owned. Simpson himself offered a series of blatantly transparent lies through which he lost credibility with the jury. For example, asked how many times he had struck his wife, Simpson replied, "Never."

The case against Simpson was brilliantly marshaled by Fred Goldman's attorney Daniel Petrocelli. In addition to the new photographic evidence, Petrocelli uncovered more evidence about Simpson's motive. Simpson's one-time girlfriend, Paula Barbieri, admitted that she had broken up with O. J. in a message left on his telephone answering machine the morning of the murders. Johnnie Cochran had insisted in the first trial that Simpson had broken off his relationship with Paula, but in fact the reverse was true.

Paula Barbieri left O. J. because she realized he still loved Nicole. Indeed, in a famous interview with *Esquire* years after the murders, Simpson allowed in hypothetical terms that if he had killed his ex-wife it would have been because he loved her too much. Nicole had not only broken off with O. J. but his obsession with her had also cost him his relationship with Paula. Returning from a bad round of golf on June 12, 1994, only to receive the phone message from Paula ending their relationship, Simpson was consumed by rage and humiliation.

In contrast to the prosecution in the criminal case, Petrocelli presented a clear and coherent case. He also exploited the opportunity to take apart Simpson on the stand. "It comes down to this," Petrocelli explained to the jury in his summation. "There's blood, there's hair, there's fiber, there's cuts, there's sweat suits, there's hats, there's no alibi, there's plenty of time, and there's motive." On the other side was Simpson's testimony, which lacked credibility.

The jury in the civil trial, comprised of seven men and five women—nine whites, two blacks, and a Mexican American—issued its verdict on February 4, 1997. It did so after deliberating for thirteen hours over three days—more than three times the length of time the criminal trial jury allotted to its decision making.

The Santa Monica jury issued three judgments against Simpson totaling a whopping $33.5 million. Fred Goldman and his ex-wife received more than $20 million in damages for the loss of their son. In marked contrast to judgment day in the criminal trial, Simpson stood in silence while Kim Goldman whooped, "Yes!" upon hearing the verdict. "Thank God for some justice for Ron and Nicole," Fred Goldman declared. "This is all we ever wanted." A few days later Goldman offered to drop the judgment against Simpson if he would admit his guilt (for which he could not again be tried under the Constitutional prohibition of double jeopardy) in the murders. Simpson, of course, declined.

The jury awarded Nicole Brown Simpson's estate nearly $13 million. Seeking no money of their own, the Browns had filed their complaint for damages in behalf of Simpson's own children, Justin and Sydney.

The court began to seize Simpson's assets, forcing him to sell his Rockingham home. Many experts predicted, however, that as a result of appeals and delaying tactics Simpson could avoid actually paying out even a fraction of the jury's award. Simpson complained that he was penniless, but in reality he had enjoyed ample time to hide money in offshore accounts and to transfer funds to his adult children from his previous marriage. Under California law, Simpson could and did maintain an expensive home (though not the mansion at Rockingham, which was subsequently razed), an automobile, and pension funds estimated to be worth $2.5 million. Simpson continued to find ways to make money, including making commercials—not for rental cars but, appropriately enough, for a national lawyer-referral service.

Like Lizzie Borden, Simpson found that although he had won acquittal, he would be forced to live out his life as a pariah. His upscale Hollywood friends disowned him as did his golf partners at the Riviera Country Club. Simpson continued to center his existence around golf, but now had to look for partners to join him on public courses.

In the final analysis, the Simpson affair was far more than a murder case. Public fascination with the event also reflected more than a media-driven desire for the salacious details of sex, sleaze, and murder. The trial became something of a national referendum on race and power relationships in the United States. The two murders in Brentwood became peripheral to the larger cultural drama.

The history of race relations in America has been essentially a struggle for power. For centuries, first through slavery and then through segregation, terror, and denial of civil rights, whites monopolized power. As African Americans understood from bitter experience, the police and the criminal justice system continued to oppress black people in the late twentieth century even as they continued the struggle against a racist system.

With such dynamics in place, the Simpson trial became another battleground in a seemingly endless power struggle across the pages of American history. The lesson that a majority of African Americans took from their awareness of the nation's history of racist criminal justice was the need to side with one of their own against a system that historically had repressed people of color.

The striking juxtaposition of white anger and black celebration on the part of whites and blacks, respectively, after the first trial, points to the ultimate significance of the Simpson case. Despite meaningful progress in race relations since the civil rights movement of the 1960s, the Simpson case illuminated the profound divisions that remained in American society. At century's end the words used in a federal report analyzing a wave of race riots in the mid-sixties could still be employed to describe the country. In 1967 the Kerner Commission had declared that the United States actually consisted of two nations—one black, one white—separate and unequal.

For African Americans the Simpson case became a referendum on a history of prejudice, discrimination, and mistreatment—abuses to which most whites were oblivious. To many African Americans, charges that Simpson gained his freedom by playing the "race card" had little resonance. After all, the race card in American jurisprudence had always been played from a deck stacked against them, not in favor of a black defendant. According to a survey conducted by the National Center for State Courts in and released in spring 1999, 68 percent of African Americans believed that "people like them" received unfair treatment in the criminal justice system.

Although many African Americans view white racism as the main problem of the criminal justice system, the dynamics are rapidly changing. It is true, as already noted, that a disgracefully high number of African American young men are in prison and on death row. Their plight reflects systematic discrimination and profound social problems in urban America. Most of the crimes that land people in prison are committed by African Americans, but most of those crimes are also intraracial—directed against black victims.

Authoritative studies have shown, however, that African-American defendants today are less likely than white defendants to be convicted by juries of violent crimes. Across the country prosecutors are reporting more difficulty obtaining convictions against African Americans based on testimony by white policemen. Juries are increasingly practicing nullification. As legal scholar Susan Estrich has noted in *Getting Away With Murder* (Harvard University Press, 1998), "The Simpson case, for all its uniqueness, captured too well the ills of the system; it is in all the ways that it is not unusual that the case teaches us the most."

The Simpson case traumatized Americans, not simply because of the verdict that was rendered but because it brought into the open deep divisions over race. These divisions not only undermine the administration of justice, but if left unbridged will remain a menace to domestic tranquility.

V CONCLUSION: SENSATIONAL MURDER AND AMERICAN JUSTICE

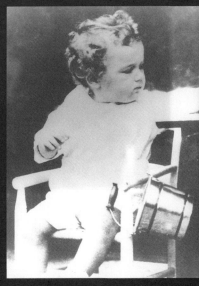

V CONCLUSION: SENSATIONAL MURDER AND

AMERICAN JUSTICE

This study of four sensational murder cases in American history illuminates the vulnerabilities of the criminal justice system, especially in high-profile cases. Celebrity trials, with their feverish media coverage, place inordinate pressures on those responsible for administering criminal justice. As we have seen in all four cases, police, attorneys, judges, and juries often succumb to those pressures, particularly in sensational murder trials.

Murder within the family taps into public fascination with the human penchant for evil, the quest to understand the primordial killer that still lurks in the hearts of certain men and women. Such cases, especially when they involve a national celebrity such as Charles Lindbergh or O. J. Simpson, instantly become sensational public dramas. They become part of American culture rather than merely of American jurisprudence.

In each of the four cases analyzed in this book, cultural perceptions unique to their place and time played a decisive role in the outcome of the murder trial. Gendered perceptions obscured the compelling evidence against Lizzie Borden and helped win her acquittal. In the Lindbergh case, the press, the public, and the state sought vengeance for the "crime of the century"—the kidnapping and murder of the infant son and namesake of a popular national hero—and denied a German immigrant defendant, Bruno Richard Hauptmann, a fair trial. In the Sheppard case, class anxieties, a McCarthy era witch-hunt atmosphere, and vicious Cleveland journalism combined to destroy an innocent man. Finally, the acquittal of O. J. Simpson stemmed from police misconduct and exploitation of profound racial divisions, the perpetual American dilemma, rather than from the evidence presented at trial.

Intense media coverage transformed these four murder cases into larger public dramas revolving around emotional cultural issues such as gender, ethnicity, class, and race. A national media circus intruded on each case and complicated the quest for justice. Packed galleries, sensational headlines, rumors, gossip, innuendo, hawking of souvenirs on the courthouse steps, and cameras at every turn created a carnival atmosphere around the courtrooms and in the culture at large. While many other nations place much tighter restrictions on media access to criminal trials, the openness of American society allows for intense publicity in celebrity trials. Whole television networks are now devoted to coverage of just such trials.

In the Lizzie Borden case, adjudicated in an era of yellow journalism, the press promoted the widespread public perception that no woman could have committed the Borden murders. Newspapers thus helped condition the community, judges, and the jury to grant "Miss Lizzie" an acquittal in 1893.

Conversely, the newspapers, now abetted by national radio coverage and newsreels, condemned Hauptmann for the kidnap and murder of the Lindbergh baby well before he went on trial in the Flemington, New Jersey, courthouse in 1935. Under intense pressure to convict and obtain the death penalty for the hated German immigrant, New Jersey police and prosecutors withheld and manipulated evidence. Although the evidence uncovered against Hauptmann was compelling, he failed to receive a fair trial. Moreover, the official abuses spurred a series of ongoing efforts to assert the existence of a conspiracy to frame and condemn Hauptmann, thus obscuring a more realistic historical assessment of the Lindbergh kidnapping.

In the Sam Sheppard case, the Cleveland newspapers, and especially the *Cleveland Press*, uncritically parroted official versions of the crime and bore responsibility, through their sensational headlines and relentless call for an arrest and indictment, for the atmosphere that made it impossible for the defendant to receive a fair trial in 1954. The Sheppard case took the controversial issue of free press-fair trial all the way to the Supreme Court. In its landmark 1966 decision, the high court established the responsibility of public officials to ensure that defendants receive a fair trial. Sheppard won an acquittal the next year. In the wake of the Supreme Court decision, police and prosecutors now had to be wary about leaking information and conducting the type of "trial by newspaper" that Cleveland authorities had orchestrated in 1954.

Despite such reforms, the challenge of conducting a fair trial in a sensational criminal case became ever more difficult in an increasingly media-saturated society. The gavel-to-gavel coverage of the Simpson trial featured a dizzying

The Simpson trial was the most heavily mediated event in the history of American criminal justice. Television networks offered "gavel-to-gavel" coverage while journalists and attorneys debated the implications of every twist and turn. Tabloid publications paid potential witnesses for their stories, often undermining the ability of the prosecution to summon them to testify in the actual trial. Helicopters, "action news" trucks and photographers crowded outside the courtrooms of both the criminal and civil trials of O.J. Simpson. Courtesy Associated Press Wide World Photos

array of network anchors, packs of reporters, legal experts on myriad channels, round-the-clock Court TV, worldwide satellite transmission, news helicopters, and a general atmosphere of tabloid journalism run amok. Both sides conducted press conferences and expended considerable energy in efforts to "spin" the momentum of the trial in their favor.

The Simpson case was a phenomenon of the postmodern era, a media event in which the lines between reality and representation became so blurred as to blend together in the public eye. Indeed, the trial went on for so long—more than a year—that the case cost millions of dollars, exhausted the attorneys, and nearly ran out of jurors. Whereas the Borden trial consumed two weeks, the

Hauptmann trial just over a month, and the first Sheppard trial two months, the Simpson trial was interminable. By the end of it the sequestered jurors were too exhausted even to enter into responsible deliberations.

The Simpson case also underscored that justice, like most things in capitalist society, can be purchased. In 1902 the great defense attorney Clarence Darrow told a group of prison inmates that their incarceration stemmed primarily from the fact that they had lacked the wherewithal to employ a good attorney. The statement contained more than a grain of truth then, but Darrow's dictim was even more true in subsequent years.

In three of the cases studied here, culminating with the Simpson Dream Team, a high-priced defense secured a not guilty verdict. Shrewd attorneys played a key role in the courtroom victories of Lizzie Borden, Sam Sheppard in his second trial, and O. J. Simpson. Bruno Richard Hauptmann, universally condemned, poorly represented, and denied access to exculpatory evidence, never stood a chance.

Every year across the United States, in tens of thousands of little known cases, defendants lacking the means to provide themselves with an aggressive courtroom defense are convicted on less evidence than Lizzie Borden or O. J. Simpson confronted. As these cases underscore, American justice is all too often dispensed on the basis of wealth, race, and class. The first Sheppard trial showed that class prejudices—popular resentment of a wealthy elite—can sometimes work against rather than in favor of a defendant. For the most part, however, wealth and elite status lend themselves more to courtroom victories than defeats.

As long as it carries a price tag, justice in America will remain an elusive quest. Egalitarianism under the law will be an ideal, and a rather distant one at that, rather than a reality of America's democratic society.

These four sensational murder cases underscore the crucial role that police misconduct and judicial incompetence can play in courtroom proceedings. Police forces made significant errors in all four cases. The Fall River, Massachusetts, police failed to make an adequate and timely search of the Borden home and botched their handling of the murder weapon. The much maligned New Jersey State Police, together with the FBI and wood and handwriting experts, eventually uncovered the decisive evidence that broke the Lindbergh case. Before that, however, they allowed the crime scene to be trampled outside the home, eliminated any hope of eliciting a confession from Hauptmann by subjecting him to a violent third degree, and gave Lindbergh himself far too much authority over the kidnap investigation.

Police in the Sheppard case committed a cardinal error, leaping to the conclusion that the physician had killed his wife to the exclusion of all other possibilities. Meanwhile, the man who in all likelihood actually murdered Marilyn Sheppard, and who had appeared on the original list of possible suspects, remained free to kill again, and again, and again.

Police errors in the Simpson case opened the door that Johnnie Cochran then tore off its hinges in securing a not guilty verdict for his client. Crime scene errors, inadequate supervision of evidence, demonstrable racism, and brazen "testilying" backfired against the police and against the administration of justice.

We can hope that the Simpson case, by putting the police themselves on trial, might send a message to police forces around the country and spur needed reforms. Predominantly white police forces, notorious for targeting minority suspects—while justifying the practice as "profiling," are not likely to curb their abuses overnight. Indeed, even after the lessons on police misconduct offered up by the Simpson case, a special task force had to be appointed to probe another series of Los Angeles Police Department abuses in the late 1990s. In the worst scandal in the history of the LAPD, the investigation uncovered evidence of alleged unjustified shootings, beatings, drug dealing, evidence planting, false arrests, witness intimidation, and perjury. With such abuses occurring on a regular basis, we can assume that Los Angeles juries will continue to doubt the credibility of police testimony and to practice nullification in criminal cases. As a result, guilty offenders may be expected to continue to go free.

Corrupt and deceitful police forces must be called to account across the country. At the same time, cops need to receive better training in investigative techniques and legal procedures or they will continue to make crucial crime scene blunders. A case in point was the botched handling of the crime scene in the sensational Jon Benét Ramsey murder case in 1996 in Boulder, Colorado. The death of the prepubescent blond beauty queen may never be solved as a result of the crucial crime scene errors reminiscent of those that occurred in each of the four cases analyzed in this book.

These four case studies do not inspire confidence in the quality of judges in

26

sensational criminal trials. The judges in the Lizzie Borden case ignored legal precedent and overstepped their bounds in order to mold opinions in such a way as to ensure her acquittal. In the Lindbergh case, Judge Trenchard handled a difficult challenge well in many respects, yet in the final analysis he was a willing participant in the railroading of Hauptmann. Judge Blythin judged Sam Sheppard "guilty as hell" before even hearing the evidence in the case. Presiding over the trial in the midst of his own reelection campaign, Blythin orchestrated a case that a higher judicial authority described as a "mockery of justice." Judge Lance Ito, mesmerized by the national media spotlight in the Simpson case, played to the cameras and lost control of the trial. His dilatory handling of the trial facilitated a miscarriage of justice.

As in the case of police misconduct, there is no reason to suppose the problem of judicial incompetence will be remedied anytime soon. Judges, ever eyeing the next reelection campaign or political appointment, will continue to make decisions that pander to community prejudices. For that matter, attorneys will continue to value a courtroom victory over a genuine quest for justice. Newspaper, tabloid, and television reporters will continue to intrude themselves as deeply as possible into the courtroom, especially in high-profile cases, with little concern about the impact of their actions on the judicial process. And the public will continue to seize the opportunity offered by celebrity trials to wage its cultural battles, manifest its prejudices, and display its prurient interests.

Criminal justice, especially in sensational celebrity murder cases, cannot but reflect the larger cultural milieu in which it unfolds. These cases illuminate a unique style of American justice, one that reflects the freedom inherent in the nation's democratic culture, but one whose outcomes are often flawed and dissatisfying. To the extent that these four cases represent the quest for ideal justice, their legacy can only be described as disturbing.

CRITICAL BIBLIOGRAPHY

General Sources

In recent years historians have begun to pay more attention to murder cases as a legitimate focus of scholarly inquiry. In *Murder Most Foul: The Killer and the American Gothic Imagination* (Cambridge: Harvard University Press, 1998), cultural historian Karen Halttunen analyzes popular fascination with murder narratives from the colonial era through the nineteenth century. Similar themes, though focused more specifically on gender, are explored by Patricia Cline Cohen in *The Murder of Helen Jewett: The Life and Death of a Prostitute in Nineteenth-Century New York* (New York: Alfred A. Knopf, 1998) and Amy Gilman Srebnick in *The Mysterious Death of Mary Rogers: Sex and Culture in Nineteenth-Century New York* (New York: Oxford University Press, 1995). Robert Harriman's *Popular Trials: Rhetoric, Mass Media, and the Law* (Tuscaloosa: University of Alabama Press, 1990) helps explain why sensational trials resonate with the public.

Sources on the Borden Case

The Fall River Historical Society (FRHS), located in a beautifully preserved mansion on Rock Street near downtown Fall River, Massachusetts, houses primary sources on the Borden murder. Researchers can access police reports on the murder and subsequent investigation; a transcript of the preliminary hearing; a complete trial transcript; and myriad newspaper accounts.

Edwin H. Porter's classic account, *The Fall River Tragedy: A History of the Borden Murders* (Portland, Maine: King Philip Publishing Co., 1985), originally published in 1893, is also available at the FRHS. Curator Michael Martins and archivist Jamelle Lyons can also make available to researchers other helpful sources, including city directories and some excellent local histories and document collections on Fall River life during the late Victorian era. The FRHS also has published several volumes pertaining to the crime. Particularly useful is *The Commonwealth of Massachusetts vs. Lizzie A. Borden: The*

Knowlton Papers, 1892–1893, edited by Michael Martins and Dennis A. Binette (Fall River: Fall River Historical Society, 1994). This rich collection of documents, letters, and evidentiary reports came from the files of prosecuting attorney Hosea Morrill Knowlton. The book contains an excellent biographical glossary of all the major figures in the Borden case. Soon to be published by the FRHS is a volume of the papers of Lizzie Borden's first attorney, Andrew J. Jennings, of Fall River.

A useful guide to an abundant secondary literature is Robert A. Flynn, *The Borden Murders: An Annotated Bibliography* (Portland, Maine: King Philip Publishing Co., 1992). The book surveys nonfiction, fiction, reference, and miscellaneous works, including poetry, music, and artistic renditions of the Borden saga.

A classic account is Edward Pearson's *The Trial of Lizzie Borden* (New York: Doubleday, 1937; Notable Trials Library Edition, with a foreword by Alan Dershowitz, 1991). Fascinated with the case for years, Pearson wrote numerous articles on the Borden murders. Pearson writes with percipience and occasional humor, but above all, like Edwin Porter, with a clear-eyed focus on the incriminating evidence against Lizzie Borden.

Another excellent study is Robert Sullivan's *Goodbye Lizzie Borden* (Brattleboro, Vt.: The Stephen Greene Press, 1974). Sullivan, himself a former Massachusetts Superior Court judge, offers exhaustive research, insight into Massachusetts law, and keen evaluations of the performance of the attorneys and judges in the case.

Sullivan's arguments echo the conclusions of a brilliant early legal scholar, John H. Wigmore, who dissected the evidence immediately after the Borden trial. A law professor at Northwestern University, Wigmore was long recognized as one of the nation's preeminent experts on evidence. His "The Borden case," published in the *American Law Review* 27, no. 6 (Nov.–Dec. 1893): 819–45, is still well worth reading.

By far the best combination of legal and cultural analysis is Cara W. Robertson's "Representing 'Miss Lizzie': Cultural Convictions in the Trial of Lizzie Borden," *Yale Journal of Law and the Humanities* 8 (summer 1996):351–416. This perceptive account argues convincingly that because of the gendered depiction of "Miss Lizzie" that prevailed in the Fall River courtroom, securing her conviction became "a cultural impossibility."

Another useful source is *Lizzie Borden: A Case Book of Family and Crime in the 1890s,* edited by Joyce G. Williams, J. Eric Smithburn, and M. Jeanne Peterson (Bloomington, Ind.: T.I.S. Publications Division, 1980). This study focuses on the social milieu of Victorian America, contains a copy of the inquest transcript (as do the Pearson and Sullivan books), and, most useful, offers fully reprinted newspaper accounts from local and national publications, ranging from the *Fall River Globe* to the *New York Times.*

There are some interesting essays in an otherwise uneven volume, *Proceedings: Lizzie Borden Conference,* edited by Jules Ryckebusch (Bristol Community College, Fall River,

Among the most useful essays in the book is Joyce Williams's analysis of Lizzie's shoplifting. See also the excellent academic study by Elaine S. Abelson, *When Ladies Go A-Thiev-
ing: Middle-Class Shoplifters in the Victorian Department Store* (New York: Oxford University Press, 1989).

Perhaps the most intriguing account of the Borden murders is Victoria Lincoln's *A
Private Disgrace: Lizzie Borden by Daylight* (New York: G. P. Putnam's Sons, 1967), which
posits that Lizzie killed her mother during an epileptic fit. Herself a Fall River native,
Lincoln more than understands Lizzie's social milieu. The book is intelligent and engaging, but many of its arguments rest ultimately on hearsay and imaginative speculation.

While Lincoln's book deserves to be read, even by those who will not embrace the
epilepsy theory, many accounts of the murders are implausible. Among these is Edward
W. Radin's *Lizzie Borden: The Untold Story* (New York: Simon and Schuster, 1961), which
fingers Bridget Sullivan as the real killer, presumably because she was furious about
being forced to wash windows on a hot day when she was feeling ill. Frank Spiering's
Lizzie (New York: Random House, 1984) offers the far-fetched argument (insofar as she
was out of town at the time) that Emma Borden, not Lizzie, killed her parents. Finally,
Arnold R. Brown, in *Lizzie Borden: The Legend, the Truth, the Final Chapter* (Nashville,
Tenn.: Rutledge Hill Press, 1991), insists that an illegitimate son of Andrew Borden's
dropped into the Second Street home to murder the Bordens.

It is unfortunate that authors and publishers attach the label of nonfiction to works
which display so little regard for historical accuracy.

Sources on the Lindbergh Case

Evidence in the Lindbergh kidnapping case is accessible to researchers at the New
Jersey State Police Museum at the NJSP Headquarters in West Trenton. The museum,
expertly attended by archivist Mark W. Falzini, contains a collection of more than a half
million documents, including the complete state police investigation; FBI documents;
the complete transcript of the Hauptmann trial; videos on the case; and thousands of
photographs and maps. The baby's sleeping suit, the kidnap ladder, ransom money,
Hauptmann's revolver, the electric chair in which he died, and other artifacts of the
"crime of the century" are artfully displayed at the State Police Museum. The former
Lindbergh estate near Hopewell and the spot where the baby's body was found are within easy driving distance of the museum. The house in which Anna and Richard Hauptmann once lived still stands in the Bronx, New York.

The best study, by far, on the kidnapping and murder, as well as the Hauptmann trial, is Jim Fisher's *The Lindbergh Case* (New Brunswick, N.J.: Rutgers University Press,
1987; reprint 1994). Fisher, a professor of criminal justice, refutes in objective fashion

many of the arguments which have been marshaled to make a case for Hauptmann's innocence.

An abridged version of the Hauptmann trial transcript, an essential source for serious students of the Lindbergh case, appears in Sidney B. Whipple, *The Trial of Bruno Richard Hauptmann* (New York: Doubleday, 1937). George Waller's *Kidnap: The Story of the Lindbergh Case* (New York: Dial Press, 1961) is still worth reading.

Many biographies on the fascinating life of Charles A. Lindbergh contain chapters on the kidnap and murder. A. Scott Berg's *Lindbergh* (New York: G. P. Putnam, 1998) is the authorized biography grounded in privileged access to Lindbergh's private papers. My own short biography, *Charles A. Lindbergh: Lone Eagle* (New York: Longman, 1996), contains a chapter on the case as well as bibliographic references to an abundant literature.

An indispensable source is law professor Lewis M. Seidman's "The Trial and Execution of Bruno Richard Hauptmann: Still Another Case that 'Will Not Die,'" *The Georgetown Law Journal* 66 (October 1977): 1–48. Based on what at the time were just-released FBI documents, Seidman reveals that the FBI, New Jersey State Police, and prosecutors conspired to prevent exculpatory evidence from being presented at Hauptmann's trial. As Seidman's analysis makes clear, the deck was stacked against the German immigrant. Laudably, however, Seidman does not embrace the syllogism that because Hauptmann failed to receive a fair trial he was therefore innocent of the crime.

The same cannot be said of a host of conspiracy theorists who have shown a marked determination to exonerate Hauptmann while unmasking a variety of "real" culprits in the Lindbergh kidnap and murder case. Anthony Scaduto's *Scapegoat: The Lonesome Death of Bruno Richard Hauptmann* (New York: G. P. Putnam's Sons, 1976) latched onto the evidence of official misconduct in the Hauptmann trial and made much of the contradictions and misstatements by eyewitnesses against the accused kidnapper. However, Scaduto went on to offer the since disproven argument that the Lindbergh baby had never been killed but was alive, well, and living in Westport, Connecticut.

Ludovic Kennedy, *The Airman and the Carpenter: The Lindbergh Kidnapping and the Framing of Richard Hauptmann* (New York: Viking, 1985) makes the most of the state's manipulation of evidence, but remains unconvincing in arguing Hauptmann's innocence. Noel Behn's *Lindbergh, The Crime* (Boston: Atlantic Monthly Press, 1993) posits, without evidence, that Lindbergh killed his own son, by accident, while staging the kidnapping as a practical joke.

Publication of Lindbergh conspiracy theories, however implausible (e.g., Anne Morrow Lindbergh's sister killed the baby in a jealous rage over Anne, and not she, having snagged Charles in marriage), has become a cottage industry. These accounts could be dismissed as laughable except when one considers that they enjoy a wide readership and may be taken seriously.

The Cuyahoga County prosecutor's office graciously provided me with access to seven thick volumes of police reports, crime scene descriptions, interviews, letters from citizens, photographs, and newspaper and magazine accounts of the Sheppard case. I would like to thank prosecutors Carmen Marino and David Zimmerman for providing me with the access to this invaluable material and for giving me a place to work in their busy public offices.

I would also like to thank Terry Gilbert, attorney for Sam Reese Sheppard, for supplying me with access to the report on the Sheppard case by AMSEC International, a private investigations firm in Middleburg, Virginia. AMSEC's "Confidential Homicide Investigation Report and DNA Supplement: Marilyn Sheppard," illuminated a great deal about Richard Eberling as well as the crime scene evidence. Gilbert also allowed me to view his videotaped interview with the Ohio prison informant, Robert Lee Parks.

The William Corrigan Papers, on microfilm at the Western Reserve Historical Society in Cleveland, proved most useful. The papers include correspondence, legal documents, briefs and appeals, transcripts of interviews, analysis of evidence by Paul Leland Kirk, and Sam Sheppard's autobiography, written during his imprisonment in the Cuyahoga County Jail.

Beyond question the best book on the Sheppard case is by Cynthia L. Cooper and Sam Reese Sheppard, *Mockery of Justice: The True Story of the Sheppard Murder Case* (Boston: Northeastern University Press, 1995). This well-researched, impassioned account offers far too much compelling evidence to be dismissed as merely a son's plea for his father's innocence.

Another important work, *The Sheppard Murder Case* (New York: McKay, 1961), by Paul Holmes, was the first to shed serious doubts on Dr. Sam's guilt. Holmes, who covered both Sheppard trials for the *Chicago Tribune*, also rushed into publication *Retrial: Murder and Dr. Sam Sheppard* (New York: Bantam, 1966) in the wake of the second trial in which Sheppard was found not guilty. Dr. Sheppard's own *Endure and Conquer* (Cleveland: World Publishing Co., 1966) was also rushed into print and is not nearly the revealing source that perhaps he could have written had he not been so devastated by the ordeal.

Jack Harrison Pollack's *Dr. Sam: An American Tragedy* (Chicago: H. Regnery, 1972), by a journalist who was Sheppard's friend, is a sensitive but now dated account. F. Lee Bailey (with Harvey Aronson), *The Defense Never Rests* (New York: Stein and Day, 1971), offers some useful recollections from the attorney who won Sheppard's freedom on retrial.

No serious student of the Sheppard case can avoid going back and reading the inflamed articles in the Cleveland newspapers at the time of the Sheppard trial. Their shameful journalism went a long way toward condemning an innocent man. Doing much better in recent years, the *Cleveland Plain Dealer* and the *Akron Beacon-Journal* have closely monitored Sam Reese Sheppard's lawsuit based on the new evidence in the Sheppard case.

Sources on the Simpson Case

A good place to begin is Jeffrey Toobin, *The Run of His Life: The People v. O. J. Simpson* (New York: Random House, 1996). An attorney and former staff member for the independent counsel's office in the Iran-Contra affair, Toobin covered the trial for the *New Yorker.*

To appreciate the full spectrum of views on the Simpson case, readers would be well advised to read carefully and compare the diametrically opposed arguments of two highly accomplished attorneys, Alan Dershowitz and Vincent Bugliosi. Dershowitz, a celebrated Harvard Law School professor and member of Simpson's team charged specifically with preparing for appeal in the event of conviction, offers *Reasonable Doubts: The Criminal Justice System and the O. J. Simpson Case* (New York: Touchstone, 1996). Dershowitz carefully avoids the conclusion that Simpson was innocent, but he does argue that the record of racism, lies, and manipulation by the LAPD presented a reasonable doubt. Thus, unlike Toobin, Dershowitz defends the legitimacy of the Simpson jury's verdict. Three Simpson jurors—Armanda Cooley, Carrie Bess, and Marsha Rubin-Jackson—echo Dershowitz's argument in their *Madam Foreman: A Rush to Judgment?* (Beverly Hills, Calif.: Dove Books, 1996).

Bugliosi, known best for his successful prosecution of the Manson "family," offers an incisive challenge to Dershowitz in *Outrage: The Five Reasons Why O. J. Simpson Got Away with Murder* (New York: Island Books, 1996). Bugliosi's legal expertise and cold logic reveal the devastating errors made by the prosecution and Judge Lance Ito.

Most of the participants in the Simpson trial—with the notable exception of Ito—quickly cashed in on multi-million-dollar book contracts. In *Without a Doubt* (New York: Viking Penguin, 1997), Marcia Clark (with Teresa Carpenter) blames racial politics and jury nullification for the state's defeat, thereby ignoring the role that the prosecution's blunders, including her own, played in losing the Simpson case. *In Contempt* (New York: Harper-Collins, 1996), by Christopher Darden (with Jess Walter), comes to similar conclusions, but offers an engaging account of Darden's uniquely challenging role as both an African American and a member of the Simpson prosecution team. On the other side of the aisle, Johnnie Cochran (with Tim Rutter) presents the victor's version of the Simpson case in *Journey to Justice* (New York: Ballantine Books, 1996).

For a readable and expert analysis on DNA evidence, both as a general phenomenon as well as its role in the Simpson case, see the book by New York attorney Harlan Levy, *And the Blood Cried Out* (New York: Avon Books, 1996).

In the unlikely event that anyone wants to hear more words from Mark Fuhrman, they are accessible in his *Murder in Brentwood* (Washington, D.C.: Regnery, 1997). Fuhrman, now a convicted felon for committing perjury in the Simpson case, apologizes for his racist utterings, admits to being ashamed, and offers an insider's analysis of the police handling of the case. In *Evidence Dismissed: The Inside Story of the Police Investigation of O. J. Simpson*, Detectives Tom Lange and Philip Vannatter (with Dan Moldea) are most interested in salvaging their own reputations and making a buck.

In *Triumph of Justice: The Final Judgment on the Simpson Saga* (New York: Crown Publishers, 1998), Daniel Petrocelli (with Peter Knobler) offers the most complete and compelling account of the motives for murder, the evidence against Simpson, and the keys to an effective legal strategy in the civil case.

As of this writing, academic analysis of the Simpson case had only begun to emerge. An excellent starting point, however, is the sociological analysis by Darnell M. Hunt in *O. J. Simpson: Facts and Fictions* (New York: Cambridge University Press, 1999).

A massive literature addresses the timeless issue of race relations in American history. A thoughtful recent meditation, written in the wake of the Simpson trial, is David K. Shipler's *A Country of Strangers: Blacks and Whites in America* (New York: Knopf, 1997).

INDEX

SERIES ON LAW, POLITICS AND SOCIETY

Jack Gieck, **LICHFIELD:** THE U.S. ARMY ON TRIAL

Walter L. Hixson, **MURDER, CULTURE, AND INJUSTICE:** FOUR SENSATIONAL CASES IN AMERICAN HISTORY